Documents in Contemporary History

General editor
Kevin Jefferys
Faculty of Arts and Education, University of Plymouth

British defence policy since 1945

This book aims to provide an introduction, based on excerpts from original sources, to the controversies and dilemmas that have confronted those making and implementing British defence policy since the end of the Second World War.

Ovendale explores the policy dilemmas caused by Britain's parallel commitments to continental Europe and to a global foreign policy, the legacy of her imperial past. He also examines the decision in 1957 to rely on the nuclear deterrent, abolish conscription and move away from a maritime strategy; and the role of the Treasury in dictating the limits of British defence policy.

The book draws on newly released documents from the Public Record Office, London, the Australian Archives and American and other sources.

This book will provide valuable source material for sixth form students, undergraduates, and those studying defence issues in military colleges; as well as those who have a general interest in seeing how British defence policy evolved.

Ritchie Ovendale is Reader in International Politics at the University of Wales, Aberystwyth

CN00553629

Documents in Contemporary History is a series designed for sixth-formers and undergraduates in higher education: it aims to provide both an overview of specialist research on topics in post-1939 British history and a wide-ranging selection of primary source material.

Already published

Kevin Jefferys   *War and reform: British politics during the Second World War*

Forthcoming

Sean Greenwood   *Britain and the European integration since the Second World War*

Steven Fielding   *The Labour Party since 1951*

Stuart Ball   *The Conservative Party, 1940–1992*

Chris Wrigley   *British trade unions since 1945*

Harriet Jones   *The politics of affluence, Britain 1951–64*

Rodney Lowe   *The classic welfare state in Britain*

Documents in Contemporary History

British defence policy since 1945

Edited by

Ritchie Ovendale

Professor of International Politics, University of Wales, Aberystwyth

Manchester University Press

Manchester and New York

Distributed exclusively in the USA and Canada by St. Martin's Press

Published by Manchester University Press
Oxford Road, Manchester M13 9NR, UK
and Room 400, 175 Fifth Avenue, New York, NY 10010, USA

Distributed exclusively in the USA and Canada
by St. Martin's Press, Inc., 175 Fifth Avenue, New York,
NY 10010, USAA

British Library Cataloguing-in-Publication Data
A catalogue record for this book is available from the British Library

Library of Congress Cataloging-in-Publication Data
British defence policy since 1945 / edited by Ritchie Ovendale.
     p. cm. — (Documents in contemporary history)
    ISBN 0–7190–4014–0 (Hbk). — ISBN 0–7190–4015–9 (Pbk)
     1. Great Britain—Military policy.   2. Great Britain—Politics and
government—1945–   I. Ovendale, Ritchie.   II. Series.
UA647.B948   1994
355'033541—dc20   94–12637
                                                                         CIP

ISBN 0–7190–4014–0 *hardback*
     0–7190–4015–9 *paperback*

Typeset in Linotron Sabon
by Northern Phototypesetting Co. Ltd, Bolton
Printed in Great Britain
by Bell and Bain Ltd, Glasgow

Contents

Acknowledgements

I should like to thank my colleagues in the Department of International Politics, University of Wales, Aberystywth, for their help, and in particular Professor John Garnett, Dr Colin McInnes, Dr Len Scott, Professor Steve Smith and David Steeds. Mrs. Donna Griffin word-processed a great deal of the text with cheerfulness and humour. Mr Meirion Derrick of the Hugh Owen Library, University of Wales, Aberystwyth, used his expertise to trace documents for me.

Stephen R. Ashton drew my attention to some recently released documents in the Public Record Office, London, on the policy of the Eden government.

Some of the research for this book was made possible by grants from the British Academy and its Small Grants Fund in the Humanities.

I am grateful for permission from the following to cite from copyright material: the Controller of Her Majesty's Stationery Office for Crown copyright material held in the Public Record Office, London, as well as the Official Report of Lords and House of Commons Debates and other parliamentary papers, including the reports of Select Committees, and the Ministry of Defence for Defence Open Government Documents; to David Higham Associates for permission to quote from Hugh Dalton, *High Tide and After: Memoirs 1945–1960*, originally published by Frederick Muller; to A. P. Watt Ltd, on behalf of Viscount Montgomery of Alamein, CBE, to include excerpts from *The Memoirs of Field-Marshal the Viscount Montgomery of Alamein, KG*, originally published by Collins; to the Department of the Prime Minister and Cabinet and the Department of Defence of the Government of Australia to reproduce and publish material currently held by the Australian Archives; to Macmillan London Ltd, to reproduce an extract from the Harold Macmillan Archives, Macmillan to Queen Elizabeth II, 21 December 1962, quoted by Alistair Horne, *Macmillan 1957–1986*; and Harper Collins Publishers Inc, New York, for permission to reprint material from Harold Macmillan, *Riding the Storm*, copyright © 1971 by Thompson Newspapers Ltd, index copyright © 1971 by

Acknowledgements

Macmillan & Co. Ltd; to Hamish Hamilton Ltd for extracts from Richard Crossman, *The Diaries of a Cabinet Minister*, Volume I, *Minister of Housing 1964–1966* (Hamish Hamilton, 1975); to Virgin Publishing Ltd for the extracts form Christopher Grayling and Christopher Langoon, *Just another Star? Anglo-American Relations since 1945*, published originally by Harrap, 1988; and to the Labour Party for excerpts from their publications.

I should also like to thank Michelle O'Connell for her good humour and hard work in securing these permissions.

Chronology of events

1945

July
A Labour government is elected in Britain with Clement Attlee as Prime Minister and Ernest Bevin as Foreign Secretary.

August
Atomic bombs dropped on Hiroshima and Nagasaki hasten the conclusion of the war in the Far East.
The United States Congress ends Lend Lease to Britain.

September
British troops reoccupy former colonial territories of Britain, France and the Netherlands.

October
The Haganah, Irgun and Stern gang implement their plan to co-operate in mounting a terrorist campaign to wear down British morale in the Palestine mandate.

December
Egypt requests the revision of the Anglo-Egyptian treaty of 1936.
Britain secures a loan from the United States on favourable interest terms.

1946

February
Mutinies in the Indian navy and air force.

5 March
Churchill makes his 'Iron Curtain' speech at Fulton, Missouri.

July
Menachem Begin and the Irgun, with the co-operation of the Haganah, blow up the King David Hotel in Jerusalem, one wing of which was used as British army headquarters.

1 August
McMahon Act, restricting the disclosure and exchange of information on atomic energy, becomes law in the United States.

September
Montgomery meets the American Joint Chiefs of Staff on board the USS *Sequoia* and lays foundation of post-war Anglo-American military agreements.

Communist insurrection starts in French Indochina.

1947

10 January	A group of British ministers decides that Britain should build its own atomic bomb.
March	The withdrawal of British troops from Egypt to the Canal Zone is completed.
	The United States Congress approves the Truman Doctrine.
April	Britain refers the Palestine mandate to the United Nations.
May	The United States takes over part of the British commitment in Greece.
June	Bevin helps to prepare West European nations for the Marshall Plan for European Recovery.
15 August	India achieves independence, followed by massacres in the newly created states of India and Pakistan.
29 November	General Assembly of the United Nations votes for the partition of Palestine. Britain abstains, and starts military withdrawal from the mandate.

1948

25 February	Communist coup in Prague, and the Soviet Union assumes control of Czechoslovakia.
March	Brussels treaty signed.
14 May	Final evacuation of British troops from Palestine.
June	With the Communist uprising a state of emergency is declared in Malaya.
24 June	The Soviet Union severs the rail, road and water routes between the Western zones in Germany and Berlin.
15 July	The National Security Council agrees to dispatch B-29 'atomic bombers' to Britain from where they could reach Moscow.

1949

4 April	North Atlantic Treaty signed in Washington by twelve governments.
August	The Soviet Union explodes its first atomic bomb.
September	Britain devalues sterling.
October	Chinese People's Republic proclaimed.

1950

June	Britain accelerates its rearmament programme.

Chronology of events

July
British Cabinet agrees to the formation of a brigade group to operate in Korea under American command as part of the United Nations forces in the Korean War. Period of National Service in Britain extended to two years.

December
First V bombers are ordered for the Royal Air Force.

1951

May
Muhammad Mossadeq, the Prime Minister of Iran, secures the passage through the Iranian parliament of a Bill nationalising the Anglo-Iranian Oil Company. The British Cabinet considers military action, but Washington approves of the nationalisation, urges restraint and sends a mediator to Tehran.

9 October
Egypt denounces the 1936 Anglo-Egyptian treaty.

16 October
Cairo formally rejects proposals for a Middle East Command.

26 October
Churchill heads a new Conservative government.

1952

January
Conservatives slow down rearmament programme.

April
The North Atlantic Treaty Organisation is formed.

October
Following the Mau Mau uprising a state of emergency is declared in Kenya.

Britain tests its first atomic bomb at Monte Bello.

November
The United States tests its first hydrogen bomb.

1954

July
British Cabinet agrees to the building of a British hydrogen bomb.

8 September
South East Asia collective defence treaty signed in Manila by Britain, Australia, France, New Zealand, Pakistan, the Philippines, Thailand and the United States.

October
German Federal Republic accedes to the Brussels treaty.

19 October
Anglo-Egyptian treaty signed, allowing for the British evacuation of the Suez base.

1955

April
Start of Greek-Cypriot EOKA terrorist campaign in Cyprus led by Archbishop Makarios and Colonel George Grivas.

4 April
Britain joins Turkey and Iraq in the Baghdad Pact. Pakistan and Iran join later.

Chronology of events

6 April	Eden becomes Prime Minister.
1956	
June	Eden institutes a review designed to take into account Britain's economic circumstances, to cover changes in domestic and overseas policy and adjustments in Britain's defence programme.
October–November	Anglo-French invasion of Egypt and occupation of part of Suez Canal.
1957	
March	Eisenhower and Macmillan meeting at Bermuda restore Anglo-American special relationship which had been devalued by Eisenhower when he became President with his insistence that Britain was merely one among a number of allies.
April	Sandys defence review, based on the abolition of National Service made possible with a reliance on nuclear weapons, published.
May	Britain tests its first hydrogen bomb on Christmas Island in the Pacific.
October	With the Russian launch of Sputnik Eisenhower tells Macmillan in Washington that the Anglo-American relationship is one of mutual interdependence. Eisenhower indicates that the McMahon Act will be amended.
1958	
July	Hashemite dynasty overthrown in Iraq. A jointly planned Anglo-American invasion of Jordan and the Lebanon is successfully mounted.
1959	
August	The name Central Treaty Organisation (CENTO) given to the Baghdad Pact; this follows Iraq's withdrawal in March 1959.
1960	
3 February	Macmillan in his 'Wind of Change' speech to the South African parliament signals the British abdication in Africa.
March	Macmillan negotiates an agreement with Eisenhower that in return for the purchase of the American Skybolt

	missile Britain will allow the Americans to use Holy Loch in Scotland as a submarine base. First Campaign for Nuclear Disarmament (CND) Aldermaston march takes place.
September	The Trades Union Congress votes for a policy of unilateral British nuclear disarmament.

1961

July	Britain initiates a successful military operation to prevent an Iraqi invasion of Kuwait.

1962

September	A pro-Nasser revolution in the Yemen is followed by the involvement of British troops in quelling revolts in the Aden Protectorates and Aden.
December	Britain intervenes in the rebellion in Brunei. Macmillan meets Kennedy at Nassau and secures the submarine-launched alternative to Skybolt, Polaris.

1963

April	Start of Indonesian 'Confrontation' with Malaysia.
July	White Paper establishes a single Ministry of Defence in Britain.
December	A state of emergency is declared in Aden. Makarios requests British military assistance in Cyprus.

1964

January	British troops help to put down mutinies in former British territories in East Africa.
16 October	Harold Wilson becomes Labour Prime Minister with Denis Healey as his Secretary of State for Defence.
November	Against the background of a crisis over sterling Healey initiates a defence review.

1965

April	The TSR2 fighter aircraft is cancelled.
November	Britain takes no military action when the Unilateral Declaration of Independence (UDI) is made by Rhodesia.

1967

July	Announcement made that Britain will withdraw from East of Suez by the mid-1970s.
18 November	Sterling is devalued.
29 November	Britain evacuates Aden and the National Liberation

Front proclaims the independent People's Republic of
Southern Yemen.

1968
January Announcement made of the acceleration of the
withdrawal from East of Suez by the end of 1971.
NATO strategic doctrine changes from 'Massive
Retaliation' to 'Flexible Response'.

1969
August British troops intervene in Northern Ireland in an
attempt to restore order.

1970
December Joint Anglo-American announcement that work will
start in March 1971 on an Anglo-American base in the
Indian Ocean to be financed by the Americans.

1972
January Strategic Arms Limitation Talks (SALT) 1 agreement
signed.

1973
January Britain joins the European Economic Community (EEC).
April The decision is taken to initiate the Polaris improvement
programme with the United States.

1974
March Wilson's Labour government initiates a defence review
designed to maintain NATO as the lynchpin of British
security and to reduce commitments outside the alliance
so as to avoid overstretching Britain's forces.

1976
February Sterling crisis.

1978
April President Carter cancels the neutron bomb project and
strains Anglo-American relations. Prime Minister James
Callaghan and Chancellor Helmut Schmidt of West
Germany had co-operated with Carter in 1977 over
NATO's policy to deploy the neutron bomb in Europe.

1979	
January	At Guadeloupe a NATO 'Twin Track' response to the deployment of Soviet SS-20 missiles targeted on Western Europe is evolved. American cruise missiles will be deployed in Western Europe and there will be negotiations with Moscow to eliminate all intermediate-range missiles. Carter also indicates that he is prepared to offer Britain Trident.
June	The SALT II treaty is signed but not ratified.
1980	
July	Mrs Margaret Thatcher's government announces its decision to buy Trident I C4 missiles from the United States.
1981	
June	The review of the Defence Secretary, John Nott, is published. It reduces the size of the surface fleet and enhances the 'maritime-air and submarine effort'.
1982	
March	Britain agrees to buy Trident II D5 from the United States.
April to June	The Falklands War.
1984	
January	Start of cruise missile deployment in the United Kingdom.
July	Publication of Michael Heseltine's proposals to reform the Ministry of Defence on the basis of functional efficiency.
1986	
June	Heseltine resigns over the Westland affair.
1987	The Minister of Defence, George Younger, cancels the contract with the General Electric Company for the Nimrod warning system, and orders the aircraft that the Royal Air Force prefers, the Boeing airborne warning and control system (AWACS).
1988	
June	The Labour leader, Neil Kinnock, initiates a move away from unilateralism.

Chronology of events

1990

June With the end of the Cold War, at the Turnberry meeting of NATO foreign ministers, Britain accepts the need for a more political role for the alliance.

25 July The Defence Secretary, Tom King, announces to the House of Commons that the British Army of the Rhine (BAOR) will be scaled down and the armed forces substantially reduced. This initiates the 'Options for Change' programme.

1991 Early in the year Washington announces that it is abandoning the Poseidon base at Holy Loch, and that it is also withdrawing the F–111 bombers.

January–February Britain's role in the Gulf War shows the enduring strength of the Anglo-American special relationship in defence. It also leads to an evaluation of Britain's combat forces.

1992

7 July The Defence Secretary, Malcolm Rifkind, outlines a defence review suited to Britain as a middle-ranking European power. But he emphasises that Britain still has worldwide responsibilities.

1993

5 July While further reducing the British armed services the Defence Statement stresses that Britain, following its role with the United Nations in the former Yugoslavia, has a part to play in international peacekeeping missions. It abolishes the distinction between 'in area' and 'out of area' operations and tries to resolve the conflict between the continental commitment and Britain's wider interests.

Introduction

In recent years scholars researching British defence policy have been preoccupied with certain controversies. They have concentrated, in particular, on the debate as to whether Britain should maintain a continental strategy based on the defence of Europe, and later, commitments under the North Atlantic Treaty Organisation (NATO), or a defence policy which emphasised more a maritime strategy and considerations outside the confines of continental Europe. Another issue of controversy is the development of Britain's independent nuclear deterrent, and the extent to which Britain should rely instead on conventional weapons. An adjunct of this is the importance of the special relationship with the United States in Britain's defence planning, and the extent to which Britain became dependent on American nuclear weapons, especially after 1957. Then there are the claims that British defence policy has been driven by financial restrictions and the dictates of the Treasury.[1]

In considering these debates scholars have sometimes been frustrated in their searches for the original sources. Some have complained about the delays in transferring the minutes of the Chiefs of Staff meetings to the Public Record Office in London – these minutes initially took more than the usual thirty years plus one after the date of the document to arrive – and about the closure for fifty years of the Defence Policy and Global Strategy papers of the early 1950s. Even before the Chiefs of Staff papers were transferred there were often copies of the Chiefs of Staff minutes available in the Foreign Office papers or other collections in the Public Record Office. The Defence Policy and Global Strategy Papers have now

---

[1] See the 'Guide to further reading' for details.

been opened, with a few deletions. There is a wealth of primary material available to the student of post-1945 British defence policy. Even for the period for which the most of the official material remains closed, the published defence White Papers, particularly those from the early 1980s onwards, which are extensive documents with statistical appendages, defence Open Government documents from the Defence Council on debates over the Polaris and Trident missiles, published minutes of the Parliamentary Defence Committee hearings on various matters like the Westland helicopter affair in the mid-1980s, the reports from the National Audit Office on issues such as the control and management of the Trident programme, the parliamentary debates, as well as revealing published diaries of participants, are rich sources.

The primary sources, those which offer the first available information of the event, are the historian's raw material. But it must be remembered that these primary sources do not give an exact record. They are already one remove from the event. It is the duty of the historian to examine the source to see how good a record of the event that source is likely to provide. Witnesses often exaggerate their own role, and this is something the historian has to consider when analysing material. It is often evident in diary accounts. Some accounts are a deliberate distortion.

The primary source, the historical record, is both selective and subjective. Hansard is not an accurate record of what was said in the House of Commons: members have the right to change the text of their speeches. Cabinet minutes, minutes of Chiefs of Staff meetings and the like, are only summaries of what was said. As comparison with diary accounts often reveals, a great deal is left out. Despatches are often sent by officials with particular objectives in mind and distort the account of events accordingly. It is essential to bear in mind the distinction between an 'event', what happened in the past, which is finite, immutable, and unknowable, and the record of that event, the historical fact, which is already at least one remove from that event. What the historian handles is the record.[2]

The historian is also a fallible human being, with his or her own prejudices, and, being a product of a particular society at a particular

---

[2] The classic work on textual criticism is Ch. V. Langlois and Ch. Seignobos, trans. by G. G. Berry, *Introduction to the Study of History* (London, 1898); the modern manual is Jacques Barzun and Henry F. Graff, *The Modern Researcher*, revised edition (New York, 1970).

time, is likely to reflect the prejudices and preoccupations of that time rather than of the time that he or she is writing about.[3]

When selecting material the modern historian is often confronted with the problem of too many sources rather than too few. The Public Record Office, London, is reported to house the British records that have been retained of the Second World War on five miles of shelving. And of course only a small proportion of records are selected for preservation.

Few, if any, today would accept the possibility of finite history. E. H. Carr in *What is History?*, published in 1961, pointed to Lord Acton's hopes at the height of Victorian optimism that the *Cambridge Modern History* he was editing would be the opportunity to 'bring home to every man the last document, and the ripest conclusions of international research'. Acton anticipated that although 'ultimate history' would not be possible in his generation 'we can dispose of conventional history, and show the point we have reached on the road form one to the other, now that all information is within reach, and every problem has become capable of solution'. Carr points to Professor Sir George Clark's comments sixty years later on Acton's beliefs in the introduction to the second *Cambridge Modern History*. Clark argues that historians expect their work to be superseded again and again: 'They consider that knowledge of the past has come down through one or more human minds, has been "processed" by them, and therefore cannot consist of elemental and impersonal atoms which nothing can alter.' Clark explains further that, faced with this, scholars have become sceptical and some have accepted the doctrine that 'since all historical judgements involve persons and points of view, one is as good as another and there is no "objective" historical truth'.[4]

Recent obsessions with systems, the rise and fall of empires, generalisations drawn from the past to apply to the future,[5] make it

[3] See R. G. Collingwood, *The Idea of History* (London, 1961), pp. 205–31; Carl Becker, 'Everyman his own historian', *American Historical Review*, 37, 1931–2, pp. 221–36; Charles Beard, 'Written history as an act of faith', *American Historical Review*, 39, 1933–4, pp. 219–31.

[4] E. H. Carr, *What is History?* (London, 1961), pp. 7–8. See also R. J. B. Bosworth, *Explaining Auschwitz and Hiroshima: History Writing and the Second World War 1945–1990* (London, 1993), pp. 23, 27–30, 45, 107, 137.

[5] Paul Kennedy, *The Rise and Fall of the Great Powers. Economic Change and Military Conflict from 1500 to 2000* (London, 1988); Gordon Martel, 'The meaning of power: rethinking the decline and fall of Great Britain', *The International History Review*, XIII, 1991, pp. 662–94.

important for a student approaching sources to be wary of the temptation of generalisation. If it is acknowledged that it is impossible to find out what happened in the past it is difficult to generalise about what may have happened. The historian may have a general hypothesis to which he or she applies to the sources, but the concern is to use the general hypothesis to discover the unique event.[6]

Some go so far as to assert that lessons can be drawn from a series of unique events that can be applied to the future. But even the great systematiser, Arnold Toynbee, with his study of the rise and fall of civilisations, insisted that because something had happened in the past there was no certainty that it would happen in the future: civilisations were not necessarily destined to decline and disintegrate.[7] The insistence that an event is inevitable is the prerogative of the Marxist school of historians,[8] and maybe those who hold Calvinist beliefs of predestination. Similarly explanations of events in terms of 'causes' have increasingly been questioned, and apart from practising Marxist historians, with their concept of determinism and cause and effect, Western historians have inclined to the use of the word 'origin'.[9]

While keeping in mind Professor Sir George Clark's observations on the limitations of ultimate history, it might be more encouraging when starting to scrutinise documents, and to apply techniques of criticism to them, to remember the observation of Marc Bloch, a member of the French resistance captured by the Nazis who wrote his 'reflections on the nature and uses of history and the techniques and methods of the men who write it' in a prison camp before being executed in 1944: 'The past is, by definition, a datum which nothing in the future will change. But the knowledge of the past is something progressive which is constantly transforming and perfecting itself.'[10] It is, however, essential not to get too carried away, and always to bear in mind the limitations of the exercise. As has been observed in a

[6] Carey B. Joynt and Nicholas Rescher, 'The problem of uniqueness in history', *History and Theory*, I, 1961–2, pp. 151, 153–4.

[7] Arnold Toynbee, abridged by D. C. Somervell, *A Study of History*, I (London, 1947), p. 254.

[8] See Edmund Wilson, *To the Finland Station. A Study in the Writing and Acting of History* (London, 1974).

[9] See Sir Isaiah Berlin, 'Historical inevitability', and Ernest Nagel, 'Determinism in history', in Patrick Gardiner (ed.), *The Philosophy of History* (London, 1974), pp. 161–215.

[10] Marc Bloch, trans. Peter Putnam, *The Historian's Craft* (Manchester, 1992), p. 48.

classic American study: 'What is meant by credibility is not that it actually happened, but that it is as close to what actually happened as we can learn from a critical examination of the best available sources. The historian thus establishes *credibility* or *verisimilitude* (in the special sense of conformity with a critical examination of the sources) rather than *truth*.'[11]

Many of the primary sources which describe the British move towards a continental commitment with the joining of the Cold War in the decade following the end of the Second World War are now freely available. There is an obvious temptation to draw parallels between the defence policy of that period and the one that evolved with the end of the Cold War in the early 1990s: during both periods defence policy reflected Britain's world-wide commitments and the belief that Britain had to play a role disproportionate to its power and resources.

In September 1945, after the conclusion of the war in the Far East with the explosion of the atomic bombs at Hiroshima and Nagasaki, the British Chiefs of Staff decided that the possession of atomic weapons was not likely to make any difference to strategic planning in the immediate future, that the only major enemy in the immediate future was the Soviet Union, and that following the British experience at Mons in the First World War and at Dunkirk in the Second World War British troops should not serve again on the European continent. Land and air support might be permissible, but that was all. The Chiefs of Staff, at a time when Britain's dependence on Middle Eastern oil increased dramatically, moved towards a defence policy based on the three pillars: defence of the United Kingdom and its development as a base for an offensive; defence of the sea lanes; and defence of the Middle East as both an offensive and a defensive base.[12]

This policy, which made defence of the Middle East coextensive in importance with defence of the United Kingdom itself, had to be implemented against the background of Zionist terrorism in the Palestine mandate, designed to wear down British morale. Palestine, together with the Suez base, was the main area of a British military

[11] Louis Gottschalk, Clyde Kluckholm and Robert Angell, *The Use of Personal Documents in History, Anthropology, and Sociology; prepared for the Committee on Appraisal of Research of the Social Science Research Council* (New York, 1945), p. 35.
[12] Public Record Office, London, CAB 128/11, fos 7–8, CM6(47)3, Confidential Annex, 15 January 1947.

presence in the Middle East following the withdrawal from Egypt announced in 1946. After the hanging of two British servicemen and the booby-trapping of their bodies by the Irgun under Menachem Begin, and the subsequent outbreaks of antisemitism in Britain and the widespread disillusionment over the deaths of conscript troops in Palestine, the Cabinet decided on 29 September 1947 that Britain could not stay on in the Palestine mandate and had to withdraw.[13] Britain was able to sustain its strategic policy only because the Americans agreed to uphold rather than undermine Britain's position in the Middle East.[14]

With the joining of the Cold War the refusal to have a continental commitment was challenged by the Chief of the Imperial General Staff, Field-Marshal B. L. Montgomery, early in 1948.[15] It was not until 23 March 1950 that the Chiefs of Staff requested an assurance that Britain would send a corps of two infantry divisions to the European continent if there were a war with the Soviet Union.[16] In October 1950, when the Americans became part of European defence, with the 'Europe first' policy that evolved with the Korean War, instead of just being committed to go to the defence of Europe, British land troops were effectively consigned to the European continent.[17] Indeed it was only on 30 September 1954 that Anthony Eden, the Foreign Secretary, announced that Britain would maintain for an indefinite period four divisions in Europe and the tactical air force. Eden did this following the collapse of the proposed European Defence Community, on which the American administration had based its European policy, to allay threats of an American withdrawal from Europe and to calm French fears about German rearmament.[18] Britain assumed a continental commitment at a time when the development of the hydrogen bomb rendered large bases

[13] See Ritchie Ovendale, *Britain, the United States, and the End of the Palestine Mandate* (Woodbridge, Suffolk, 1989), pp. 181–216.
[14] Public Record Office, London, FO 371/61114, AN4017/3997/45/G, Record of informal political and strategic talks in Washington on Middle East held from 16 October to 7 November 1947, Top Secret.
[15] Public Record Office, London, FO 800/452, fos 19–30, Def/48/5, COS(48)26(0), Memorandum by Montgomery on the problem of future war and the strategy of war with Russia, 30 January 1948; see Ritchie Ovendale, *The English-Speaking Alliance. Britain, the United States, the Dominions and the Cold War 1945–51* (London, 1985), pp. 68–84.
[16] Public Record Office, London, CAB 131/8, DO(50) 5th mtg, 23 March 1950.
[17] Ovendale, *The English-Speaking Alliance*, pp. 218–20.
[18] Public Record Office, London, CAB 127/27 Pt 2, CC62(54)1, Secret, 1 October 1954.

like the Suez base in the Middle East too exposed, and British strategy was moving away from giving the Middle East the priority it had enjoyed at the end of the Second World War.

Over the following two decades British defence planning increasingly emphasised the European priority. In the 1940s the Chiefs of Staff had viewed the Cold War not just in European but in global terms. This was also reflected in the Defence Policy and Global Strategy Papers of 1950, as amended in 1951, and in 1952.[19] In the 1940s and 1950s British conscript troops fought in imperial and colonial wars in Malaya, Cyprus, Kenya and Egypt, and were used in operations in Jordan and elsewhere. Some of these engagements could be viewed in Cold War terms: in Malaya British troops fought the Communist insurgents partly because of the country's strategic significance, to some extent to secure for Britain's economy the dollar earnings from Malaya's rubber and tin, but also to enable an independent Malaya to come into being; after the statement in the House of Commons on 28 July 1954 that 'there are certain territories in the Commonwealth which, owing to their particular circumstances, can never expect to be fully independent'. Britain fought the Greek-Cypriot terrorist organisation EOKA (the Greek initials of the words National Organisation of Cypriot Fighters) to maintain a territory thought to be essential for strategic reasons.[20] But in Kenya British troops were employed to enable the British settlement initiated by the post-war Labour government to continue, a settlement thought to be in the interests of both Britain and Africa; and in Egypt force was used to implement Anthony Eden's vision as Prime Minister seeing the 1950s, and Nasser, through the spectacles he had worn in the 1930s as Foreign Secretary when Mussolini had been allowed to occupy Abyssinia – what Eden saw as the need to stop a dictator when it was desirable and still possible.[21]

In 1961 Britain initiated a successful military operation to prevent an Iraqi invasion of Kuwait, and the following year British troops were involved in quelling revolts in the Aden Protectorates and Aden itself. In 1963 British troops went to the assistance of Archbishop Makarios in Cyprus, and in January 1964 they helped to put down

[19] Ovendale, *The English-Speaking Alliance*, pp. 273–89; William Jackson and Lord Bramall, *The Chiefs. The Story of the United Kingdom Chiefs of Staff* (London, 1992), pp. 283–93.
[20] Brian Lapping, *End of Empire* (London, 1985), pp. 320–2.
[21] See Ritchie Ovendale, *The Origins of the Arab–Israeli Wars*, 2nd edition (London, 1992), p. 182.

mutinies in former British territories in East Africa. On the whole these operations were successful, and members of the armed services began to argue that Britain could play a vital role in what effectively were peacekeeping operations in what became known as 'out of area' ventures. Indeed the Americans indicated to the new Labour government of Harold Wilson in December 1964 that Britain's forces would be more useful to the alliance outside Europe in places like Hong Kong, Malaya and the Persian Gulf than in West Germany.[22]

Initially the new Labour government decided to keep Britain's peacekeeping role East of Suez, but against the background of a crisis over sterling the Secretary of State for Defence, Denis Healey, initiated a defence review which led to the announcement in July 1967 that Britain would withdraw from East of Suez by the mid-1970s. In January 1968 this was brought forward to the end of 1971. Although it had intended to do so, Edward Heath's Conservative government did not reverse the decision: it was advised that local rulers in Arabia would resent the reinstitution of what could be considered a British imperial presence.

The emphasis went right over to the continental commitment: in March 1974 Wilson's second Labour government initiated a defence review designed to maintain the North Atlantic Treaty Organisation as the lynchpin of British security and to reduce commitments outside the alliance. This policy was seriously challenged in 1982 with Argentina's seizure of the Falkland Islands. The Sandys White Paper of April 1957[23] had initiated a British defence policy that moved away from a maritime strategy towards the emphasis on a continental commitment at the expense of safeguarding British interests outside the NATO area. At the time the First Sea Lord, Earl Mountbatten, fought to maintain the Royal Navy, whose future he thought was at stake.[24] Two decades later Enoch Powell criticised the Sandys policy in the House of Commons in January 1977 when he argued that the philosophy and shape of the defence forces needed to be remoulded and primacy given to the maritime element.[25] In the 1980s the Chiefs of Staff developed plans for mounting operations

---

[22] Richard Crossman, *The Diaries of a Cabinet Minister*, I, *Minister of Housing 1964–66* (London, 1976), pp. 93–5.

[23] *Cmnd 124, Defence. Outline of Future Policy* (London, 1957).

[24] Jackson and Bramall, *The Chiefs*, p. 319.

[25] *United Kingdom Parliamentary Debates, House of Commons*, 5th Series, Volume 923 (London, 1977), cols 1468–9.

outside the NATO area.[26] The 1993 Statement on the Defence Estimates with its elimination of the distinction between in and out of area,[27] by implication, aimed to resolve what had been a dilemma in British defence policy since 1945: whether to give priority to the continental (European) commitment or whether to pursue a policy which sustained worldwide commitments.

The other great issue confronting those controlling British defence policy in the post-1945 era was whether Britain should develop its own atomic and later nuclear weapons. The Foreign Secretary of the 1945–51 Labour governments, Ernest Bevin, was determined that Britain should remain a 'great Power'. It needed the bomb to do this, and, when frustrated by the American refusal to honour earlier agreements about post-war collaboration, after the McMahon Act became law on 1 August 1946 in the United States with its restriction on the exchange of nuclear information between the United States and other countries, the decision was formally made by a group of ministers on 10 January 1947 that Britain should build its own atomic bomb. This was a decision taken by a socialist government which feared the Soviet Union.

It was a government which in 1949 opted for the Anglo-American special relationship as the cornerstone of Britain's foreign and defence policy. The Cabinet, though aware of the difficulties of relying on an ally who, as the Palestine experience had shown, could allow a policy inimicable to its own interests as well as to those of its principal ally to be dictated by a minority pressure group, and which had been unreliable on the subject of nuclear collaboration, accepted the conclusion of William Strang's Permanent Under Secretary's Committee that Western Europe and the Commonwealth together were not strong enough to withstand the Soviet menace: Britain had to rely on the United States.[28] It is evident that as early as February 1946 Bevin had opted for the Anglo-American military alliance.[29] It became his ambition to have American troops on British soil as the front line of the United States' defence against the Soviet Union. He

[26] Jackson and Bramall, *The Chiefs*, pp. 426–8.

[27] *Cm 2270, Defending Our Future. Statement on the Defence Estimates 1993* (London, 1993), para. 116.

[28] See Ritchie Ovendale, 'William Strang and the Permanent Under-Secretary's Committee', in John Zametica (ed.), *British Officials and British Foreign Policy 1945–50* (Leicester, 1990), pp. 212–27.

[29] Public Record Office, London, FO 800/451, fo. 44, Def/46/3, Bevin to Attlee, 13 February 1946.

achieved this during the Berlin blockade with the arrival of American B-29 'atomic' bombers on British soil and the subsequent establishment of American bases in Britain.[30] Though the initial B-29s had not been converted to carry atomic bombs, Bevin was elated at the deterrent effect, and in December 1950 regretted that President Harry S. Truman's statement about the use of atomic bombs in Korea had limited that option.[31]

The British Defence Policy and Global Strategy Paper of 1950 envisaged a 'deterrent phase' in the Cold War, one achieved by the American atomic bomb.[32] With the development of the hydrogen bomb and Britain's decision to develop its own version, British defence policy moved more and more away from the conclusions of the Chiefs of Staff as late as January 1947 that it should not be affected by atomic weapons, and towards what became known as nuclear deterrence. This was partly as a result of technical developments and partly a consequence of what the Treasury and others saw as a cheaper option to the massive expense of conventional warfare at a time when the British people were turning inwards and demanding a higher standard of living at home.

The Sandys White Paper of April 1957, which emphasised nuclear deterrence and abolished conscription, was possible only because of the revival of the Anglo-American special relationship by President Dwight D. Eisenhower in the aftermath of the Suez crisis, and his apparent penance over his role in forcing Britain to withdraw from the Suez Canal in November 1956. Eisenhower later described his handling of the Suez crisis as 'his major foreign policy mistake'.[33] Shortly after becoming President Eisenhower had demoted Britain from being the special ally to being merely one among a number of allies.[34] Eisenhower had revived the special relationship at his meeting with the Prime Minister, Harold Macmillan, at Bermuda in

[30] Ovendale, *The English-Speaking Alliance*, pp. 78–80; see generally Avi Schlaim, *The United States and the Berlin Blockade, 1948–1949. A Study in Crisis Decision-making* (Berkeley, California, 1983).

[31] Public Record Office, London, FO 800/465, fos 249–58, FR/50/23, Record of meeting of Attlee and Bevin with French Prime Minister and Minister of Foreign Affairs, Top Secret, 2 December 1950.

[32] *Documents on British Policy Overseas*, Series II, Volume IV (London, 1991), p. 414.

[33] Jonathan Aitken, *Nixon. A Life* (London, 1993), p. 244.

[34] Ritchie Ovendale, 'Egypt and the Suez Base agreement', in John W. Young (ed.), *The Foreign Policy of Churchill's Peacetime Administration 1951–1955* (Leicester, 1988), pp. 135–57, at pp. 138–42.

March 1957. Later, in October of that year, against the background of the panic over the launch of the Soviet sputnik, Eisenhower indicated that the Anglo-American relationship was to be one of mutual interdependence and that the McMahon Act was to be further amended. Britain was able to move over to reliance on American nuclear weapons, obtained at low cost, and – as established at the Nassau meeting between Macmillan and President John F. Kennedy in December 1962 at which Macmillan secured the submarine-launched American missile, Polaris – apparently to maintain the independent British nuclear deterrent.

Harold Wilson's Labour government, while hinting that the British deterrent might not be as independent as was assumed by the Conservatives, in 1966, having taken the decision not to buy the Poseidon submarine system from the Americans, started to collaborate secretly with the Americans on a project called 'Chevaline' to upgrade Polaris. It was feared that the anti-ballistic missile system around Moscow could intercept Polaris, and that the decoy and deceptive techniques envisaged in Chevaline would be necessary. It was only in 1981 that the House of Commons first heard of the Chevaline project when the Conservative Secretary of State for Defence, Francis Pym, announced that the project had by that stage cost around £1 billion.[35] It was a Labour Prime Minister, James Callaghan, who in 1979 offered to deploy cruise missiles in Britain to counter the Soviet intermediate-range SS-20 missiles, and was offered Trident as a replacement for Polaris by the American President, Jimmy Carter.[36]

At this time a division was emerging between the Labour government and the Labour Party on the issue of nuclear weapons. The issue of NATO's deployment of the neutron bomb, a weapon designed to minimise the destruction of buildings, over which Callaghan and Chancellor Helmut Schmidt of West Germany had co-operated with Carter in 1977, roused the long-dormant British peace movements. Carter's unilateral abandonment of the project in April 1978 strained Anglo-American relations. Opinion polls in Britain increasingly reflected unease over the likelihood of a nuclear

---

[35] *House of Commons. Ninth Report from the Committee of Public Accounts. Session 1981–82. Ministry of Defence. Chevaline Improvement to the Polaris Missile system* (London, 1982).

[36] James Callaghan, *Time and Chance* (London, 1987), pp. 554–8; Denis Healey, *The Time of my Life* (London, 1990), p. 456.

war. Membership of the Campaign for Nuclear Disarmament (CND), which had dwindled to just a few thousand after the huge support evidenced in the early 1960s with the Aldermaston marches, grew to around a quarter of a million in late 1981. This pressure resulted in a Labour defence policy from 1980 to 1989 which was contradictory: while committed to full membership of NATO the Labour Party was at the same time pledged to a non-nuclear defence policy which included the manifesto commitment at the 1983 and 1987 general elections that the United States would be required to remove its nuclear weapons from Britain. But after repeated election defeats Neil Kinnock managed to lead his party in 1989 to a policy that proclaimed the retention of nuclear weapons as a way of promoting world-wide nuclear and conventional disarmament.[37]

The Conservative governments of Margaret Thatcher and John Major, while emphasising the need for flexibility in Britain's military response and both fighting and preparing for conventional wars, maintained the British nuclear deterrent. The 1992 defence White Paper made provision for the purchase of four Trident nuclear submarines, sustaining Trident as a central element of British defence policy. The 1993 paper disclosed that three destroyers and frigates as escorts, acting in an anti-submarine warfare role, were required for the nuclear ballistic missile submarine deterrent. The tensions that developed, particularly in the Labour Party, over the maintenance of Britain's independent nuclear deterrent have not led to its being abandoned in the post-Cold War era in favour of a defence policy relying on conventional weapons.

The defence cuts of the 1990s, in some ways precipitated by a domestic economic crisis as well as the perception of the different strategic situation brought about by the end of the Cold War, are symptomatic of a British defence policy which particularly since the time of the Korean War has been driven by economic necessity. With allied intelligence estimates suggesting that North Korea's invasion of South Korea was a Communist strategy designed to entice Western forces to the Far East and so enable Soviet troops to destabilise Western Europe, the British and American Combined Chiefs of Staff recommended a British rearmament programme that would cost £6,000 million over three years. Washington would contribute to this programme, but the extent of American support

---

[37] See Dan Keohane, *Labour Party Defence Policy since 1945* (Leicester, 1993).

was not spelt out. The proposal would have increased defence expenditure from around 6 to 12 per cent of the British gross domestic product (GDP). The sum was reduced to £4,700 million or 10 per cent of GDP by Whitehall. Sterling, however, came under pressure with the nationalisation in May 1950 of the Anglo-Iranian Oil Company and the subsequent need to spend dollars on American oil, as well as with the outflow of sterling precipitated by the United States' stockpiling of raw materials.

When he came to power in October 1951 Winston Churchill initiated an investigation into how to economise on British military commitments. The Defence Policy and Global Strategy Paper of 1952 which was the result was in turn undermined by R. A. Butler, the Chancellor of the Exchequer, determined on further economies, and his Treasury advisers, assisted by Duncan Sandys, the Minister of Supply. On becoming Prime Minister in January 1957 Harold Macmillan chose Sandys to devise a defence policy based on the nuclear deterrent and the abolition of conscription, a policy that would enable huge cuts in defence and the release of skilled man-power into a consumer economy at a time when the British people were clamouring for an increase in the standard of living. Within eleven weeks Sandys had devised a revolutionary programme which he laid before Parliament on 4 April 1957 to general acclaim. This paper, which marked a radical departure from the maritime strategy on which a great deal of British defence had been based in the past, was opposed by Earl Mountbatten, the First Sea Lord. The British move towards a policy of nuclear deterrence was, in many ways, determined by economic necessity.[38]

When Labour returned to power, following the sterling crisis in the autumn of 1964, the Chancellor of the Exchequer, James Callaghan, reduced the defence estimates by 20 per cent, limiting expenditure to £2,000 million (at 1964 prices). This meant a cut of 40 per cent in equipment programmes and the questioning of pro-jects like the fleet carrier CVA 01 and the TSR2 fighter plane, as well as the immediate cancellation of the supersonic version of the Harrier aircraft, the P1154, and a transport plane, the HS681. The defence review that followed, necessitated by these economies, was published in February 1966. The review implied that Britain could carry out major military ventures only in co-operation with its allies;

[38] Jackson and Bramall, *The Chiefs*, pp. 266–321.

with the envisaged withdrawal of the aircraft carriers Britain could no longer mount military operations unless provided with facilities by the appropriate states; and Britain would not maintain defence facilities in an independent state if that state objected. There was still to be a presence East of Suez for a while.

After the general election of March 1966 Harold Wilson, as Prime Minister, was forced to resist a Labour Party parliamentary resolution deploring the continued presence East of Suez. More significant, however, was the seamen's strike and the consequent sterling crisis in July 1966, which resulted in a Treasury demand for a cut in overseas expenditure of £100 million, most of which had to come from defence. This demand was met relatively painlessly with economies made possible by the ending of the campaign in Borneo. But it was not enough: against the background of pressure from the left wing of the Labour Party, and Britain's second application to join the European Economic Community, Denis Healey as Secretary of State for Defence required the Chiefs of Staff to look into British withdrawal from East of Suez. Although the Foreign Office disapproved, the Chiefs of Staff thought withdrawal logical, and with the British economy further afflicted by a drain on dollars needed to buy oil with the closure of the Suez Canal following the Six Day War, the withdrawal East of Suez was announced in a supplementary statement on defence made in July 1967 which envisaged a reduction in the strength of the army from 200,000 to 165,000 by 1971.

Defence retrenchment was briefly halted when the Conservatives were elected in 1970 but, with the dramatic rise in oil prices following Arab use of the oil weapon after the 1973 October War between Israel and Arab states, the miners' strike and the three day week during the winter of 1973–4, Denis Healey, the Chancellor of the Exchequer in Wilson's second Labour government, initiated studies to reduce defence expenditure from 5.5 per cent to between 4 and 4.5 per cent of GDP. With the expiry of the Malta Facility Agreement in 1979 the only world-wide commitments Britain had were in Gibraltar, Hong Kong, the Falkland Islands, Belize and the Cyprus sovereign base areas. With the sterling crisis of 1976, and the cut in government expenditure demanded by the International Monetary Fund which resulted in further reductions in defence expenditure, morale in the services deteriorated and skilled personnel left to go to the private sector where they could earn more money at a time when the government's pay policy meant that service pay had fallen far behind comparable professions. The firemen's strike, which lasted from November 1977 to January 1978, and the subsequent pay award led to a phased increase in service pay.

When the Conservatives were voted back in 1979 the Treasury was able to show that in NATO terms British defence expenditure was on a growth curve of 3.5 per cent per annum. This was first reduced to a 3 per cent annual increase, and then to 21 per cent over a seven year period, eliminating the compounding of the annual interest. The Secretary of State for Defence, John Nott, in his defence White Paper of June 1981 initiated a review which reduced the real growth in defence expenditure to around 7 per cent over the three years since the 1979 general election. This reduction was possible mainly because of cuts in the navy. The Falklands War followed and the experience arrested the drift, initiated by the Sandys White Paper of April 1957, away from a maritime strategy towards the continental commitment at the expense of Britain's interests outside the NATO area. Nott's December 1982 defence White Paper on the lessons of the Falklands campaign referred to the intention to devote substantially more resources to defence with the object of increasing mobility and flexibility.

Returned by the British public in the general election of 1983 in which the Falklands factor had played a part, Mrs Thatcher accepted the NATO 3 per cent growth rate up to the end of 1986. 'Out of area' studies in the subsequent defence statement pointed to the need to improve the flexibility and mobility of British forces assigned to NATO so that they could be used in out-of-area crises like the Falklands War.[39] The 1987 White Paper on defence emphasised the importance of out-of-area operations and emphasised that 'we must aim to use our defence resources as effectively as we can in support of our interests throughout the world'.[40] The defence budget was cut by 5 per cent; it was argued that Michael Heseltine's managerial reforms would increase efficiency and make this possible. In 1984 defence took up 5.2 per cent of the GDP; by 1985 this had fallen to 4.3 per cent.[41]

The 'Options for Change' policy initiated in 1990, possibly to meet financial pressures, possibly to ensure a peace dividend with the

[39] *Ibid.*, pp. 356–435.
[40] *Cm 101–1, Statement on the Defence Estimates 1987* (London, 1987), p. 24.
[41] Jackson and Bramall, *The Chiefs*, pp. 435–7. •

end of the Cold War, and subsequent defence statements in 1992 and 1993 envisaged a drop in defence expenditure by around 12 per cent in real terms between 1990–1 and 1995–6, representing around 3.2 per cent of GDP. It has been argued that for Britain the peace dividend has been negligible.[42] There is, however, the obvious dilemma. Previous defence cuts have often been challenged by events: the announcement of the British withdrawal from East of Suez in 1967 possibly led to disruption in the Gulf area; Nott's cuts in the navy of 1981 were followed by the Falklands War and a return to a maritime strategy; 'Options for Change' was followed by the Gulf War and this emphasised the inherent instability of the post-Cold War world and the dangers of cashing in the peace dividend too early; Britain's commitment to the United Nations operation in Bosnia led to the reprieve of two infantry battalions in 1992.

The financial constraints imposed on British defence policy in the post-1945 era reflect to some extent the changes in its organisation. This period saw an increase in civilian control of the military. The first move in this direction was the White Paper on the Central Organisation of Defence in October 1946, which established a Ministry of Defence. In effect, however, the Chiefs of Staff could by-pass the Minister of Defence, and the three service ministers, who had their independent parliamentary appropriations, could ignore him.[43]

When Harold Macmillan became Prime Minister in 1957 he decided that it was necessary to give reality to the powers of the Minister of Defence to ensure that the envisaged review of defence policy was carried through. Macmillan gave Duncan Sandys authority, subject to the Defence Committee of the Cabinet, to decide the size, shape, organisation and disposition of the armed forces. Further provision was made for the Chief of Staff, Sir William Dickson, to act both as Chief of Staff to the Minister of Defence and as Chairman of the Chiefs of Staff Committee.[44] There was opposition to these arrangements from both the military and Whitehall but Sandys's White Paper of July 1958 on *The Central Organisation of Defence* confirmed the increased powers given to the Minister of Defence, and also made him responsible to the Prime Minister for military operations. The post of Chairman of the Chiefs of Staff

[42] *The Times*, 8 July 1992, Editorial.
[43] Cmd 6923, *Central Organisation for Defence* (London, 1946), p. 6.
[44] Harold Macmillan, *Riding the Storm 1956–1959* (London, 1971), p. 244.

Committee was retitled and became 'Chief of Defence Staff'.[45]

This move towards the centralisation of defence was confirmed in July 1963 when a White Paper was published envisaging a unified Ministry of Defence with authority vested in a single Secretary of State for Defence. The existing service ministries would become Army, Navy and Air Force Departments.[46] These provisions were implemented, and on 1 April 1964 the Defence Council was established, chaired by the Secretary of State for Defence, and responsible for the defence of the realm, which includes the running the armed forces. The Defence Council has as members: the Ministers of State for Defence; the Permanent Under Secretary of State; the Chief of the Defence Staff and the Vice-Chief of the Defence Staff; the Parliamentary Under Secretary of State; the Chief Scientific Adviser; the Chief of Defence Procurement; the Second Permanant Under Secretary of State; the Chief of the Naval Staff; the Chief of the General Staff; and the Chief of the Air Staff.

[45] Jackson and Bramall, *The Chiefs*, pp. 321–2.
[46] *Cmnd 2097, Central Organisation for Defence* (London, 1963).

1

The Three Pillars: defence of the United Kingdom, the Middle East, and the sea lanes, 1945–47

At the end of the Second World War Britain was, in effect, bankrupt. Against the background of the overriding need to rebuild Britain economically, Clement Attlee's Labour government faced a new strategic situation. Jet engines, rockets, guided missiles and the atomic bomb practically eliminated the sea as a significant defence. If the Soviet Union were the most likely enemy, the British navy would be of limited use against a landlocked power. This meant that, despite the financial straits, the army would have to be maintained. In addition Britain had the victor's obligations to occupy Japan, Germany, Austria, Venezia Giulia and Greece. In the end Britain also retained troops for several years in the former Italian colonies, and for a while in south Vietnam and Indonesia. Troops were also needed to keep order against terrorism in Palestine. The Labour governments retained conscription in peacetime. This was seen as necessary. By December 1946 Britain needed 400,000 more troops than had been anticipated; the British military establishment totalled almost 1,500,000. During the fiscal year 1946, 18.7 per cent of men were in military service; in comparison only 10 per cent of American men were under arms. That year Britain's defence expenditure accounted for 18.8 per cent of the national income; in the United States it was only 10.6 per cent. Attlee was even forced to slow down demobilisation.

The Chiefs of Staff were convinced that British armies should not fight again on the European continent. They evolved a military policy which re-established the Three Pillars strategy under which the security of the British Commonwealth depended on: protecting the United Kingdom; maintaining vital sea communications; and securing the Middle East as a defensive and striking base against the Soviet Union. With the withdrawal from Egypt Palestine assumed renewed importance in British strategic thinking. Attlee wanted to withdraw from Palestine, and reach an accommodation with the Soviet Union. The Chiefs of Staff and the Foreign Office opposed this. In January 1947 the Cabinet endorsed the Three Pillars strategy.

Faced with American isolationism, and a refusal on the part of the American administration to continue atomic weapons research collaboration with Britain, the British Foreign Secretary, Ernest Bevin, opted for the Anglo-American special relationship as the way to counter the Soviet threat. As early as February 1946 Bevin had ideas for integrating British and American armaments. The Chief of the Imperial General Staff, Viscount Montgomery, to Attlee's alarm, pursued the military links with the United States in September 1946. The informal Anglo-American military alliance was in effect in place by the end of 1946, ahead of the political alliance.

1.1 *1945 17 August* Attlee's expectations of continued atomic weapons research collaboration with the United States

> Initially the development of the atomic bomb had been regarded as an equal partnership, and President Franklin D. Roosevelt and Winston Churchill had agreed at Quebec in 1943 that the collaboration should continue after the end of the war. This was reaffirmed in 1944. Prompted by the Chiefs of Staff, Clement Attlee, the new Labour Prime Minister, raised the issue with President Harry S. Truman of the United States on 17 August 1945, urging that means should be sought to enable the frank collaboration and exchange of information to be continued.

During the course of the present struggle now brought to a victorious conclusion, there has grown up a close collaboration between the United Kingdom and United States Governments and agencies concerned with the development of new and improved weapons and techniques. Both countries have benefited immeasurably from this frank exchange of information and personnel, and the close collaboration of the British and United States forces in the field have [*sic*] thereby been facilitated.

2. I am strongly of the opinion that means should be sought to enable this frank collaboration and exchange of information to be continued, now that the Japanese war is at an end, as part of the general collaboration between the United States and the United Kingdom upon which the peace of the world ultimately depends. I recognise that there are considerable difficulties to be overcome in that it is difficult to draw a line between developments for defence purposes and those of commercial application, but whatever

arrangement is made will have to pay regard to legitimate commercial interests.

3. I very much hope that you will agree with me that these difficulties should be overcome and that continued collaboration in research and development in the defence field should be authorised. My proposal is that you and I should issue directives authorising this collaboration and instructing our representatives to get together and to work out methods for the solution of the commercial difficulties.

Public Record Office, London, FO 800/512, fo. 8, US/45/7, Attlee to Truman, Telegram No. 8436, Personal and Top Secret, 17 August 1945. *Printed in Documents on British Policy Overseas*, Series I, Volume II (London: HMSO, 1985), pp. 522–3.

1.2   *1945   8 September*   Palestine Committee of the Cabinet and the strategic significance of the Middle East

> At the end of the Second World War the Middle East, to the British military mind, had an importance second only to that of the United Kingdom. The experience of Mons and Dunkirk lingered. British land armies should not again fight on the European continent. That was a job for Europeans. Air and naval support might be possible, but that was all. Britain could not stop the advance of Soviet armies across the continent. Only the United States could do that. The security of the British Commonwealth depended on protecting the United Kingdom, maintaining vital sea communications and securing the Middle East as a defensive striking base against the Soviet Union. The existence of the atomic bomb did not affect this strategy. As strategic planners began to assess the situation after the devastation of Hiroshima and Nagasaki, the British military presence in the Middle East was considerable. Britain exercised sovereignty over the island of Cyprus in the Mediterranean and controlled the port of Aden in the Gulf of Aden.

Great Britain's Position in the Middle East

27. The attitude of the Arab States to any decision which may be reached [on Palestine] is a matter of the first importance. The Middle East is a region of vital consequence for Britain and the British Empire. It forms the nodal point in the system of communications, by land, sea and air, which links Great Britain with India, Australia

and the Far East; it is also the Empire's main reservoir of mineral oil. It contains the area of the Suez Canal and its terminal ports; our main naval base in the Eastern Mediterranean at Alexandria; the oilfields in Iraq and Southern Persia, the port and installations at Abadan, the pipe-line from Northern Iraq to Haifa and the port and installations at Haifa itself; and the whole line of communications by land and air running from the Mediterranean sea-board through Palestine, Trans-Jordan and Iraq to the Persian Gulf.

28. In spite of the importance of the Middle East to the Empire, the island of Cyprus is the only territory in the region over which we hold full sovereignty. Palestine is a mandated territory, and its future is subject in some considerable measure to international agreement. All the other Middle Eastern countries are independent States except Trans-Jordan, whose independence will very soon be equally complete. Protection of our vital interests depends, therefore, upon the collaboration which we can obtain from these independent States.

29. At present, our prestige in the Middle East stands immensely high and our relations with the Rulers of the various States are friendly and cordial. But Arab sentiment is notoriously changeable, and any action by Great Britain which the Arabs deemed injurious to their interests might transform it almost overnight. Unfortunately, the future of Palestine bulks large in all Arab eyes and is a subject of deep moment to the Arab League, the formation of which has greatly increased both the power and will of the individual States to resist the implementation in the Middle East of policies to which they object. To enforce any such policy, and especially one which lays us open to a charge of breach of faith, is bound seriously to undermine our position and may well lead not only to widespread disturbances in the Arab countries but to the withdrawal of the co-operation on which our Imperial interests so largely depend.

Public Record Office, London, CAB 129/2, fo. 20, CP(45)156, Great Britain's position in the Middle East, Secret, 8 September 1945.

1.3 *1945* *4 October* Cabinet conclusions about the strategic significance of the Middle East

The Cabinet endorsed the views of the Chiefs of Staff on the strategic importance of the Middle East.

6. The Cabinet considered a memorandum by the Foreign Secretary . . . submitting recommendations on Middle East policy based on the discussions at the Conference held in September with British Representatives in the Middle East.

The Foreign Secretary [Ernest Bevin] said that, in his view, it was essential to broaden the basis of British influence in the Middle East by developing an economic and social policy which would make for prosperity and contentment in the area as a whole. It would be the object of this policy to remedy the mal-distribution of purchasing power in the Middle East communities and to raise the standard of living of the masses of the people. The Middle East Supply Centre had, during the war, pursued a policy of economic co-ordination throughout the Middle East and the good work which it had started should not be lost. We had to face a threatening situation in Palestine, an agitation in Egypt for the withdrawal of our forces, and the difficulties with France in the Levant. If, however, we could promote economic development and social reform in the area these military and political problems would be more easily solved.

So far as concerned defence, the Chiefs of Staff were considering the possibility of basing in British territory, rather than in Egypt, the forces required for the protection of the Middle East. If this could be arranged, responsibility for the defence of Egypt could be shared by a common agreement which would leave with us the responsibility for the defence of the Suez Canal area. . . .

(b) *The Chief of the Imperial General Staff* [Sir Alan Brooke, later Viscount Alanbrooke] said that the Chiefs of Staff were continuing to examine the problems of defence in the Middle East. While the Mombasa area was in many ways suitable as a base, there were difficulties with regard to road and rail communications and port facilities. A joint arrangement with the Government of Egypt on the lines indicated by the Foreign Secretary would be desirable from the point of view of the defence of the Suez Canal.

Public Record Office, London, CAB 128/1, fos 81–2, CM28(45)6, Secret, 4 October 1945.

1.4 *1946 13 February* **Bevin's choice of the Anglo-American alliance and ideas for integrating British and American armaments**

Bevin chose the Anglo-American alliance. He wrote to Attlee:

3. I believe that an entirely new approach is required, and that can only be based upon a very close understanding between ourselves and the Americans. My idea is that we should start with an integration of British and American armaments and an agreement restricting undesirable competition between our respective armament industries. The next step would be the adoption of parallel legislation in both countries to give their governments real control over the production of arms. The final stage would be the necessary conventions.

Public Record Office, London, FO 800/451, fo. 44, Def/46/3, Bevin to Attlee, 13 February 1946.

1.5 1946 February Attlee proposes withdrawal from the Middle East

The Chancellor of the Exchequer, Hugh Dalton, wrote in his memoirs that some of the Cabinet met at Chequers in the middle of February 1946 and that the Prime Minister introduced an interesting line of thought. Dalton recorded in his diary on 9 March 1946:

Attlee is pressing on the Chiefs of Staff and the Defence Committee a large view of his own, aiming at considerable disengagement from areas where there is a risk of clashing with the Russians. We should pull out, he thinks, from all the Middle East, including Egypt and Greece, make a line of defence across Africa from Lagos to Kenya, and concentrate a large part of our forces in the latter. In view of India's uncertain attitude in future, we should put a large part of Commonwealth defence, including many industries, into Australia. We should put a wide glacis of desert and Arabs between ourselves and the Russians. This is a very fresh and interesting approach, which appeals to me.

Hugh Dalton, *High Tide and After. Memoirs 1945–1960* (London: Frederick Muller, 1962), p. 105.

1.6   *1946   2 April*   The Chiefs of Staff and fears of Russian expansion if Britain move out

Negotiations about the British withdrawal from Egypt and discussions over Palestine took place against the background of the decision of the Chiefs of Staff on 2 April 1946 that if Britain moved out of certain parts of the world in peacetime, the Soviets would move in. The British Chiefs of Staff thought in terms of what later became known as the 'domino theory' when applied to Asia.

Strategic position of the British Commonwealth
Report by the Chiefs of Staff

The Prime Minister has asked for an appreciation of the strategic position of the British Commonwealth in the light of our resources and of modern conditions of warfare.

We have accordingly reviewed our strategical requirements throughout the world, confining ourselves to the fundamental issues involved, so as to present a broad picture of what, from the defence point of view, our vital interests are.

We have related this examination primarily to a possible policy discussed by the Prime Minister. This policy we understand to be that we should concentrate our preparations in peace and our defence in war upon those areas and communications which are vital to us. The implication is that these are the United Kingdom, the American continent and the White Dominions. As a corollary to this we should cut our commitments in other parts of the world which are nearer to the areas of potential conflict. . . .

2. A conflict with Russia is the only situation in which it at present seems that the British Commonwealth might again become involved in a major war. In such a conflict it would be vital to obtain the early and wholehearted participation of the United States on our side. We have, therefore, in the following review, considered our strategical position, having particular regard to the possibility of a war in which the British Commonwealth and the United States, with such allies as they could obtain, were confronted by Russia and her satellites. . . .

10. A policy of concentrating upon the defence of our main support areas would result in adding to the Russian-controlled area and therefore to the war-making potential at her disposal, the following:

24

(a) All Europe less the United Kingdom.
(b) North-West Africa.
(c) The Middle East and North-East Africa.

11. These additions to Russian-controlled territories would have a far-reaching effect on the security of our sea communications. . . .

Under the circumstances, it is doubtful whether the industrial potential of the United Kingdom could be sustained. The threat to its sea communications, coupled with the direct threat by air attack and long-range bombardment from the mainland of Europe, would introduce a grave risk that the United Kingdom would be reduced to a Malta-type existence, contributing little to the main war potential. . . .

Areas of Strategic Importance other than the Main Support Areas

15. From the preceding section it is clear that, if we concentrate our preparations in peace upon our main support areas only, we should be at a very grave disadvantage from the start of a conflict. We must, therefore, consider the extent to which we should maintain our influence in additional areas which will enable us to:

(a) Ensure the security of our main support areas.

(b) Ensure that at the start of a conflict we have sufficient depth in front of our vital areas to allow the necessary time both for us to mobilise our own forces and for the resources of the United States to be brought into play.

(c) Deny to the probable enemy the opportunity of developing in peace important additional resources and war potential.

(d) Attack areas of importance to the enemy at the outbreak of war.

16. In considering our strategic requirements forward of our main support areas, the main factor to be taken into account is the very great numerical superiority in land forces which the Russians would be likely to enjoy in the event of war. . . .

Middle East

20. It may be argued that we can afford to abandon this area, that we should thereby place between ourselves and a potential enemy large tracts of difficult country, and thus compel him, in order to extend his influence further, to fight at the end of long and difficult lines of communication, and that we are unlikely in any case to be able to hold the area in war.

21. The strategic importance of the Middle East lies in the following facts:

(a) It forms the land-bridge between the continents of Europe, Asia and Africa and controls the Eastern Mediterranean and one of the main gateways into the Indian Ocean. It offers therefore the easiest route for a European-Asiatic Power into the African continent.

(b) Control of the area Egypt–Palestine would provide the Russians with a ready-made base area which could be built up by short sea route from Russia itself and which then would enable them to extend their influence both westward and southward into Africa. Such an extension would prejudice our position both in North West Africa, the importance of which we have already shown, and in the Indian Ocean. It would be the first step in a direct threat to our main support area of Southern Africa.

(c) Control of the Middle East will give us the essential depth in front of our main support area in Southern Africa and the highly important area of India to give us the time necessary to organise the defence of these areas.

(d) Of those areas in which we can reasonably expect to maintain our influence in peace, the Middle East is the nearest to the important Russian industrial and oil-producing areas of Southern Russia and the Caucasus. It is also an area from which many other important industrial centres of Russia could be subjected to long-range attack. Our Middle East air bases are therefore a valuable deterrent to Russian aggression.

(e) The immense importance to us of the oil supplies of this area has been stressed in a recent paper by the Minister of Fuel and Power. We should clearly do our utmost to maintain our position in the area as long as we can in war and should certainly do so in peace. . . .

Conclusions

27. We conclude that:

(a) The main support areas upon which our war effort must be based will be the United Kingdom, the American Continent, Southern Africa and Australia. The security of these areas is essential.

Every effort should be made to develop and stabilise India as an additional main support area.

(b) The sea and air communications between our main support

areas in the Atlantic, Pacific and Indian Oceans are of vital importance.

Communications through the Mediterranean, though not vital, are of great importance particularly in relation to economy of shipping.

(c) By concentrating in peace upon our main support areas only, we should place ourselves in an unfavourable strategic situation at the start of any future conflict. We must, therefore, establish and maintain our influence in other areas of strategic importance since we must assume that, if we do not, our influence will be supplanted by that of Russia, whom we must at present consider as our most probable potential enemy.

(d) These additional areas are Western Europe including Scandinavia; the Iberian Peninsula and North West Africa; the Middle East, particularly Egypt and Palestine; India and South East Asia.

If these areas were to fall under Russian domination:

(i) The security of the United Kingdom would be directly threatened.

(ii) Our vital sea communications, particularly those in the Atlantic would not be secure.

(iii) We should lack the essential depth in front of our vital areas to allow the necessary time both for us to mobilise our own forces and for the resources of the United States to be brought into play.

(iv) We should have relinquished to Russia important sources of man-power and war potential.

(v) We should be deprived of bases outside the United Kingdom from which the threat of air action would be a deterrent to Russian aggression and from which we could, at the outset of a war, conduct offensive operations, which might indeed be the only effective means of defence open to us.

28. Our main strategic requirements are based principally upon facts of geography and the distribution of man-power and natural resources which do not change. We consider therefore that the basic principles of our strategy set out above will not be radically altered by new developments in methods or weapons of warfare.

(Signed) Alanbrooke,
Cunningham of Hyndhope,
Tedder.

Public Record Office, London, CAB 131/2, DO(46)47, Strategic Position of the British Commonwealth, Top Secret, 2 April 1946.

1.7 *1946* *1 May* **Britain's frustrated hopes for atomic weapons research collaboration with the United States**

> Britain hoped to construct large-scale atomic energy plants, and Bevin and the Chiefs of Staff discounted Truman's case that a plant in Britain would be vulnerable, presumably either to enemy attack or to sabotage. But the Foreign Secretary was prepared to consider the erection of the plant elsewhere. The American administration, however, lent its support to the McMahon Bill in Congress, which proposed restrictions on the disclosure and exchange of information on atomic energy. The Bill became law on 1 August 1946. Britain felt that this Bill went back on the undertakings that had been given. On 10 January 1947 a group of British ministers decided that Britain should build its own atomic bomb.

Prime Minister. I notice that in his minute to you of April 25th on Atomic Energy, the Dominions Secretary mentions that expert view considers it essential that we should have one pile in this country and a second, e.g. in Canada.

2. I refrained at our meetings with the Dominion Prime Ministers from expressing my view on this question, since I did not know your mind on it. I hold the view strongly that our main atomic energy development ought to be placed at the Victoria Falls. This location is protected, has the necessary water and electric power and would ensure the necessary production. It should enable us to assure the safety of the Pacific and the Indian Oceans.

3. I do hope you will hold out for this proposal. [Jan C.] Smuts [the South African Prime Minister], I think, would agree with it.

Public Record Office, London, FO 800/438, fo. 107, Ate/46/7, Bevin to Attlee, 1 May 1946.

1.8 *1946* *24 May* **Strategic importance of Palestine**

> So far as the Chiefs of Staff were concerned the strategic importance of Palestine could not be questioned.

The conclusion of the Chiefs of Staff in D.O.(46)67 of the 24th May is that we must have full military rights in Palestine. We must be in a position to locate in Palestine any forces which we consider necessary and we must have complete control of the organisation of the defence of the area.

The above conclusion raises two problems – (1) with the Americans; and (2) with U.N.O.

As regards (1) the Anglo-American Committee on Palestine have made recommendations, the implementation of which by us alone would impose intolerable financial and military burdens on this country. . . .

As regards (2), Palestine is a mandate, and we have already said that it is our policy to transform mandates into trusteeships. We have stated that our eventual aim in Palestine was to prepare a trusteeship agreement for that territory. In order to ensure that the Chiefs of Staff's requirements are met, we should have to see that the terms of the trusteeship were satisfactory to ourselves. Under the Charter, the terms of the trusteeship have to be agreed between 'the States directly concerned' who remain to be determined in the case of Palestine. Zionism will make it difficult to get a trusteeship agreement, but if the United Kingdom become sole trustee, it should be possible to meet the military requirements of the Chiefs of Staff.

If it is impossible to reach agreement on the trusteeship, His Majesty's Government presumably would have to continue to administer the country under the existing mandate.

Public Record Office, London, FO 371/52527, E5065/4/31G, Minute by R. G. Howe, Assistant Under Secretary of State at the Foreign Office, 25 May 1946.

1.9   *1946   September*   Collaboration between British and American armed forces

Talks between Field-Marshal Montgomery, by then Chief of the Imperial General Staff, and the American Chiefs of Staff came about partly as a result of the crisis in August 1946 that followed Soviet demands on Turkey for a base in the straits between the Black Sea and the Mediterranean and the subsequent firm stand by the Americans, and partly through a suggestion from the Joint Chiefs of Staff that British representatives should attend their meetings. On 29 November 1946 the Joint Chiefs of Staff approved a British proposal for Anglo-American–Canadian long-term military planning. In Washington, American, British and Canadian military experts discussed arms standardisation, weapons research and common tactical doctrines. Britain had offices in the Pentagon, close to the Joint Chiefs of Staff; the British Joint Staff Mission handled matters of common interest. The Combined Chiefs of Staff, in some ways the only Anglo-American organisation that survived the end of the Second World War, continued until 1949, when the North Atlantic Treaty was signed. Britain and the United States had an informal military agreement by December 1946.

I arrived in the United States on the 10th September. . . .

I saw the President the next morning; we were alone. I opened the conversation by saying that Eisenhower and I considered the time had come to begin discussions covering the whole field of defence. Seeing at once that I was on very receptive ground, I went on to tell the President of [William Lyon] Mackenzie King's [the Prime Minister of Canada] approval. I finally said that if the Heads of State would merely give their approval, the military staffs would get on with the job at once. The President replied without hesitation: 'That's O.K. by me, go right ahead.' . . .

After leaving the White House I went back to Eisenhower and told him of my talk with the President. He was delighted and at once began to arrange for me to meet the American Chiefs of Staff. He had to be careful and so the meeting was to be represented as a social gathering on board the S.S. *Sequoia*. . . .

The next day, the 16th September, we boarded the *Sequoia* for our 'social gathering' on the Potomac. The American Chiefs of Staff were represented by Admiral Leahy who was present in his capacity as Chief of Staff to the President, General Eisenhower, Admiral Nimitz, and General Spaatz. We reached agreement that discussions should begin as soon as possible and should cover the whole strategic concept of the West in a third World War, together with the best way of handling the business of standardisation and combined action. It was agreed that the first meeting might well be held in Washington and that a planning staff from Canada should be included. . . .

And so ended a remarkably successful visit – successful beyond my wildest dreams. It had been established that the continued functioning of the machinery of the Combined Chiefs of Staff was accepted without question by the President and the American Chiefs of Staff. . . .

The fact remained that within a matter of a few days I had managed to obtain the approval of the Heads of State and the Chiefs of Staffs of Canada, America and the United Kingdom to the opening of military discussions on a wide basis, and this should now lead to the unification of the defence policy and plans of the British Empire and the United States before another war was thrust on us. Indeed, such unity might well prevent the outbreak of just such a war.

Bernard Law Montgomery, *The Memoirs of Field-Marshal the Viscount Montgomery of Alamein, K.G.* (London: Collins, 1958), pp. 440–3.

1.10   *1946   October*   **British defence policy planning and management**

> The intention of the White Paper on the Central Organisation of Defence, presented to Parliament in October 1946, was to give the head of the newly created Defence Ministry executive authority. In effect, however, the Chiefs of Staff could by-pass the Minister of Defence, and the three service ministers, who had their independent parliamentary appropriations, could ignore him. The 1946 White Paper outlined the basis for the management and planning of British defence policy in the aftermath of the Second World War.

19. *Outline of New Organisation Proposed.* After reviewing the development of our defence organisation over the last forty years and its practical performance under the test of two major wars, His Majesty's Government are satisfied that there are no grounds for any drastic re-casting of the main structure of the organisation as it exists today. Some changes are, however, required in order to consolidate the advances which have been made in recent years under the compulsion of war or of the threat of war. Above all, experience during these years has shown the need of a Minister who has both the time and the authority to formulate and apply a unified defence policy for the three Services; and it is proposed that this need should be met by the creation of a Minister of Defence.

20. The form of the new organisation proposed may be summarised as follows:

(a) The Prime Minister will retain the supreme responsibility for defence.

(b) The Defence Committee, under the Chairmanship of the Prime Minister, will take over the functions of the old Committee of Imperial Defence, and will be responsible to the Cabinet both for the review of current strategy and for co-ordinating departmental action in preparation for war.

(c) A new post of Minister of Defence, with a Ministry, will be created. The Minister of Defence will be responsible to Parliament for certain subjects . . . affecting the three Services and their supply. In addition, he will be Deputy Chairman of the Defence Committee; and he will also preside over meetings with the Chiefs of Staff whenever he or they may so desire.

(d) The Chiefs of Staff Committee will remain responsible for preparing strategic appreciations and military plans, and for submitting them to the Defence Committee; and the Joint Staff system will be retained and developed under their direction.

(e) The Service Ministers will continue to be responsible to Parliament for the administration of their Services in accordance with the general policy approved by the Cabinet and within the resources allotted to them.

Cmd 6923, Central Organisation for Defence (London: HMSO, 1946), p. 6.

1.11   *1946   1 December*   Attlee and accommodation with the Soviet Union

> Against a background of parliamentary criticism of British policy towards the Soviet Union, Attlee wrote to Bevin, who was in New York, speculating on the extent to which Soviet policy was dictated by expansionism and how far 'by fear of attack' by Britain and the United States.

I do not think that the countries bordering on Soviet Russia's zone viz Greece, Turkey, Iraq and Persia can be made strong enough to form an effective barrier. We do not command the resources to make them so. If it were possible to reach an agreement with Russia that we should both disinterest ourselves as far as possible in them so that they became a neutral zone, it would be much to our advantage. Of course it is difficult to tell how far Russian policy is dictated by expansionism and how far by fear of attack by the U.S. and ourselves. Fantastic as this is, it may very well be the real grounds of Russian policy. What we consider merely defence may seem to them to be preparations for an attack. The same kind of considerations apply to the proposals by the U.S.A. for Air bases in Canada which the Russians might regard as offensive in intention.

I think, therefore, that we have got to be very careful in taking on military obligations in Greece and Turkey when the U.S.A. only gives economic assistance.

There is a tendency in America to regard us as an outpost of America, but an outpost that they will not have to defend. I am disturbed by the signs of America trying to make a safety zone around herself while leaving us and Europe in No Man's Land.

While, I think, we should try to find out what the Americans are prepared to do, we should be careful not to commit ourselves.

Public Record Office, London, FO 800/475, fos 59–60, ME/46/22, Attlee to Bevin, Private and Personal, 1 December 1946.

1.12   *1947   5 January*   **Attlee's opposition to the Chiefs of Staff's 'strategy of despair'**

> Attlee persisted that he wanted to try for an accommodation with the Soviet Union. He sent his thoughts to the Foreign Secretary:

1. The broad conclusions of the Chiefs of Staff and of the Imperial Defence College are:

(a) That the U.K. which is the heart of the Commonwealth is extremely vulnerable to modern attack by long range weapons and that our present knowledge does not provide any effective method of passive defence.

(b) Therefore the only way to prevent such an attack is by a threat of counter attack so formidable that a potential enemy will be deterred through fear of his own losses.

(c) The only possible enemy is Russia.

(d) The only bases from which Russia could be attacked are situated in the Near East.

(e) Therefore the maintenance of British influence and consequently British forces in the Near East are essential to our safety.

(f) As a corollary we must secure our oil supplies in the Near East and endeavour to secure our communications through the Mediterranean, if at all possible.

2. The consequence of this appreciation means heavy military commitments which must be considered in relation to our man power and our economic resources.

It also means that we have to support a number of states in the Near East[:] Turkey, Greece, Iraq, Persia, Lebanon, Syria, Egypt and Transjordan and also to maintain our position in Palestine.

This brings us into a sphere of competition for political and economic influence with the U.S.S.R.

This needs very careful consideration. . . .

7. We, therefore, endeavouring to keep our influence over this congeries of weak, backward and reactionary States have to face the U.S.S.R. organised under an iron discipline, equipped with the weapon of a revolutionary doctrine liable to attract the masses, strategically well placed for penetration or attack and with only a limited number of its key points open to our attack.

8. In order to gain this advantage we shall be committed:

(a) To the maintenance of considerable forces overseas. Two divisions in Palestine. Powerful Air Forces somewhere in the area for a striking force.

(b) The control of the Mediterranean with naval forces and with air forces sufficient to keep the route open. We should have to try to keep the Dardanelles closed. We should have to watch for the development of naval forces in Jugo-Slavia and Albania. We should have only Malta and Cyprus of our own to depend on. We should have to be on good terms with Spain.

(c) In the event of failure which I consider possible if not indeed probable we should have to supply these forces from round the Cape. It is unlikely that we shall be able to use India as a base.

(d) We shall have to spend large sums of money in bolstering up these weak States. Even if we can provide the resources it will take a long time for them to fructify. Meanwhile the U.S.S.R. will not be idle.

9. For the reasons set out above I regard the strategy outlined

above as a strategy of despair. I have the gravest doubts as to its efficacy. The deterrent does not seem to me to be sufficiently strong. I apprehend that the pursuit of this policy so far from preventing may precipitate hostilities.

10. Unless we are persuaded that the U.S.S.R. is irrevocably committed to a policy of world domination and that there is no possibility of her alteration, I think that before being committed to this strategy we should seek to come to an agreement with the U.S.S.R. after consideration with Stalin of all our points of conflict.

Public Record Office, London, FO 800/476, ME/47/1, fo. 2, Attlee to Bevin, Top Secret, 5 January 1947; fos 3–9, Memorandum by Attlee on Near East policy.

1.13   *1947   8 January*   The Chiefs of Staff and the importance of Palestine to Middle East defence

The Chiefs of Staff decided to point out to Attlee the importance of Palestine in any Middle East defence scheme.

Middle East and Eastern Mediterranean
Prime Minister's minute of January 5th.

Points which Chiefs of Staff are Taking Up
1. Importance of Palestine in Middle East defence scheme.
2. Defensive as well as offensive aspect of (1). (Prime Minister apparently considers that Chiefs of Staff dispositions are purely offensive).
3. Chiefs of Staff's plan is to complete small military establishments to be increased in case of emergency, and
4. Importance of retaining friendship of Arab world so as to assure the stability of our bases.
5. Oil stocks in the United Kingdom. (Prime Minister apparently thinks all stocks can now be kept in the U.K.).

Public Record Office, London, FO 800/476, ME/47/2, Note by Dixon based on information from Sir Norman Brook, 8 January 1947, Top Secret.

1.14   *1947*   *15 January*   The Three Pillars strategy

The debate over Palestine resulted in the enunciation of the Three Pillars defence strategy to the Cabinet. This remained the basis of British defence policy until 1952.

The Prime Minister [Clement Attlee] then asked for the views of the Chiefs of Staff on the strategic importance of Palestine as a factor in the defence of the British Commonwealth.

The Chief of the Air Staff [Lord Tedder] said that it was the considered view of the Chiefs of Staff that there were three cardinal requirements for the future defence of the British Commonwealth – (i) the defence of the United Kingdom and its development as a base for an offensive; (ii) the maintenance of our sea communications; and (iii) the retention of our existing position and influence in the Middle East. These were the three vital props of our defensive position: they were all interdependent and if any one were lost the whole structure would be imperilled. Further, these were the fundamental principles of our defensive strategy. They would be unaffected by any technical changes in the nature and use of weapons. Equally, they remained unaffected whatever assumption was made about the potential enemy.

It was essential to our defence that we should be able to fight from the Middle East in war. It followed that we must maintain our foothold there in peace, for without that we should be unable to develop with sufficient speed a strong military position there in war. This did not mean that large forces must be stationed there in peace: we must, however, retain there bases and other facilities which, though lightly manned in peace, could be used for the rapid deployment of greater force against a threat of war. The importance of our ability to move forces rapidly to check a threat of aggression had been strikingly demonstrated by the recent despatch of a force to Basra. In future we should not be able to use India as a base for such deployment of force: it was the more essential, therefore, that we should retain other bases in the Middle East for this purpose.

Palestine was of special importance in this general scheme of defence. In war, Egypt would be our key position in the Middle East; and it was necessary that we should hold Palestine as a screen for the defence of Egypt. In peace, since we had undertaken to withdraw from Egypt, we must be able to use Palestine as a base for the mobile reserve of troops which must be kept ready to meet any emergency throughout the Middle East.

Public Record Office, London, CAB 128/11, fos 7–8, CM6(47)3, Confidential Annex, 15 January 1947.

1.15   1947   27 January   Anglo-Soviet military alliance versus Anglo-American standardisation

When Field Marshal B. L. Montgomery visited Moscow early in January 1947 there was a 'flurry of Anglo-Soviet goodwill'. On 27 January Bevin recorded that Britain should handle the approach of the Russian government in such a way that 'it does not affect our relations with the Americans'.

5. It is therefore necessary to consider the connexion between these proposals for negotiating a revision of the Anglo-Russian Treaty, including the military clauses, and the conversations which the Chiefs of Staff have been having with the Americans about standardisation and exchange of information. I understand that the Chiefs of Staff have heard from Washington that the United States Chiefs of Staff have approved the proposals in the Minister of Defence's paper D.O.(47).6. and are ready to implement them as soon as they hear from us and the Canadians that we are prepared to go ahead. I consider that we should agree to do so. If we now start negotiations with the Russians and at the same time stall on the talks with the Americans, I am afraid that the Americans will conclude that we have gone over definitely to the Russian camp and have lost interest in military co-operation with them. This might mean that we should lose the agreement with the Americans altogether, I feel that this would be a disaster. I believe that arrangements of this kind with the Americans are essential to our security and that they are in no way in conflict with the United Nations Charter. Furthermore, I think that such measures would lead to proper State control of the armaments industry both here and in America and would help to prevent an armaments race between our two countries. They would also be the beginning of a system whereby all armaments were on a common footing throughout the world, thus eliminating the secrecy in military equipment which gives rise to so much suspicion and danger of war.

Public Record Office, London, FO 800/502, fos. 51A–2, SU/47/14, Memorandum by Bevin on the question of an Anglo-Soviet military alliance, and Anglo-American standardisation, Top Secret, 27 January 1947.

1.16   *1947   6 February*   Importance of Palestine with the evacuation of Egypt

> The Chiefs of Staff reiterated their insistence that Britain had to be able to station forces in Palestine. Air bases were needed for imperial communications. With Egypt being evacuated, apart form the Canal Zone, Palestine was the only area able to accommodate Britain's Middle East reserve.

The Chiefs of Staff have considered the Joint Memorandum by the Secretary of State for Foreign Affairs and the Secretary of State for the Colonies on Palestine. . . . Their views were as follows.

2. In their report on the Strategic Requirements for Palestine (DO(47)3), the Chiefs of Staff concluded that:

> 'The preservation of our strategic position in the Middle East as a whole would be gravely prejudiced if our right to station British forces in Palestine were not retained.'

This view was endorsed by a Staff Conference, presided over by the Prime Minister on the 13th January.

The Chiefs of Staff entirely adhere to the above quoted opinion.

3. Turning to paragraph 11 of the Joint Memorandum, the Chiefs of Staff feel that there are two basic principles to be preserved. First, it is essential that during the interim period of Trusteeship, we should retain our military rights in Palestine, and secondly, we should take steps to ensure that thereafter, we can acquire our military rights in Palestine.

4. The Chiefs of Staff note that if acquiescence to the plan by neither of the two parties is in prospect, the only course then open to His Majesty's Government would be to submit the problem to the United Nations, but making no positive recommendations.

5. The Chiefs of Staff consider that from the military point of view, this would almost certainly entail the loss of all, or practically all our military rights in Palestine within a very short space of time. This contingency is envisaged in paragraph 11 of the Joint Memorandum.

6. Finally, the Chiefs of Staff consider that the setting up of a time limit to the period of Trusteeship of five years, has dangers from the military point of view. Within that period, it is unlikely that a stable State will be set up in Palestine with whom we could negotiate a satisfactory Treaty. For this reason therefore, the Chiefs of Staff would prefer that the period of Trusteeship should be left indefinite, but that it should be subject to review, say in five years time.

Public Record Office, London, PREM 8/627, Pt 6, COS161/7, Note by L. C. Hollis, 6 February 1947.

1.17   *1947   19 September*   The Chiefs of Staff and withdrawal from Palestine

The United Nations Special Committee on Palestine, in a majority report, recommended in effect the partition of Palestine and the creation of a separate Zionist state. In a memorandum of 18 September the Chiefs of Staff emphasised again that Britain's strategic position made it essential that the goodwill of the Arab states, and the Muslim world as a whole, was retained. The final report of the Joint Planning Staff, dated 19 September, argued that Britain's position in the Middle East and the possibility of recovering some of the military requirements would depend on the extent to which the British withdrawal from Palestine could be made acceptable to the Arab world.

14. We conclude that:

(a) If the announcement of our intended withdrawal induces the Arabs and Jews to co-operate and further, if the two communities invite us to assist them in forming a new constitution for the country, we would be well placed to satisfy our strategic requirements.

(b) Should this not occur the extent of our short term military problem will depend on whether:

(i) We cease immediately to administer Palestine and confine ourselves to keeping such order as is necessary in order to ensure our withdrawal and then only in those portions of the country in which we may concentrate whilst effecting that withdrawal.

In this event we shall be faced with a difficult military operation of withdrawal with accompanying loss in life and property, but reinforcements would not be required.

(ii) We announce a specific date after which we shall cease to administer the country and will commence our withdrawal, but up to that specific date we endeavour to maintain law and order throughout the whole country.

In this event very substantial reinforcements will be required but the continued maintenance of law and order might provide an eleventh hour opportunity for an Arab and Jew settlement.

(c) After our withdrawal the state of Palestine would be chaotic and we will fail to obtain our military requirements. In addition we will lose our oil installations in that country.

(d) The final effect of our position in the Middle East and, hence, the possibility of recovering some of our military requirements, will depend on the success with which our withdrawal can be made acceptable to the Arab world.

Public Record Office, London, FO 371/61789, JP(47)131 (Final), Report by the Joint Planning Staff on the implications of withdrawal from Palestine, Top Secret, 19 September 1947.

1.18   *1947   16 October – 17 November*   Agreement with the Americans over the Middle East

> At this point the Americans began to acknowledge to Britain the importance, for the West, of Britain's strategic position in the Middle East. Informal political and strategic talks were held in Washington between British and American officials. The reason for these meetings was the American fear of the repercussions of the withdrawal of British troops from Greece. Bevin did not want a combined Anglo-American policy for the Middle East: the Foreign Secretary still saw it primarily as an area of strategic and economic interest to Britain. Both Truman and the British Cabinet endorsed the recommendations of the officials, though there was no formal agreement.

On the instructions of their respective Governments, United States and United Kingdom representatives, including Service advisers, have reviewed the strategic, political, and economic problems in the Middle East, as well as certain strategic and political problems in the Eastern Mediterranean.

The conversations opened on October 16th and closed on November 7th, 1947. . . .

As a result of these conversations, the United States representatives have decided to recommend the adoption of a policy towards the area based on the general principles set forth below. The United Kingdom representatives have likewise indicated their intention to recommend to their Government a policy based on the same principles.

1. The security of the Eastern Mediterranean and of the Middle East is vital to the security of the United States and of the United Kingdom and to world peace.

2. This policy can be implemented only if the British maintain their strong strategic, political and economic position in the Eastern Mediterranean and the Middle East, including the sea approaches to the area through the Straits of Gibraltar and the Red Sea, and if the British and American Governments pursue parallel policies in that area.

3. It follows from the above that both Governments should endeavour to prevent either foreign countries, commercial interests, British or American or other, or any other influences from making capital for themselves by playing off one of the two countries against the other in the Eastern Mediterranean and the Middle East. It should be the parallel and respective policies of the two Governments to adopt the general principle that they will endeavour to strengthen each other's position in the area on the basis of mutual respect and co-operation. It should be contrary to the policy of either Government to make efforts to increase its country's influence at the expense of the other. Likewise, the policy of the two countries should be to strengthen and improve each other's position by lending each other all possible and proper support. This support should also apply to the retention or development of strategic facilities, including civil air development.

Public Record Office, London, FO 371/61114, AN4017/3997/45/G, Record of informal political and strategic talks in Washington on Middle East held from 16 October to 7 November 1947, Top Secret.

2

The English-speaking alliance: defence policy and global strategy, 1948–51

Bevin was the architect of the Western alliance. He evolved a global strategy under which the democratic nations, Britain, the European democracies, the United States and the Dominions should co-operate to meet the Soviet threat. With the Americans moving towards joining their first peacetime 'entangling alliance' (the North Atlantic Treaty) there was division between the Chiefs of Staff as to whether British troops could be committed to the European continent again. The defence of the Middle East remained of cardinal importance, and Commonwealth assistance was seen as being essential. In the Chiefs of Staff papers on defence policy and global strategy of 1950 and 1951 the line was extended from the Middle East and the United Kingdom to part of the European continent. The Communist uprising in Malaya made the Cold War in Asia a reality for Britain in 1948. But in June 1950 the Chiefs of Staff argued that the front line of the Cold War in Asia lay in Indochina. They hoped that the Pacific Dominions would play a role in Asia. Malcolm MacDonald, the British Commissioner General in South East Asia, enunciated the domino theory for Asia long before President Dwight D. Eisenhower.

With the American stand on the outbreak of the Korean War it seemed to Britain that the United States was finally prepared to face up to its world-wide responsibilities. The *pax Britannica* became in effect the *pax Americana*. Although the Chiefs of Staff were reluctant to send troops, Britain did so following the advice of the British ambassador in Washington, Sir Oliver Franks, that in Korea the American government and people had 'instinctively followed their high destiny in the world', that they felt 'lonely', and that Britain should offer to send land forces to reassure them. In early 1951 an anti-American revolt led by John Strachey was quelled and the 1949 conclusion of William Strang's Permanent Under Secretary's Committee reaffirmed: Britain, the countries of Western Europe and the Commonwealth could not stand up to the Communist threat on their own. The full participation of the United States was 'essential to sustain the free world which Soviet Russia is trying to undermine'. What Britain had to do was to 'exert sufficient control over the policy of the well-intentioned but inexperienced colossus on whose co-operation our safety depends'. The Labour government felt that it was helped in this by the responsibilities undertaken by Australia and New Zealand working with the United States in the Pacific. The tripartite pact, ANZUS, was regarded by Attlee and most of his colleagues as being in line with their idea of the evolution of the modern Commonwealth in which member states would take the lead in areas of their particular interest.

2.1 *1947   17 December* Bevin's plan for an association of Western democratic countries and the Dominions

> On the evening of 17 December Bevin outlined the gist of a policy that he was formulating to deal with what Walter Lippman, the American columnist, a few months earlier had described as the 'Cold War'.

The Secretary of State [Ernest Bevin] said that the problem was to decide what we should now do. He had discussed the position with M. [Georges] Bidault [French Foreign Minister] that morning. His own idea was that the problem should not be isolated into a mere quarrel between the western Powers and the Soviet Union. The issue, to use a phrase of the American Ambassador's, was where power was going to rest. His own idea was that we must devise some western democratic system comprising the Americans, ourselves, France, Italy etc. and of course the Dominions. This would not be a formal alliance, but an understanding backed by power, money and resolute action. It would be a sort of spiritual federation of the west. He knew that formal constitutions existed in the United States and France. He, however, preferred, especially for this purpose, the British conception of unwritten and informal understandings. If such a powerful consolidation of the west could be achieved it would then be clear to the Soviet Union that having gone so far they could not advance any further. . . .

The Secretary of State said that they would also have to consider the problem of security in which France was even more vitally interested than we were. There had been some idea of a three-Power treaty on the lines of the original Byrnes Treaty. He himself thought it might be better to have some treaty or understanding which also brought in Benelux and Italy. The essential task was to create confidence in western Europe that further communist inroads would be stopped. The issue must be defined and clear. . . .

Summing up, the *Secretary of State* said that he now felt that the spiritual consolidation of western civilisation was possible, and France could then come back as a great Power. The form in which it should be done required more study and nothing would be lost if we spent a few days in discussions between our officials. He had in mind confidential Anglo-American discussions on the same lines as the recent talks we had had about the Middle East. But there should above all be no public pronouncements about future plans until we had our ideas clear.

Foreign Relations of the United States 1947, II (Washington: United States Government Printing Office, 1972), British memorandum of conversation, undated, pp. 815–17.

2.2   *1948   30 January*   Montgomery and future war with the Soviet Union

Montgomery, the Chief of the Imperial General Staff, questioned the premiss of British defence policy agreed to the previous year.

Chiefs of Staff Committee
The Problem of Future War and the Strategy of War with Russia
Memorandum by C.I.G.S.

It is clear that in any future war which we can at present envisage, the enemy would be Russia.

We must therefore examine the problem and must set out, and agree, the broad lines or a strategy for the British Commonwealth in the event of war with Russia. Until this is done, we shall make no progress in our work. . . .

The enemy at the Gates

7. It is now clear that in any future war which we can at present envisage, the enemy would be Russia.

In view of existing conditions in Russia it is unlikely that such a war would break out before about 1957, and possibly not before 1960.

If we are to survive such a conflict we must be prepared and ready; now, as never before, real preparedness is vital to survival.

We must therefore examine the problem and must set out, and agree, the broad lines of a strategy for the British Commonwealth in the event of a war with Russia.

In this memorandum the problem, is dealt with in relation to some date between 1957 and 1960; but our preparations must take into account the possibility of an earlier outbreak.

The problem is urgent because the decisions we reach will affect the organisation of our national forces, now under review. . . .

Development of our Strategy

29. Provided we can retain the necessary air bases, we should from the outset be able to make use of our technical superiority to exert very considerable pressure upon Russia. In the initial stage this will be done almost exclusively by air action, the effectiveness of which will depend upon the use of atomic weapons and upon arrangements to bring American air forces into action at the very beginning and in advance of other forces of U.S. assistance.

The vital bases from which this air action must be launched are:

North-west India.

The Middle East.

The United Kingdom.

30. Following the initial stage, the next step will be for our allies, particularly the U.S. and Dominions, to build up their strength in order that, with them, we may go over to the general counter-offensive.

Where the emphasis of this build-up will be and therefore the shape and direction of the counter-offensive, will depend greatly on the results of the initial stage, i.e.

(a) Whether the Western Union has held;

(b) Whether the situation of the U.K. is such that it can form a main offensive base.

(c) The situation in the Middle East. . . .

Conclusions

32. In order to be successful in the initial stage we must:

(a) Be ready to exert our maximum effort at the start.

(b) Reduce the length of this stage to a minimum by ensuring the earliest possible entry of the United States into the War.

(c) Build up a strong Western Union and have an agreed strategy that the nations of this Union will fight as far east as possible e.g. on the Rhine.

(d) Organise the defence of the U.K. so that it can survive even if the Western Union does not hold.

(e) Keep open the Atlantic communications and do our utmost to keep open those through the Mediterranean.

Persuade the U.S.A. that whether she is in the war from the outset or not, she will allow no 'monkeying about' by any potentially hostile power in the Atlantic or Pacific oceans. This would help us enormously.

(f) Ensure that we have sufficient strength from Commonwealth resources to hold the position in the Middle East until American aid can become effective.

(g) Keep on good terms with the Arab countries. The more Treaties we can have with Arab countries the better.

Public Record Office, London, FO 800/452, fos 19–30, Def/48/5, COS(48)26(0), Memorandum by Montgomery on the problem of future war and the strategy of war with Russia, 30 January 1948.

2.3   *1948*   *2 February*   **Britain and the continental commitment**

Sir John Cunningham, the First Sea Lord, warned the Chiefs of Staff that it had been Britain's traditional policy in the past to avoid continental commitments: 'Twice in the past we had given a guarantee to assist a continental nation to the limit of our power by the provision of land forces. On both occasions we had suffered severely, first at Mons and more recently at Dunkirk.' But Montgomery insisted that the Western Union powers alone would not be able to stop the Russians from overrunning Europe. The Western Union had to have the full assistance of Britain and the British Commonwealth. He insisted that a Western Union could be created and supported only if Britain gave 'a guarantee to support those countries to the limit of our power by the provision of land sea and air forces'. Because of the implications of this difference of opinion Tedder referred the matter to A. V. Alexander, the Minister of Defence.

At the Chiefs of Staff today we discussed what brief should be given to our representative should he be required to go to Washington for talks on policy in Western Europe.

The broad strategy in [the] event of a war with Russia is set out in D.O.(47) 44 which was approved at a Staff Conference with the Prime Minister on 11th June, 1947. In this paper we recommended that 'every effort should be made to organise an association of Western European Powers, which would at least delay the enemy's advance across Europe'. . . . We also said 'We must encourage the building up of a strong Western Region of Defence, with France is its keystone, and ensure that Germany does not become a Russian satellite'. . . .

On the basis of that memorandum separate estimates were prepared of the land, sea and air forces required to implement that policy. These estimates were subsequently costed and totalled over £1,100 million for an average year.

That policy and those estimates allowed for land/air operations in [the] Middle East but *not* on the continent of Europe.

Today's discussion has re-introduced the question as to whether or not we should, in addition, commit ourselves to, and provide for, land operations in Western Europe, and showed a divergence of opinion between the C.I.G.S. [Montgomery] on the one hand and First Sea Lord [Sir John Cunningham] and myself on the other, which we were unable to resolve.

We are entirely agreed as to the importance of giving all possible help to the West European Powers: the steps already taken towards integrating the Air Defence of France, Belgium and Holland with our own are consistent with this policy.

C.I.G.S. holds that we should now decide, and tell the Americans, that, irrespective of any American plans, we intend to support the Western Powers on the Continent with all our forces: that unless we do this the Western Union will collapse.

The First Sea Lord and I consider it premature to come to such a decision. In our view, our policy regarding operations in Europe can only be decided in collaboration with the Americans, and in any case a policy of engaging in a Continental war must first be related to its effect on our ability to meet our other commitments. We therefore consider that our representative should discuss with the Americans our mutual support of the Western Union without in any way committing us to specific land operations in Europe.

47

Public Record Office, London, FO 800/452, fo. 46, Copy of a minute from
the Chief of the Air Staff to the Minister of Defence dated 2 February 1948.

2.4 1948 *4 February* Attlee's opposition to a continental commitment

On 4 February Attlee, Bevin and A. V. Alexander, the Minister
of Defence, met the Chiefs of Staff.

The Prime Minister [Clement Attlee] said that he would like first to
hear the views of the Chiefs of Staff.

Lord Tedder [Chief of the Air Staff] recalled that in May 1947, the
Staff Conference had approved a paper on Future Defence Policy
(D.O.(47) 44) in which the basic requirements of our strategy had
been defined as the defence of the United Kingdom and a firm hold on
the Middle East – with the development of those two areas as
offensive bases – and the control of sea communications. Operations
with land forces on the Continent at the outbreak of war had not
been contemplated. Following agreement on this policy, the Chiefs
of Staff had made an estimate of the forces necessary to implement it,
as a result of which it was found that the annual cost of the defence
policy would be some £1,100 million. Consequently, the forces had
had to be drastically cut. He and the First Sea Lord, therefore
considered that it would prove both financially and economically
impossible to place an army on the Continent on the outbreak of
war, especially as in any future war we should have to be prepared
for full-scale operations from the beginning. He pointed out that it
was not only additional land forces that would be required; additional supporting air forces would also be required. Furthermore it
was open to doubt whether it was militarily sound to attempt to hold
an enemy, with such predominant superiority in man power, on the
Continent.

On the other hand, the Chiefs of Staff had been in favour of 'a
strong Western Region of Defence, with France as its keystone' but
he thought our support to such a Western Union should be limited, in
Western Europe, to naval and air support, both of which would be of
great value. Military assistance by the United Kingdom to a Western
Union must be determined by what we could afford. We could
provide a great deal of advice on organisation and training in all

48

arms. The Navy could and was doing much to reorganise, train and equip the French navy so that joint operations would ultimately be possible. The R.A.F. were doing much the same, and discussions had proceeded on the integration of air defence systems. The Army, in particular the C.I.G.S., was doing much in advising the French on how to rebuild their Army. All this action was an assurance of our full support, but he could not believe the Western Union would collapse if we withheld a specific promise to fight on land on the Continent.

Sir John Cunningham [First Sea Lord] agreed with the Chief of the Air Staff. Any contribution we might make would be so small, when compared to Continental armies, that its provision would be indecisive. Our traditional policy was to encourage and assist our Continental allies to provide land forces but to refrain from engaging in any land operations ourselves at the outset, in order to leave ourselves free to wield our maritime power. Nowadays, of course, we could use air power as well, and he feared that any commitment to engage in land operations was bound to detract from our air and sea power. The only times that we had broken away from our traditional policy had led to the tragedies of Mons and Dunkirk.

Lord Montgomery [Chief of the Imperial General Staff] said that he took the opposite view from that expressed by the Chief of the Air Staff and the First Sea Lord. He would, however, like to make it clear that he envisaged only defensive action with land forces on the Continent. Our main weapons for winning the war must be over-whelming air power and he regarded any land offensive to invade Russia from the west as out of the question. But a successful defence of the Rhine would be of immense value to the defence of this country and our sea communications. Furthermore, we should need bases on the Continent from which to develop our air power. He did not think any Western Union could be achieved unless we joined in with land forces, for France and the Benelux countries needed vigorous leadership before they would plan successfully to defend themselves. He had made some preliminary study of what forces would be required for a European alignment and had concluded that the Rhine was the most practicable one. He estimated that Russia would not be able to deploy more than thirty-three Divisions on the Rhine a fortnight after the outbreak of war, or more than seventy-three a month after the outbreak. To hold an attack of this order on the Rhine would require twenty-three Divisions by D+14 and forty-eight Divisions by D+30. From his contacts with the French he believed that France alone could provide thirty Divisions on the outbreak of war. He was convinced that Western Europe had enough manpower to keep the enemy out, provided their forces were properly organised, trained and led. They would have to be equipped mainly from the United States. He did not think more than two divisions would be required from this country and this force could be provided from the army we were already planning, for he had always foreseen that two divisions would have to go overseas at the outbreak of war. All that would be required before war broke out would be some additional administrative backing.

The Prime Minister said that previously the Staff Conference had accepted the fact that the whole of Europe might be overrun by the enemy – for they had been informed that the Western Powers would be very weak – and he was disturbed at this new idea that we might send land forces to the Continent. He had understood that our conception had been to develop a counter-offensive from the Middle East. Considerable land and air forces would be required in the Middle East to do so and he did not see how we could support forces on the Continent as well. Previous experience had shown how Continental commitments, initially small, were apt to grow into very large ones. In any case he did not think that the countries of a Western Union would be much encouraged by the offer to help them with land forces if it transpired that our contribution was to be limited to only one or two Divisions.

He was also disturbed at the suggestion in the paper by the Chief of the Imperial General Staff that we ought to build up the strength of Germany once again. He thought it dangerous to hold that Russia was the only potential enemy, and he suggested that the Chiefs of Staff might have expressed the same view in 1922. Our defence policy should not be too rigid; a future world war need not necessarily begin in Europe, for it might break out in the Far East between Russia and America; nor did he like the conception of holding a specific line on the Continent. For all these reasons, he was opposed to giving any definite assurance as to how we should participate in a future war; in any case he would like to know what American intentions were.

The Secretary of State for Foreign Affairs [Ernest Bevin] said that he had held up the projected talks in Washington for the time being because the Americans had not yet made up their minds as to what their own policy would be and he did not want to begin discussions on any false assumptions. Our aim must be to prevent war; he did not want to repeat the mistake that had been made before the last war when the Government of the day had failed to provide forces either to prevent war or for proper defence. When war had broken out we should not again have a breathing space in which to build up our strength so we must be ready beforehand and America must be prepared to come in at once. He intended to make it clear to the Americans that we could not act as a mercenary army or defensive outpost for them. He believed that American military authorities were already aware that their security lay in taking action at once wherever it might be.

His approach to the problem of the creation of a Western Union was somewhat different from that of any of the Chiefs of Staff. He preferred to think of the forces of the Western Union as being one force. He thought the Western Union had sufficient manpower to withstand attack and that the way to work out what forces they could provide should be on a budgetary basis. National pride must be overcome and all their resources must be pooled. He believed in fact that there was already a close link between [the] French and British navies and he would like to see the same with the air forces. An approach on these lines would lead to the result that the continental countries would provide the bulk of the manpower for the land forces.

He had always envisaged that the Rhine might be a dividing line between the Western democracies and their opponents, but he thought that this was not the way in which to approach the problem. The first step should be to see what forces could be provided by the method he had suggested, and then to see how best they could be used. If, when the forces had been worked out, we found that we had land forces to spare, he had no fundamental objections to their fighting on the Continent. He would like the Chiefs of Staff to consider how the forces of the United Kingdom, France, the Benelux countries and possibly Italy should be organised and rationalised so as to form one effective whole. He would then make America face the fact that they had got to be in any future war from the beginning. Mr. [George] Marshall [Secretary of State] had already spoken to him of the possibility of rationalising the British and American forces, for the full weight of taxation to support the Marshall plan was likely to lead to cuts in their present expenditure on defence.

Defence arrangements however formed only one facet of the Western Union as he saw it. He was trying to arrange for close links between the countries concerned in banking, finance and currency, and for economic links with Africa and with the Commonwealth. Collaboration in defence would be complementary to all these.

The future of Germany caused him much concern for both east and west were now being forced into a position of courting Germany and we might find it impossible to avoid building her up again until once again she became a menace. This was another reason for organising some sort of regional defence organisation in Western Europe which might perhaps be framed within the Charter of the United Nations.

The Minister of Defence [A. V. Alexander] said he favoured the Foreign Secretary's approach to Western Union military collaboration on a budgetary basis. He had thought the Chief of the Imperial General Staff had made out a strong case for being prepared to send land forces to the Continent to ensure formation of a Western Union. But he believed the estimate of forces required might prove optimistic and, having regard to the present economic outlook, he feared that we might not even be able to maintain our present cadres. He thought that France and the Benelux countries might find provision for defence equally difficult and that we should have to make it clear that in planning joint defence with them that we were thinking a number of years ahead. He thought it important to prevent Europe being overrun, for with an enemy in France, our naval ports would suffer severe attack and we would have much difficulty in sustaining our production. . . .

In further discussion it was decided that the conception of sending land forces to the Continent at the outbreak of another war could not be accepted as part of our defence policy without further study but our approach to this problem should be on the lines suggested by the Foreign Secretary. As the first step towards this, the Chiefs of Staff should prepare an estimate of the forces that would be required in peace if we were to be ready to send a force of the order of two divisions, with supporting air forces, to the Continent at the outbreak of war.

The Staff Conference:

(a) Took note that the proposed talks in Washington on defence arrangements in connection with a Western Union were postponed for the time being.

(b)   Took note that, without further study, no change would be made in our defence policy to include the conception of taking part in land operations on the Continent on the outbreak of war.

(c)   Invited the Chiefs of Staff to examine and report their recommendations on very broad lines as to the organisation and rationalisation of the armed forces to be contributed by Western European Nations for the Defence of the Western Union, using the assumptions recorded in discussion.

(d)   Agreed that in the course of the examination in (c) above there should be included an estimate of the extra commitment involved in the provision of two divisions to take part in a continental land campaign at the outbreak of a war.

Public Record Office, London, FO 800/452, fos 47–52, Def/48/7, COS(48)16, 4 February 1948.

2.5   1948   22 March–1 April   The Pentagon talks and the involvement of the Americans in Western defence

Delegates from Britain, Canada and the United States met in the Pentagon between 22 March and 1 April. The Americans blocked French participation on the grounds of security. One of the British delegates, however, was Donald Maclean, the Soviet spy, and it seems from an article in the Polish press of 4 April that the Soviets knew what went on. Bevin's triple system of alliances was abandoned. It was evident that if the United States were to join any defence system it would have to be in association not only with certain selected Western European democracies but if practicable with all of them. If possible, Italy would have to be admitted. Furthermore, a defence organisation was eventually envisaged under Article 51 of the United Nations charter which acknowledged the right of individual and collective self-defence, covering all the Middle Eastern states and Greece. The Americans also wanted further defence agreements under this article covering South East Asia and eventually the whole of the Far East. In the end the issue focused on whether the Americans should propose a collective defence agreement for the North Atlantic area as a whole or whether a presidential declaration of support of the Western European democracies would be enough. Bevin thought that the Russians would not be deterred by a presidential declaration, and in any case Britain would be lucky if Truman and the leaders of the Senate pronounced in favour of 'a treaty binding the United States for the first time in her history to accept positive obligations in the way of the defence of her natural associates and friends'. Bevin reported to Attlee:

You will remember that on . . . 10th March you approved my telegram No. 2768 of that date to [Lord] Inverchapel [British ambassador to the United States] on the question of our next moves in the organisation of security. We invited the Americans to enter into secret talks with ourselves and the Canadians in order to examine my proposals for American support of the Five Power Treaty, the creation of an Atlantic defence system and possibly a Mediterranean system. . . .

2. I now attach for your information . . . a copy of the final document which the United States negotiators agreed to refer to their political chiefs as a State Department paper, making no reference whatever to any conversation with the Canadians and ourselves. *I would emphasise most strongly that the Americans rely on us to see that no whisper of these conversations gets out from this end*, and I need hardly say that if there were any such leak the result might be fatal so far as the proposals for any defence arrangements are concerned. In any case we are not, of course, committed by the attached paper, though we have expressed general approval of it as something which the Americans might suitably put up to their chiefs. When and if it is approved by the President and by the Senatorial leaders concerned it will represent the instructions to the United States representative at the meeting which is shortly to take place in Washington between the United States, United Kingdom and France and Benelux. The Americans have told us, however, that in the process of getting agreement it is quite possible that the present paper may suffer material changes, and in any case the chances of eventual agreement by the United States Government on a proposal for a Treaty are now reckoned as little better than fifty fifty.

3. Though you have been following the correspondences yourself, I should like to remind you very shortly how the present situation has developed. When I sent my telegram No. 2768 I was thinking broadly of a triple system, namely:

(i) The United Kingdom–France–Benelux system with United States backing. (This of course blossomed out into the Five Power

Treaty signed at Brussels.)

(ii) A scheme of Atlantic Security 'with which the United States would be even more closely concerned'. (You will remember in this connexion the anxiety expressed to us by the Norwegians early in March about the soundings which the Soviet Government had begun to make in relation to Norway, which seemed rather similar to their renewed pressure upon Finland.)

(iii) A Mediterranean security system which would particularly affect Italy.

4. When these problems were thrashed out in the discussions in Washington, however, the Americans represented strongly:

(a) that the United States were not prepared to accede to the Five Power Treaty, though they were prepared to issue some residential declaration assuring support to the five countries if attacked;

(b) that the members of an 'Atlantic' system which included the United States would consequently receive a far wider assurance of United States support than any member of the Five Power group which was not in the 'Atlantic' system;

(c) that in these circumstances it was fairly clear that if America was going to come into a defence system at all it would have to be in association, not only with certain selected Western European democracies, but if possible with all of them;

(d) that this being so, Italy, the only doubtfully 'Atlantic' state, would have, if possible, to come into the system too and that the idea of a special 'Mediterranean' system would consequently have to be abandoned;

(e) that in place of the latter there might eventually be constructed some defence system under Article 51 covering all the Middle Eastern states and also Greece; but

(f) that this was scarcely practical politics at the moment and consequently that at least Greece, Turkey and Iran ought to be covered by some interim Anglo-American declaration.

5. I should add that the Americans were very keen on the eventual conclusion of further regional defensive agreements under Article 51 covering, for instance, South East Asia and eventually the whole Far East as well. They would not, I think, object to the phrase 'all free nations' which occurs in paragraph 5A in the attached document being altered to 'all nations'. But they held that the conclusion of any system embracing China, to say nothing of India and Pakistan, is impracticable at this moment, and that the mere fact that progress is

at present impossible in other directions should not deter us from at least attempting to construct the best possible system in the Atlantic area.

6. The really big question therefore for us to decide now is whether, in the light of the U.S. attitude as revealed in Washington, we believe that it would be to our advantage if the Americans were to propose a collective defence agreement for the 'North Atlantic' area, or whether, on the other hand, some Presidential declaration of support for the Western European democracies would be enough. I have myself no hesitation whatever in saying that we shall be lucky if the President and the American senatorial leaders pronounce in favour of a treaty binding the United States for the first time in her history to accept positive obligations in the way of the defence of her natural associates and friends. A Presidential declaration would, as has been pointed out many times, only bind the President; and even if it were issued after full consultation with other political figures, we could have no assurance of permanence in the event of any change in the political situation. It seems to me that though such a declaration may be all that the United States may feel able to do in the way of assuring the signatories of Brussels and other Western European democracies, it is not something which on the face of it is very likely to deter the Soviets from taking further steps, indirect if not direct, in their path of expansion.

Public Record Office, London, FO/800, fos 67–73, US/48/32, Bevin to Attlee, Top Secret, 6 April 1948.

2.6   *1948   13 November*   American bases in Britain and the issue of British knowledge of American plans for the use of the atomic bomb in war

With the blockade of Berlin Bevin urged the Americans to take military measures by increasing the airlift to the city, and sending B-29 bombers to Britain. The National Security Council on 15 July agreed to dispatch these 'atomic bombers' – the bomb bays of the initial aircraft had not been converted to carry atomic bombs – to Britain, from where they could reach Moscow. Sixty bombers were sent to East Anglia, and the first American Strategic Air Command base was established on British soil. The Cabinet did not accept the principle that there should be a permanent American base in Britain, and the matter was not reported to Parliament. At the end of 1949, in any case, Britain was prepared to formalise the American presence in 'an adequate, proper and agreed arrangement'. The Royal Air Force did not know what plans the Americans had for the use of the atomic bomb in war.

In answer to a question from Mr [James V.] Forrestal [United States Secretary of Defence], *Lord Tedder* [Chief of the Air Staff] said that the British Chiefs of Staff still considered defence of the Middle East as of the highest importance; they placed it in the same category as the defence of the United Kingdom as one of the fundamentals of our defence policy. He thought that, providing the troops and the aircraft could be got there in time, there was no reason why the Middle East should not be held, and indeed he thought that, in view of the difficult nature of the country, the enemy might be prevented from capturing Persia. . . .

Lord Tedder said that the Royal Air Force were in the dark about American plans for use of the atomic bomb in war. Indications they had been given were on very broad lines. It was important that the Royal Air Force should know, if possible, certain technical details. It was quite possible that a future war might occur at a time when British bombers had reached a stage of development that made them more suitable for certain tasks than American bombers. It was therefore desirable that British bombers be designed to be capable of carrying the U.S. atomic bomb.

Mr Forrestal explained that originally it had been held that the law concerning atomic energy forbade the preparation of military plans for the use of the atomic bomb. The result was the planning had only begun quite recently. He thought that the law would permit the necessary technical details to be given to the Royal Air Force since it could be held that this contributed to the security of the United States. On the other hand, in giving the necessary information about military plans, and technical details in connection with those military plans, it might be impossible to avoid disclosing information about atomic energy development generally. This was a matter on which civilian, as opposed to military, opinion in the United States would be unwilling to encourage the British. There was a strong feeling in some quarters in the United States that the building of an atomic pile in the United Kingdom was a duplication of effort which was not justifiable from the economic point of view.

Public Record Office, London, FO 800/454, fos 50–5, Def/48/39, Misc/M(48)39, 13 November 1948.

2.7   *1948   October*   The Dominions and Western defence

At the Conference of Commonwealth Prime Ministers in October 1948 Bevin tried to involve the Dominions in Western defence. The British Chiefs of Staff suggested to the Dominion Prime Ministers that, in the event of war, five aims should be pursued in co-operation with the allies: to secure the integrity of the Commonwealth countries; to mount a strategic air offensive; to hold the enemy as far east as possible in Western Europe; to maintain a firm hold on the Middle East; and to control sea communications. The early support and action of the United States had to be ensured. The Commonwealth had to co-ordinate defence plans with the Western Union. The allied scientific and technical lead had to be maintained and increased. The Australian Defence Committee commented on these views:

Part 1 – General Defence Policy and Strategy

International Factors – United Kingdom's Views
  1. The outstanding factors . . . may be summarised as follows:
  (a) The establishment of collective security under the United Nations has not been achieved. It has proved impossible for the Security Council to reach agreement on the question of establishing United Nations security forces, and the inability of the Soviet Government to agree to negotiate in the Atomic Energy Commission or in the Commission for Conventional Armaments has contributed powerfully towards the disruption of international confidence.
  (b) Soviet policy and aims are a threat to all free nations who are in danger of being subjugated one by one.
  (c) Soviet policy, if pursued, will inevitably lead to a clash.
  (d) Soviet armed forces could engage in a land war at any time. The probability of the Soviets engaging in a major war before 1956 may be conditioned by adverse economic factors, and, for a time, confident of attaining her primary objectives rapidly, economic considerations would not in themselves be enough to prevent her from doing so.

2. Faced with this situation, the Western Powers feel that it is of paramount importance that all like-minded governments could cooperate in building up collective security from another angle, that of regional security. This is contemplated in Article 51 of the United Nations Charter. Political agreement for a Regional plan for Western Europe has been reached with the Governments of the United States of America and of the countries of Western Europe. This will enable long-term and emergency planning with these Governments to take place.

In the United Kingdom view, as the planning with the United States and the Western European countries proceeds, corresponding planning should take place with the Commonwealth. . . .

Aspects of Defence Co-operation

9. The United Kingdom Chiefs of Staff consider that the two main aspects of defence co-operation are:

(a) The co-ordination of general issues affecting all Allies, e.g. the fundamental objectives of defence policy and strategy, the utilisation of resources, dispersal, etc.

(b) The planning of action in the various regions. . . .

Strategic Objectives in War

14. The United Kingdom Chiefs of Staff suggest that, if war occurs, the following aims should be pushed in co-operation with all Allies:

(i) Secure the integrity of Commonwealth countries.

(ii) Mount a strategic air offensive.

(iii) Hold the enemy as far east as possible in Western Europe.

(iv) Maintain a firm hold on the Middle East.

(v) Control essential sea communications.

15. As has been indicated above, the integrity of Australia and New Zealand from the military aspect will depend in the long run on the outcome of comprehensive operations such as those mentioned in sub-paragraphs (ii), (iii) and (iv) above. It is agreed that the control of essential sea communication will be a basic requirement in Allied strategy.

The United States, as is indicated in the United Kingdom paper, is affected by the Soviet threat in both the European and Pacific regions. Action which may be taken by the United States of America in the Pacific will be of major importance to Australia.

The degree to which Australia could contribute to overall strategy in war would depend on Allied measures which may be taken in Pacific and South East Asia and which could directly or indirectly secure the position of Australia and New Zealand. A correct balance must be struck between Australia's contribution to overall strategy on which ultimate safety depends and on local defence measures. Both of these measures are essential to achieve the aim of securing the integrity of the Australia area, as envisaged by the United Kingdom Chiefs of Staff in paragraph 14(i) above.

Essential Measures in Peace:
16. The United Kingdom Chiefs of Staff suggest also essential measures required in peace to allow Commonwealth countries to fight successfully in the event of war, as follows:

(i) To prepare common strategic objectives and co-ordinated plans.

(ii) To possess balanced armed forces ready for immediate use on the outbreak of war with the necessary resources to support them.

(iii) To maintain co-operation between all members of the Commonwealth in all aspects of defence.

(iv) To ensure the active and early support of the United States.

(v) To co-ordinate defence plans with the Western Union.

(vi) To maintain and increase Allied scientific and technical lead.

Australian Archives (ACT), Shedden Papers, A5954, 1790/3, Defence Committee minute No. 252/1988, Defence discussions at Prime Ministers' Conference, October 1948 (11 November, 1948), Attachment A, Report by the Defence Committee on United Kingdom paper PMM(48)1, The world situation and its defence aspects.

2.8   1949   *February*   Defence talks with the Dominions

Following the Commonwealth Prime Ministers' Conference, bilateral defence discussions and strategic plans were started between Britain, Australia and New Zealand. Talks began with South Africa in 1949. In February that year the British Chiefs of Staff maintained that the close co-operation between the British Commonwealth and the United States, together with the development of the Western Union and the European Recovery Programme, were most disquieting to the leaders of the Soviet

Union. Given the prevailing balance of strength, the Soviet Union would pursue a policy of Communist penetration aided by economic distress rather than open warfare. The Chiefs of Staff Committee prepared an appreciation for discussion with the Dominions.

The Soviet armed forces, despite certain deficiencies, could embark on a land war at any time and would, at least in the early stages, have the advantage of numbers against any likely combination of opposing forces. In any major war, however, that started before 1956/60, at any rate, the initial advantage could be increasingly counter-balanced, as hostilities continued, by the incompleteness of Russia's industrial plan. Moreover, the strategical air situation is, at least at present, unfavourable to the Soviet Union; her air striking force and air defences are still comparatively backward despite the efforts she is making. She can thus not yet adequately protect those centres of population and industry which are within range of air attack. Her future readiness to embark upon a major war is likely, therefore, to be conditioned by the relative efficiency of her air strength.

8. We consider it improbable that the Soviet Union will have sufficient atomic bombs for some years to offset the allied preponderance in that weapon, though as time passes, she may have a stock capable of neutralising small areas such as the United Kingdom. It is a reasonable deduction that a realisation of her relative backwardness in atomic development may cause, or has caused, the Soviet Union to hasten her preparedness to wage biological warfare. Although there are no raw material difficulties comparable to those for atomic development, biological warfare presents many technical problems.

9. Failing the early development of biological or other weapons of mass destruction to a point which she believed would ensure her rapid victory, the Soviet Union's economic situation is likely to militate strongly against her provoking a major war until, at any rate, the aims of the second post war Five-year Plan have been achieved. . . .

15. The close co-operation between the British Commonwealth and the U.S.A. together with the development of the Western Union and the European Recovery Programme are most disquieting to the Soviet leaders. Given the present balance of strength, the Soviet

Union will pursue a policy of Communist penetration aided by economic distress rather than of open war.

Australian Archives (ACT), Shedden Papers, A5954, 1797/1, Strategical planning in relation to co-operation in British Commonwealthy defence – Appendix G(1), Defence appreciation as a basis for military planning between Commonwealth staffs – The threat to world security – United Kingdom Chiefs of Staff Committee paper COS(49)49, 9 February 1949.

2.9   *1949   23 March*   The Chiefs of Staff and Asia

The British Chiefs of Staff, when consulted about the situation in South East Asia, advised that the spread of Communism into southern China would mean unrest, and consequently an increased security commitment throughout South East Asia.

I transmit to Your Excellency herewith a further Memorandum on the implications on British policy and interests in the Far East of a Communist domination of China.

2. As foreshadowed in my previous Memorandum, I have consulted the Chiefs of Staff on the military implications of the situation and the possibility of co-ordinating military measures within the region to meet any possible strategic threat. They have reached the following general conclusions:

The spread of Communism into Southern China will cause increased unrest and consequently an increased security commitment throughout South East Asia. It will also increase the threat to our sea communications in war, which would be particularly serious if Formosa were to come under Soviet domination, and increase the difficulties of delivering the air offensive from the Japanese islands. In consequence, the forces required in the area in both peace and war would be increased. Should the Russians establish bases in Southern China, the threat to South East Asia and to our sea communications might become serious. If Communism successfully spreads into the Indian sub-continent, our whole position in South East Asia would become untenable. They go on to suggest that until all countries interested in the area have agreed on a policy for the Far East, the only military consultative and information organisation which is likely to be effective is the exchange of intelligence information on

Communist activities and the exchange of police information.

Public Record Office, London, FO 371/75743, F3507/1015/10G, P. W. Scarlett (Foreign Office) to Sir Oliver Franks (Washington) for the attention of Bevin, Secret, 23 March 1949.

2.10   *1949   30 April*   **The Permanent Under Secretary's Committee and the Middle East**

> The North Atlantic Treaty was signed in Washington on 4 April by twelve governments. Bevin felt that the pact has 'steadied the world'. At this time Britain's overall position in the Middle East was assessed by the newly formed Permanent Under Secretary's Committee under Sir William Strang in April 1949.

(For the purpose of this paper, the Near East is considered to include Greece, Turkey, the Arab countries, Persia, the Persian Gulf, Israel, Egypt and Cyrenaica.) . . .

Strategic Importance

3. The Near East is important strategically because it shields Africa; is a key centre of land and sea communications; and contains large supplies of oil, particularly in Persia, the Persian Gulf, Saudi Arabia and Iraq. Above all, in the event of attack on the British Isles, it is one of the principal areas from which offensive air action can be taken against the aggressor. The strategic key to this area is Egypt, to which there is no practical alternative as a main base.

4. If the Near East is to be denied to an enemy in wartime, at least two conditions are necessary:

(a) Certain peacetime facilities which include the maintenance of airfields and stores.

(b) The goodwill of the inhabitants.

5. It is also extremely desirable that we should possess the right of entry or reinforcement in case of apprehended emergency. Otherwise, we might be obliged to enter or reinforce certain countries either without right or too late.

General Conclusion from the above

6. The desire of His Majesty's Government is accordingly that the Near East should be stable, prosperous and friendly, and to have

defence arrangements with some or all Near East countries which will afford the best prospect of being able to deny as much as possible of the Near East to an enemy in time of war. This is the established policy of His Majesty's Government, who have accepted the thesis that the security of the Near East is vital to the security of the United Kingdom.

The United States

7. It must be recognised that it would be impossible for His Majesty's Government to hold the Near East in a major war without the assistance of the United States. It is therefore necessary not merely that the United Kingdom and the United States should not be rivals in the Near East, working one against the other, but that the two countries should as far as possible have a common policy.

8. Apart from the problem of Palestine, American policy towards the Near East has for some time past been crystallising on lines similar to our own. In particular there is a common approach to the problems of Greece, Turkey and Persia, to defence, and to the promotion of social and economic advancement. The United States Government has undertaken to help His Majesty's Government to maintain their position in the Near East. On Palestine alignment of policy is now much nearer. . . .

General Strategic Approach

24. In the event of war there is no alternative to the use of Egypt as the main base. Cyrenaica and Transjordan can afford adjuncts but not a substitute. Airfields are important in Iraq and desirable elsewhere, particularly in Saudi Arabia, in Dhahran (where there is a United States airfield), and in Cyprus. Air warning facilities and possibly airfield and port facilities are desirable in Syria and the Lebanon. The United States wish for a fighter base in Tripolitania or Cyrenaica.

Problems of Defence

25. It is for consideration whether the objective of preventing the Near East from falling under Communist domination would be promoted by the conclusion either of a Near East Pact somewhat on the lines of the Atlantic Pact, or alternatively by some other and new form of treaty or agreements. . . .

Africa

54. Dr Malan has recently indicated that South Africa would be willing to join the Atlantic Pact if invited and has also made an alternative suggestion for an African Pact, of which the United States, the United Kingdom, the Union of South Africa and European countries with possessions in Africa (presumably France, Belgium, Portugal and perhaps Italy) would be members. Whether he contemplates the inclusion of Egypt is not clear.

55. Since the Near East is the shield of Africa it would be somewhat illogical to conclude an African Pact unless it were to be accompanied or followed by a Near East Pact. But it is, of course, possible to contemplate an African Pact coupled with political and defence arrangements for the Near East in a form other than a Near East Pact. Dr Malan's suggestion also points to the possibility of the inclusion of South Africa in a Near East Pact, which might in fact take the form of a Near East and African Pact. The ideas need further exploration.

Public Record Office, London, FO 800/455, fos 191–6, PUSC(19)Final, Near East, Top Secret, 30 April 1949.

2.11   *1949   5 May*   Containment of Communism in Asia

With the rapid advance of the Communists in China, the British Defence Co-ordination Committee in the Far East suggested the urgent need for diplomatic, economic and military action.

For Chiefs of Staff from British Defence Co-ordination Committee
We consider that forthcoming visits to London of Commissioner General, Commander-in-Chief Far East Land Forces and Commander-in-Chief Air Command Far East will provide opportunity for useful discussion with Chiefs of Staff on general effects in South East Asia and India of recent developments in China. We feel that there is an urgent necessity to take the diplomatic, economic and military steps to form a firm containing ring against further Communist penetration. In our opinion this ring must be formed by the co-ordinated action of many countries including India, Burma, Siam, French Indo-China and Netherlands East Indies.

Public Record Office, London, FO 371/76034, F6670/1075/61G, British Defence Co-ordination Committee to Chiefs of Staff, Telegram No. SEACOS 900, Top Secret, 5 May 1949.

2.12   *1949   26 May*   The threat to Hong Kong

> Following consultations with the relevant Far Eastern British officials, the Prime Minister told the Cabinet on 26 May that failure to meet the threat to the security of Hong Kong would damage very seriously British prestige throughout the Far East and South East Asia.

The Prime Minister [Clement Attlee] recalled that on 5th May the Cabinet had authorised the despatch to Hong Kong of reinforcements sufficient to secure the Colony against internal unrest or sporadic attacks by guerillas. Since then the Communist forces in southern China had made substantial progress, and the question now arose of sending further reinforcements in order to secure Hong Kong against the risk of direct attack by these forces from the mainland. The Chiefs of Staff had advised that such an attack might be delivered at any time after September: and that, if it was to be resisted with success, an immediate decision should be taken to despatch to Hong Kong the further reinforcements set out in the memorandum by the Minister of Defence. . . .

The Prime Minister said that, from consultations which he had held with the Commissioner-General for South East Asia and the Commanders-in-Chief of the Land and Air Forces in the Far East, he was satisfied that failure to meet this threat to the security of Hong Kong would damage very seriously British prestige throughout the Far East and South East Asia. Moreover, the whole common front against Communism in Siam, Burma and Malaya was likely to crumble unless the peoples of those countries were convinced of our determination and ability to resist this threat to Hong Kong.

In their earlier discussions the Cabinet had been reluctant to commit themselves to any long-term policy in respect of Hong Kong; and the Prime Minister had therefore considered, in consultation with the Foreign Secretary and other Ministers directly concerned, how a decision to defend the Colony could be presented in such a way as to command the support of public opinion in the democratic countries of the world. He had come to the conclusion that it should be presented as a decision to resist aggression; and he recommended that support for such a policy should be enlisted from the Governments of other Commonwealth countries and of the United States.

Public Record Office, London, CAB 128/15, fos 147–8, CM38(49)3, Secret, 3 May 1949.

2.13   *1949   June–August*   Commonwealth responsibilities for the Far East

> By the middle of 1949 it was evident to British defence planners that in any major war Britain, with the limited defence forces it could afford, could not discharge unaided its responsibilities to dependencies outside certain vital strategic zones, and that it was almost certain that the Malaya–Borneo area would be in a non-British theatre of war with an American supreme commander. Consequently it was decided to encourage other members of the Commonwealth to participate in strategic planning, and to assume some responsibility for the defence of the Commonwealth in war. Particular attention was given to the Far East.

Consideration has recently been given by His Majesty's Governments in the United Kingdom and in Australia to the extent to which Australia might co-operate in Commonwealth defence in the Far East. It is assumed that, in view of the limited defence forces which the United Kingdom can now afford to maintain, this country can no longer discharge unaided in the event of a major war the defence of British Dependencies outside certain vital strategic zones. Certain zones, in which British Dependencies are situated, will certainly in a major war be in an allied rather than a United Kingdom theatre of command. For example, it is probable that both the West Indies and Hong Kong would be in a United States theatre of command and certain that the territories of Fiji and the South West Pacific High Commission would be in that of Australia and New Zealand. It is almost certain that the Malaya–Borneo area would be included in a non-British theatre of war i.e. the Supreme commander might be an American.

2. In these circumstances His Majesty's Government in the

United Kingdom have been anxious to encourage other members of the Commonwealth to participate in strategic planning and to assume a measure of responsibility for defence of the Commonwealth in war. In particular the question of Commonwealth defence co-operation in the Far East has been given the most careful consideration by His Majesty's Governments in the United Kingdom and in Australia during the past three years. The Government of Australia has now been invited, and has agreed in principle to accept responsibility for the initiation of defence planning (as distinct from operational responsibility in war) in an area of the Far East which has still to be exactly defined but which will [? may] include Malaya and the Borneo Territories. The agreement of the Australian Government to assume this responsibility is regarded as a valuable though limited [? *omit*] advance in Commonwealth co-operation for defence. As explained above no arrangements have been made about the operational responsibility for the zone in war but it must of course be envisaged that responsibility for strategic planning may lead on ultimately to that for operations.

3. During the negotiations with the Government of Australia to secure their agreement, special care was taken to safeguard the interests of the British and British-protected territories in the area. Responsibility for planning does not of course involve any executive control in peacetime; and it is also agreed that the present United Kingdom command in the Far East will not be removed either in peace or war. The special obligations which His Majesty's Government in the United Kingdom has assumed by Agreement with the Malay Rulers for the protection of the Malay States are fully recognised by the Australian Government, and His Majesty's Government in the United Kingdom has made it plain that local command in Malaya in war must remain in United Kingdom hands. The Australian Government also understands that His Majesty's Government in the United Kingdom reserves the right, if necessary, to reassure the local population in Malaya and the Borneo territories, by public statement, that they have no intention of transferring to any other country, either in peace or war, the responsibilities that now rest with the United Kingdom.

Public Record Office, London, DO 35/2273, Saville Garner to John Morrice Cairns James, 16 June 1949; 94001/26/49, Draft memorandum by Colonial Office on defence responsibilities of Australia in the Far East, Top Secret, August 1949.

2.14 *1949 August* Australia, New Zealand, and the priority of the Middle East

The Australian and New Zealand Chiefs of Staff met British planners in Melbourne between 22 and 26 August 1949. The view of the British Chiefs of Staff was endorsed that it was not possible to limit the allied war aim to the narrow one of restoring the situation to that immediately preceding the outbreak of war, or even that of driving the Russians out of territories over which they had acquired control.

It was stated in United Kingdom Paper P.M.M. (48)1, that, in the present world situation, the United Kingdom Government had thought it necessary to pursue the following policy:

(i) to stimulate political resistance to the spread of communism and to promote economic recovery in those countries threatened by it and

(ii) Recognising that no one country can safely stand alone, to join with the United States and the countries of Western Europe and the Commonwealth in organising all deterrent forces, in building up effective defences, and in working out appropriate collective security arrangements in accordance with Article 51 of the United Nations Charter.

War Aims

8. With a view to building up effective defences and working out the necessary plans, it is necessary first to determine the war aims toward which Allied strategy should be directed. In this connection we are in agreement with the following views of the United Kingdom Chiefs of Staff:

'We consider that it is not possible to limit the Allied War Aim to the narrow one of restoring the situation to that immediately preceding the outbreak of war, or even to that of driving the Russians out of territories over which they have acquired control. We therefore define the Allied War Aims as:

(a) to ensure the abandonment by Russia of further military and ideological aggression

(b) to create conditions conducive to world peace.'

Military Measures to Achieve the Aims

9. *Air Offensive.* Because of all the geographic characteristics of

Russia, and the great numerical superiority of her land forces, the only means of taking offensive action initially is by a strategic air offensive.

10. *Bases and Sea Areas Essential for the Strategic Air Offensive.* To launch an air offensive, the bases from which it must be mounted and the vital sea and air communications necessary to the maintenance of the Allied war effort must be protected. Air bases must be selected so that all the important targets in Russia are within range. Nearly all the major targets in Soviet territory could be reached from bases in Western Europe, the Middle East, Pakistan, and the Japanese Islands. At present it is not possible to plan on using Pakistan bases, at least from the outset, as there is no defence arrangement with that country. It may be, however, that the situation will change and these will become available. . . .

Conclusions on Allied Strategy

16. We are in agreement with the conclusion of the United Kingdom Chiefs of Staff, that the following military measures are essential to implement allied strategy.

(a) To deliver the strategic air offensive from the outbreak of war;

(b) To hold the air bases and sea areas essential for our air offensive. These are:

(i) the United Kingdom

(ii) the Middle East

(iii) Japan

(c) It would also be desirable to hold as bases for our air offensive:

(i) Sea areas for possible carrier offensives

(ii) Pakistan

(d) To defend the main support areas, which are:

(i) United States of America and Canada

(ii) Australia and New Zealand

(iii) South Africa and certain other parts of the African continent

(iv) The Argentine and certain other parts of South America

(e) To ensure the internal security and local defence of support areas of less importance.

(f) To hold those areas necessary to give defence in depth to allied air bases and support areas.

(g) To retain firm control of the essential sea and air communications, and of land areas necessary to ensure their control.

17. *Indian Sub-continent.* Should it be possible subsequently to

make appropriate arrangements with India and Pakistan under which the Indian Sub-continent could be included as a support area, this would be most advantageous.

The Strategic Problem in the Australian Area

... 19. The strategic importance to Russia of Europe and the Middle East is such that the major effort of her armed forces is likely to be made in these theatres. We note and agree with the views expressed by the United Kingdom Chiefs of Staff in the attachment to the United Kingdom Prime Minister's letter of 29 December 1948, that:

'... The most immediate and dangerous Russian threats will be in Western Europe and the Middle East, ...

The successful defence of the Middle East depends on the rapid build up of Commonwealth and American Forces. We estimate that we shall be hard put to deploy adequate forces in time.'

Australia is most unlikely to be an objective of high strategic priority in Russian plans. In addition, geographic factors, and the inferiority of Russian surface naval forces, decrease the probability of serious attack. The security of the Australian mainland will depend, therefore, on:

(a) the distance from Australia of possible enemy air bases; and

(b) the control and security of sea and air communications in the Pacific, South East Asian Area and Indian Ocean.

Australian Archives (ACT), A5799/15, 68/1949, Appendix C, The basic objectives of British Commonwealth defence policy and general strategy (revised 26 August 1949 following discussion between the Defence Committee and the New Zealand Chiefs of Staff).

2.15 *1950 23 March* **British commitment to send land forces to the European continent**

On 23 March 1950 the Chiefs of Staff told the Defence Committee of the Cabinet that they wanted a promise that Britain could send a corps of two infantry divisions to the European continent if there were war with Russia. It was not until October 1950, when the Americans became part of European defence instead of just being committed to go to the defence of

Europe, that British land troops were effectively consigned to the European continent.

1. *United Kingdom Contribution to the Defence of Western Europe* . . .

The committee had before them a note by the Minister of Defence . . . covering a report by the Chiefs of Staff, recommending that His Majesty's Government should give an undertaking to provide a Corps of two Infantry Divisions as a reinforcement to the British Army of the Rhine in the event of war with Russia.

The *Minister of Defence* [Emmanuel Shinwell] emphasised the importance of the decision he was now seeking from the Defence Committee. The precarious situation in which we should be placed if the Russians were to overrun Europe, and the difficulty we should find in recovering Europe from Russian occupation if we survived and had to contemplate driving them back from the Atlantic seaboard, clearly emphasised the need to hold the Russians as far to the eastward as possible in the event of war. Our ability to hold the Russians at all was dependent upon the success we achieved in building up Western European defence and this in turn depended mainly on the revival of the French Army. The morale of the French Army, at any rate in its higher ranks, was now at a low ebb and the problem for the Committee to decide was whether the promise of a United Kingdom contribution of one corps would act as a stimulant to the French and so help build up the French Army. The peoples of Western Europe feared that an occupation by the Russians might destroy their civilisation beyond hope of repair. He himself agreed with the view of the Chiefs of Staff that the moment had arrived when such a promise might have a very salutary effect and he accordingly supported their recommendation. He hoped, too, that it would encourage the United States to follow suit.

The Chief of the Imperial General Staff [Sir William Slim] said that, in the event of war, it would be vital to hold the Russians as far to the east as possible and the only prospect of our being able to do this was by building up the French Army. France had the men, and were now beginning to receive from the United States the necessary equipment. What France lacked was morale and in his view the moment had arrived when it lay within our power to stimulate that morale. It was not that the addition of a corps of two divisions would make much practical difference to the ability of the Allies to hold the

Russians on the Rhine in the event of war in the near future, and Ministers should not imagine that the promise of a corps would satisfy the French. The simple point was that it would help to remove existing suspicion and encourage the French to press on with their own preparations for defence. Thus the recommendation of the Chiefs of Staff was put forward primarily on the grounds that the promise would be in our own interest. If Ministers agreed that the undertaking should be given, the Corps of two Divisions could not, under existing arrangements, arrive on the Continent under three months and it was to be expected that the French would demand that mobilisation and transit should be speeded up. This in any case he hoped and was determined to achieve, but for the moment, under existing mobilisation arrangements, this was the best that could be done. As for the possibility of the Americans making some similar contribution, he had been assured by the United States Chiefs of Staff that it was their firm intention to send the limited land formations which they would have available in the early days to reinforce any line in Western or South Western Europe that showed a reasonable prospect of holding; and the best way of ensuring that a line would be held was by reviving the French Army to hold it. The Chiefs of Staff could think of no better way of doing this at present, without any additional financial expenditure, than making the offer of the proposed corps.

Public Record Office, London, CAB 131/8, DO(50)5th mtg, 23 March 1950.

2.16   *1950   7 June*   Defence Policy and Global Strategy, 1950

Following further bilateral conversations with individual Dominions, often with defence of the Middle East as a priority, the Chiefs of Staff on 7 June submitted a paper, Defence Policy and Global Strategy, DO(50)45. This was slightly revised in 1951 as MDM(51)2, but substantially what it outlined remained British policy into 1951, when it was changed by the new Conservative administration.

Introduction

1. Since our last review in 1947 of the strategic situation many changes have taken place, notably the formation of Western

alliances under the Brussels and North Atlantic treaties and the discovery by Russia of the atomic bomb. We now submit for the consideration of the Defence Committee a fresh review of Defence Policy and Global Strategy written in the light of these changes and from the joint point of view of a partner in a Western Alliance and a member of the British Commonwealth.

2. The British Commonwealth and the Continental Powers, whether individually or collectively, cannot fight Russia except in alliance with the United States: nor could the United States fight Russia without the help of the British Commonwealth. Today it makes no sense to think in terms of British strategy or Western European strategy as something individual and independent. Full collaboration with the United States in policy and method is vital. This truth is recognised in the most important area of conflict by the North Atlantic Treaty. But the cold war against Russian Communism is a global war as a hot war would inevitably be. After stabilisation of the European front the next most important object should be to secure an agreed Allied military strategy in the Middle East and East Asia theatres – and the machinery to implement it. It is also clearly necessary to obtain the fullest possible political, economic and military collaboration in the British Commonwealth as a whole – if possible including the countries of the Indian sub-continent, but if necessary without them. . . .

Part I – Allied defence policy and global strategy

Section 1 – General . . .

Atomic Disarmament and its Implications . . .

17. We do not now regard a shooting war as inevitable or even likely, provided the Western Allies maintain their resolution and build up their military strength. The danger of war would certainly become imminent if Russia felt herself militarily strong enough to pursue her political aims regardless of the reactions of the Western World – she might then push her policy to a point at which, as in September 1939, the Allies have no alternative to bloodless defeat except resort to force. We do not believe that Russia will feel like that or take the chance that Hitler took in 1939, as long as the Allies do not weaken. In our view America's enormous lead in the production of atomic weapons and the general scientific and industrial

74

superiority of the West will remain the most effective deterrent, the value of which will not be lessened as Russia builds up a stock of atomic bombs, as long as the Western Allies really intend – and continue to make it unmistakably clear that they intend – to use the atomic weapon immediately in reply to Russian aggression. . . .

The Three Main Theatres of War – and the Sea

20. We have said that the war, cold and hot, is indivisible and world-wide. But there are three main theatres in which Allied interests are threatened – Western Europe, the Middle East and East Asia. Against the contingency of [a] shooting war the Allies have also to provide for the protection of those sea communications which are really vital to survival and to our prospects of ever being able to bring to bear upon the enemy that offensive pressure which alone holds out hope of reasonably early victory.

Section II – Western Europe . . .

The Implementation of plans

28. Up to date, most of the activity in the North Atlantic and Brussels Treaty organisations has been confined to paper planning and the setting up of the necessary staffs and committees. This is a necessary preliminary phase and much useful ground work has been done. The time has now come when the Allies must get down to the practical implementation of these paper projects. The first deliveries of arms and equipment from America to the Western Union Powers are arriving to supplement those already provided by Great Britain. *The rate of progress in transforming paper plans into practical reality now depends in the main on finding the necessary money and industrial capacity to arm and equip the existing man-power. We are convinced that the North Atlantic system of security can become a reality but only on the basis of the principle agreed at The Hague, that the North Atlantic military establishment should be regarded as an integrated balanced force to which the individual powers should contribute those forces to which they are best suited.*

Section III – The Middle East

In the Cold War

29. The defence of the Middle East has always been one of the three pillars of British defence policy and it is of equally critical

importance in Allied strategy. It is the land bridge between Europe, Asia and Africa and a most important link in our Commonwealth system of sea and air communications. Its oil supplies are of very great importance, and, if it fell under Russian influence, the repercussions on the whole Moslem world from French North Africa through Pakistan to South East Asia would be critically serious. There can be no doubt that to retain the countries of the Middle East within the western orbit is a vital cold war measure, and we must be prepared to make military sacrifices to that end. . . .

In a Shooting War

31. In the event of a shooting war the Middle East remains of critical importance to Allied strategy for the reasons stated above with, in addition, the fact that it is a potentially important base for offensive air action against Southern Russia. Its loss would be a catastrophe not only to the British Commonwealth but also to Western Europe. The extension of Russian communist influence throughout Africa would involve the loss of the North African ports and when it reached Dakar would be a direct threat to the United States. The loss of this vast area would present us with problems after the war which we do not like to contemplate. While the loss of the Middle East would not necessarily lose us the war it would vastly increase our difficulties in winning it. If the Middle East fell we could not be considered to have won the war as long as the Russians remained there.

It follows that Allied plans must include provision for the minimum forces required to hold the Egyptian base at the opening stages of a war. The United Kingdom itself cannot afford all the forces required for the Middle East in addition to those required to defend herself and Western Europe. Additional forces must therefore be found from other parts of the Commonwealth and from the United States.

Provided sufficient forces are forthcoming we consider that the defence of the Middle East is practicable. A recent review of Russian capabilities in that area has revealed that the full threat is unlikely to develop against Egypt until considerably later than we had hitherto thought probable. . . .

United States Participation in the Middle East

35. Although it is not their intention, in the event of war in the

short term, to send any forces initially to the Middle East, we understand that the United States Chiefs of Staff still attach great strategic importance to that area and may revise their present policy when they have the resources available. It is very important from every point of view – particularly in relation to the attitude of Israel – that the United States should participate, at least with air forces and a carrier task group, in the defence of the Middle East. It would not be in the wider Allied interest for them to reinforce the Middle East at the expense of their ability to make their due contribution to the defence of Western Europe, but a small contribution to the Middle East would pay a disproportionately large dividend. . . .

Part II – British Commonwealth contribution

General

46. We now consider what contribution the countries of the British Commonwealth should make to implement the Allied strategy and defence policy defined in Part I. We have already pointed out that neither the British Commonwealth, nor the United States, nor the Continental countries can individually fight the Russians. The war effort of all the Allied Nations must therefore be fully co-ordinated. Machinery already exists in the shape of the North Atlantic Treaty Defence Organisation for integrating the war effort of the Allies in the main theatre. Both the Members of the British Commonwealth and the United States, however, have world-wide responsibilities which extend to the Middle East, to the Far East and to the Pacific. There is an urgent requirement for the estab-lishment of machinery to work out and implement British and American strategy and defence plans on a world-wide basis. The central organ of this machinery should be something on the lines of the Combined Chiefs of Staff organisation of the recent war; but arrangements should be made for the close association of other Commonwealth countries, who should share in the work of the central body when matters affecting their interests were being dis-cussed.

Cold War

47. Cold war merges imperceptibly into something very like hot war, as recent developments in Malaya illustrate. We have already stressed in Part I that first priority must be given in our defence

preparations to the cold war. We must be prepared in the interests of preventing war to take certain steps which, if we fail to prevent it, will result in our being in a somewhat more difficult position at the outset of real hostilities. The composition, distribution and to some extent the equipment of the British Army must be primarily conditioned by cold war responsibilities which must to a lesser extent also affect the other two Services. . . .

Basic Requirements of War-time Strategy

51. The basic requirements of British Commonwealth strategy in war still hold good. The three pillars of our strategy remain:

(a) The Defence of the United Kingdom and its development as an offensive base. This will require holding the enemy on a line as far East in Europe as possible.

(b) The control of vital sea communications.

(c) A firm hold in the Middle East and the development of Egypt as an offensive base. . . .

The Middle East . . .

54. . . . The retention of our position in the Middle East is of such importance to the cohesion of the British Commonwealth in cold and in hot war that we should do all in our power to encourage Australia, New Zealand and South Africa – and we hope some day in happier times Pakistan and possibly even India – to undertake firm commitments to send armed forces to the Middle East as soon as possible after the outbreak of war. . . .

55. Our existing plans provide for the despatch of a substantial proportion of Bomber Command to the Middle East on the outbreak of war. We do not now intend to do this. We regard Bomber Command as an important element in the air defence of the United Kingdom, as well as a valuable support to the forces of the Western Union – particularly in view of our inability to provide additional tactical air forces. . . .

In view of our inability to send bombers to the Middle East it is more than ever important that other Commonwealth countries and the Americans should send air forces to that theatre in the event of war.

The Far East

56. Our ability to maintain our position in the Far East in a hot

war will depend in the main on the extent to which we and the French have been able to establish internal order in our dependent territories. The external threat to Malaya from Chinese armies operating over long and difficult lines of communication is not likely to be very great. The most formidable menace will be the Fifth Column within our borders, for which the large unassimilated Chinese populations form an excellent foundation.

Our efforts in South East Asia must therefore be directed to building up the local security forces and civil administration to a point at which, with the minimum of external assistance, they can regain control of the internal situation in Malaya. We shall not be able to reinforce them in war, and must set our faces against any diversion to them of resources from the vital areas. South East Asia, though critically important, is not vital to our survival in war – as was proved last time. . . .

Australia and New Zealand have already accepted responsibility for certain aspects of defence in the Anzam area. We hope they will not allocate more than the minimum essential strength to that commitment, and will make available any surplus to reinforce the Middle East. It is important that the defence of the Anzam area should be closely linked with the United States system of defence in the Pacific.

Public Record Office, London, CAB 131/9, DO(50)45, Report by the Chiefs of Staff on Defence Policy and Global Strategy, Top Secret, 7 June 1950. Printed in *Documents on British Policy Overseas*, Series II, Volume IV (London: HMSO, 1991), pp. 411–34.

2.17   1950   *July*   The Chiefs of Staff and the outbreak of the Korean War

From Washington, with the outbreak of the Korean conflict, the British ambassador, Sir Oliver Franks, pointed to the 'steady and unquestioning assumption' that Britain was 'the only dependable ally and partner'. In Korea the American government and people had 'instinctively followed their high destiny in the world'. That was 'a very great thing for us all'. But Americans felt lonely: Britain should offer land forces to reassure them. The Chiefs of Staff did not want to do this, and the Defence Committee was worried lest the Korean conflict

diverted attention from other danger-spots in Asia, and blinded
Britain to the risks to which it was exposed in Europe.

The Prime Minister [Clement Attlee] said that the Defence Committee had that morning considered the current situation in Korea. In
view of the risks to which we were exposed elsewhere in the Far East
and South East Asia, it was not proposed that further United
Kingdom forces should be sent to Korea. It was being suggested to
the United States Government that immediate steps should be taken
to initiate an Anglo-American review of the strategic situation in the
Far East and South East Asia; and the possibilities of enlisting
military assistance from Australia and Pakistan were to be urgently
explored. It was specially important at the present time that pre-
occupation with Korea should not divert attention from other
danger-spots in these areas; and also that we should not allow the
situation in the East generally to blind us to the risks to which we
were exposed in Europe.

Public Record Office, London, CAB 128/18, fo. 6, CM42(50)3, Secret, 4
July 1950.

2.18   *1950   25 September*   Strategic importance of South Africa

On 28 September 1950 the Cabinet endorsed a paper on relations with South Africa signed by Patrick Gordon Walker, the
Secretary of State for Commonwealth Relations, which
emphasised that South Africa's goodwill was of particular
importance to Britain 'from the general strategic and defence
points of view'.

*Importance to the United Kingdom of good relations with South
Africa*
4.   Though there is thus a great deal in the policy of the present
South African Government with which we in the United Kingdom
clearly cannot associate ourselves, it is important for the following
reasons that the United Kingdom should continue to preserve good
relations with South Africa:
(i)   From the general strategic and defence points of view South
Africa's good will is of particular importance to us. If, as seems likely

at present, the Mediterranean is closed to us in any future war, the naval base at Simonstown, where the South Africans have granted us special rights, will be of vital importance to the Royal Navy, and other South African ports will be indispensable to our shipping and as staging bases for our troops. Apart from this the Union can contribute considerable military forces and we hope shortly to obtain from them a firm commitment to send troops to the Middle East in the event of war. The contribution envisaged would consist of one Armoured Division together with aircraft and naval forces. There are believed to be important deposits of uranium in the Union and the Union Government have stated that they have recently developed processes for its extraction.

(ii) The Nationalists are staunchly anti-Communist and Dr. Malan himself has more than once publicly pledged South Africa's support in any war resulting from Russian aggression; he repeated this pledge at Durban on 19th September, when he is reported as having said that they 'would ally themselves with the Commonwealth and other like-minded nations of the world in the event of a major war'. The Union Government provided air crews to assist in the air lift to Berlin when it was blockaded by the U.S.S.R., and, despite the unpopularity of the United Nations in South Africa, they have now agreed to send a squadron of the South African Air Force to co-operate with the United Nations Forces in Korea.

Public Record Office, London, CAB 129/42, fos 54–6, CP(50)217, Memorandum by Patrick Gordon Walker on relations with South Africa, Secret, 25 September 1950.

2.19   *1950   23 August*   **The English-speaking alliance**

Bevin in a conversation with the Americans Charles Spofford and Mr Justice Holmes on the need for American aid for British defence pointed out that 'Great Britain was not part of Europe; she was not simply a Luxembourg'. There was a wider consideration:

The people in this country were pinning their faith on a policy of defence built on a Commonwealth–U.S.A. basis – an English-speaking basis. People here were frankly doubtful of Europe. How could he go down to his constituency – Woolwich – which had been bombed by Germans in the war, and tell his constituents that the Germans would help them in a war against Russia? Londoners would not rely on the Germans; if the Germans come in to help, so much the better. But reliance must be placed on America and the Commonwealth. Similarly in regard to France, the man in the street, coming back from a holiday there, was almost invariably struck by the defeatist attitude of the French.

Public Record Office, London, FO 800/517, fos 114–19, Minute by Dixon of conversation between Bevin and Charles Spofford and Mr Justice Holmes, Secret, 23 August 1950. Printed in *Documents on British Policy Overseas*, Series II, Volume III (London: HMSO, 1989), p. 4.

2.20   *1950   26 September*   Britain and the crossing of the 38th parallel in Korea

Following the success of General Douglas MacArthur in mounting the United Nations landings at Inchon behind the North Korean lines, Britain took the initiative to change the nature of the Korean operation from being that of repelling the aggressor north of the 38th parallel to that of bringing about a unified Korea. Attlee outlined the policy to the Cabinet on 26 September 1950.

The Prime Minister [Clement Attlee] said that the United Nations Assembly ought now to consider the situation which might arise in the near future if the North Korean armed forces were virtually destroyed and North Korea was left in a state of chaos. It would be the duty of the United Nations to restore peace and order in the country as a whole, and to establish an independent Democratic Government for all Korea. It might well be necessary for United Nations forces to enter North Korea for the purpose of achieving these objectives. The draft resolution which the Foreign Secretary had prepared was designed to meet that situation. Since the original text was received a number of amendments had been telegraphed from New York and a revised text incorporating these . . . was handed round as a basis for the Cabinet's discussion.

In discussion the following points were made:

(a) If the United Nations forces destroyed the North Korean forces, but did not enter North Korea, Russia might occupy North Korea or anarchy might ensue. In either event it would be impossible to establish a stable administration south of the 38th Parallel. The United Nations had always desired that the artificial distinction between North and South Korea should be abolished, and world opinion was likely to accept the unification of Korea as a desirable objective. There was general agreement that military operations could not be stopped at the 38th Parallel. It would, however, be necessary to present clearly to public opinion the reasons justifying a military occupation of the whole of Korea, its temporary character and its limited objectives.

Public Record Office, London, CAB 128/18, CM61(50)2, Secret, 26 September 1950

2.21 *1950 October* The Americans insist that the Middle East is a British and Commonwealth responsibility

> In discussions with their British counterparts in Washington between 23 and 26 October, the American Chiefs of Staff reiterated that they saw the Middle East as a British and Commonwealth responsibility: the United States could make no commitment of forces for the area. The Americans thought Middle Eastern oil essential to the war effort. The Americans also agreed that Egypt was indispensable as a wartime base for forces defending the Middle East. There was also to be a study of the association of Greece and Turkey with North Atlantic Treaty planning.

Item 1
It was generally agreed that the basic difference in regard to the timing of Soviet intentions was not too important, if we agree, and we do, that the primary and important task is that both the U.S.–U.K. increase our capabilities vis-à-vis Russia as rapidly as possible.

Item 2
With regard to the several questions raised under this heading the following summary of conclusions was made:

Rearmament of Germany. That the question of how much pressure the French Government can stand on the matter of the rearmament of Germany is a delicate one and that the matter should be discussed at the meeting of the U.S. State–U.K. Foreign Office Conference, October 26th.

Forces. It is understood that the United States can make no commitment of forces for the Middle East area, in event of war, although the Strategic Air Command would strike targets which would assist in the defense in this area.

Foreign Relations of the United States 1950, Volume III (Washington: United States Government Printing Office, 1977), pp. 1686–7, Approved summary of conclusions and agreements reached at a meeting of the Chiefs of Staff of the United States and the United Kingdom, Top Secret, 23 October 1950.

2.22   1950   2 December   Atomic weapons and Korea

Attlee and Bevin met their French counterparts on 2 December. Attlee mentioned the strong feeling in Britain that atomic weapons could not be regarded on a level with other weapons. The question could not be decided on purely military grounds: 'Short-sighted decisions designed to meet an immediate situation might be fatal, and the matter must be decided at the highest political level and not by one Power alone.' The European countries would get the retaliation.

Mr Bevin said he very much regretted certain replies made to questions at a press conference which had weakened our position. During the Berlin troubles last year, the atomic question had been handled with great skill, so that the Russians really believed that if they went too far they might be subjected to an attack. The situation over Korea was of course different, but it was unfortunate that the press statement to which he referred had caused a revulsion in Allied public opinion which compelled retraction and thus weakened the deterrent effect of our possession of the atomic weapon. He felt that now, until there was a settlement, the atomic bomb must be held in the background as an ultimate reserve. Any loose talk about its use, especially at a high level, was most dangerous. The fact was that public opinion could recognise fairly clearly what were and what were not occasions on which desperate measures such as the use of atomic weapons might be justified, and certainly a conflict in which the United States were confronted with a Power like Korea would not be regarded as a case.

Public Record Office, London, FO 800/465, fos 249–58, FR/50/23, Record of meeting of Attlee and Bevin with French Prime Minister and Minister for Foreign Affairs, Top Secret, 2 December 1950. Printed in *Documents on British Policy Overseas*, Series II, Volume IV (London: HMSO, 1991), p. 235.

2.23 *1950 December* Truman's assurances on the atomic bomb

In talks in Washington Truman reassured Attlee about the 'atomic bomb'. According to the British record the President said that he regarded it as the joint possession of Britain, the United States and Canada.

The Prime Minister [Clement Attlee] said that his talks with President Truman and his advisers had been conducted in an atmosphere of frankness and candour. . . .

The Prime Minister had discussed with the President the conduct of the military operations in Korea. Some of General MacArthur's public pronouncements had been unfortunate; but he was an able commander and had conducted the earlier operations in Korea with marked success. In the later stages intelligence about the Chinese movements had evidently been inadequate; but it must be recognised that the terrain in North Korea made it possible to conceal the movement of large forces of Chinese infantry, which travelled light and were skilled in infiltration tactics. The Prime Minister had drawn attention to the need for distinguishing between politico-military decisions, in which United Nations Government should be consulted, and the purely military questions which could be left to the commander in the field; and he had given the President a memorandum suggesting improvements in the existing arrangements for liaison. . . .

President Truman had entirely satisfied him about the use of the atomic bomb. The President, at his press conference on 30th November, had not intended to make any fresh pronouncement on the subject and had never had any intention of using the atom bomb in Korea. He had assured the Prime Minister that he regarded the atomic bomb as in a sense a joint possession of the United States, United Kingdom and Canada, and that he would not authorise its use without prior consultation with the other two Governments save in an extreme emergency – such as an atomic attack on the United States which called for immediate retaliation.

The United States Government were in full agreement about the paramount importance of the defence of Europe. They had welcomed the compromise plan evolved by the Council of Deputies for enabling Western Germany to contribute military forces for the defence of Western Europe. The Prime Minister had felt that he had no alternative but to support that plan, as a means of securing the early appointment of a Supreme Commander of the European integrated force, to which he and his Cabinet colleagues attached such great importance. Some of the United States forces which had been intended for the West would now be required in the Far East, but other divisions in substitution for these, though not fully trained, would be sent to Europe in the course of 1951. . . .

The United States Government had asked that the United Kingdom Government should increase their defence effort. He had explained the military burdens which had fallen on this country since the end of the war and the difficulty of imposing further defence expenditure on the national economy. He had, however, undertaken to consider this request further; and it must be assumed that the United States Government would return to the subject at a later stage.

Public Record Office, London, CAB 128/18, fos 167–8, CM85(50)3, Secret, 12 December 1950.

2.24   *1951   January*   Importance of Suez

At the time of the Commonwealth Prime Ministers' Conference in London in January 1951 the Assistant Under Secretary for Middle Eastern Affairs in the Foreign Office, R. J. Bowker, offered the assessment of the Foreign Office and the views of the Chiefs of Staff on this area of British Commonwealth responsibility.

As I understand it, Mr. [R. H.] Scott [Assistant Under Secretary of State in the Foreign Office] does not question so much the continued importance of the Middle East, but the hitherto accepted view that the best place from which to defend it is Egypt. His main argument is that the only Middle East oil fields which we are likely to be able to hold anywhere are the fields round the Persian Gulf, which are therefore the only vital interest we have in the Middle East, and that the defence of these can best be planned from India and Pakistan, and East Africa, rather than from North Africa. The conclusion is that the role left to Egypt is merely to play its part in the local defence of North Africa and the Eastern Mediterranean, and act as a platform (too far back) from which to mount an attack on Russia.

I think the answer to this is that our Middle East Defence Plans aim at defending as much of the Middle East and of the Middle East oil as possible, and as a whole (the Outer Ring), and that in the view of the Chiefs of Staff Egypt still constitutes the only suitable wartime base from which to conduct the operations for this purpose.

For launching an attack on Russia, no doubt forward bases would be required, but so far as I know the Chiefs of Staff still regard Egypt as the best location for the necessary main base.

Apart from its oil, and the fact that it constitutes a platform from which to launch an attack against Russia's most vulnerable area (the Caucasus oilfields), the Middle East must be held as a barrier to Africa, and to deny to Russia Africa's rich resources. For this purpose again, Egypt remains the best base area.

It is true, as Mr. Scott says, that the Suez Canal has not a vital wartime importance – it was rendered unusable in the last war. But Suez remains of vast importance as the back door to Egypt and will no doubt be of great importance in the next war in servicing the vital Australian and New Zealand, and also South African, contributions to Middle East defence.

In a word, Egypt still remains the essential central point from which to defend the Middle East and all that the Middle East entails.

The Americans are just as emphatic as we about the vital importance of defending the Middle East, but regard it as a responsibility which should be borne primarily by the Commonwealth.

Public Record Office, London, FO 371/91219, E1192/11, Minute by R. J. Bowker, 10 January 1951.

2.25   *1950   December*   **Nuclear collaboration with South Africa**

South Africa was crucial for the British government's defence programme as a source of uranium. In 1946 it was agreed to set up a purification plant in South Africa. At the end of 1950, after delays following the election of the Nationalists, and difficulties with the Americans, South Africa was informed about the Combined Policy Committee and the Combined Development Agency, the prospects of atomic energy and nuclear power, and given special privileges, including access to unclassified atomic energy work in Britain and the United States. Much of this collaboration remained between British and South African scientists. The Commonwealth Relations Office wrote to the Office of the British High Commissioner in South Africa about this:

Will you please refer to my letter No. D.3450/62 of the 19th December, 1950, about giving [D. D.] Forsyth [a South African official] copies of correspondence passing between the Ministry of Supply and scientists in the Union.

2. We have now considered the matter further in consultation with the Ministry of Supply, and the following seems to be the position.

(a) *Correspondence Regarding Uranium.*   During the recent uranium negotiations in South Africa the representatives of the Combined Development Agency raised the question of direct contact on purely technical matters between responsible technical officers on the South African side and their counterparts in the United States and the United Kingdom, and an arrangement was reached . . . in a letter . . . of the 15th December, 1950. . . . The arrangement, which apparently has been discussed with the Secretary for External Affairs, is that on purely technical matters the responsible technical officers in the Union should correspond direct with their counterparts in the United States and the United Kingdom, though top secret communications should be routed through diplomatic channels. Questions of policy will be dealt with in the Mines Department and will be routed through the Department of External Affairs.

(b) *General Correspondence on Atomic Energy Matters.* Correspondence on the subject of atomic energy in general will presumably be less than that on uranium production. A certain amount of information on atomic energy in general was sent to [Brigadier

Basil] Schonland [President of the South African Council for Scientific and Industrial Research, 1945–50; Director, Atomic Research Establishment, Harwell, 1954–8] and it will continue to be sent to his successor in order to keep him generally informed on the whole picture of nuclear physics work and to stock his library. We do not imagine that Forsyth will wish to be put on the circulation list for these reports, which emanate largely from Harwell, and are highly technical in character, though should anything in particular be taken up on these reports, or any specific question be asked by either side, we should take steps to see that a copy goes to Forsyth.

3. Such an arrangement would mean that Forsyth would see correspondence on uranium matters which has a policy significance, and that he would be kept informed of any significant exchanges between the Ministry of Supply and uranium scientists on atomic energy matters in general, although he would not automatically receive unclassified reports from Harwell.

Public Record Office, London, DO 35/2494, D3450/62, Atomic energy exchange of technical information between South Africa, United Kingdom and United States, Top Secret; R. C. C. Hunt [Commonwealth Relations Office] to L. J. D. Wakely [Office of the High Commission in South Africa], Secret, 13 January 1951.

2.26   1951   29 January   Increased defence budget

Over the previous six months, particularly with the situation in Malaya and Indochina, British defence planners had placed increasing emphasis on South East Asia. More forces were needed to stop the Communist threat. More money had to be spent on defence. On 25 January the Cabinet accepted a huge increase in Britain's defence budget: £4,700 million was to be spent over the years 1951–4. Attlee outlined the programme to the House of Commons on 29 January.

The Prime Minister (Mr. Attlee): . . . At the Brussels meeting of the North Atlantic Council on 19th December, my right hon. Friend the Foreign Secretary said that, in view of the urgent need to strengthen the defences of the free world, His Majesty's Government had decided to increase and accelerate their defence preparations still further and were considering what form and direction that increased effort should take. I am now in a position to give the House a broad indication of the scale of the new defence programme which the Government have adopted. . . .

The effort we are making is an integral part of North Atlantic defence, the success of which will depend upon our defence preparations, which in their turn will depend on the mutual availability of machine tools and raw materials.

If our plan is fully achieved, expenditure on production for the Services in 1951–52 will be more than double the rate for the current year; and by 1953–54 it should be more than four times as great. By then we should have quadrupled our annual output of tanks and combat aircraft. We shall introduce new types of equipment as rapidly as possible. New types of fighter aircraft will come into service in larger numbers. Production of the twin-engined Canberra bomber will be increased, and the first order is being placed for a four-engined jet bomber. . . .

Over the whole field of military and civil preparations for defence, apart from the stockpiling programme, expenditure in the financial year 1951–52 will be in the neighbourhood of £1,300 millions. It will take time to build up defence production to the levels which we now have in mind, and expenditure on production will be on a rising curve during the next three years. If the programme is fully achieved, the total defence budget over the next three years, covering all the military and civil preparations but again excluding stockpiling, may be as much as £4,700 millions. Nearly half of this will be for production. . . .

United Kingdom Parliamentary Debates, House of Commons, 1950–51, Fifth Series, Volume 483 (London: HMSO, 1951), cols 579–84, 29 January 1951.

2.27 *1951 February* The Tripartite Pact: ANZUS

In February 1951 the Americans modified a previous suggestion and said that they would prefer a tripartite pact by which the United States, Australia and New Zealand would each undertake to go to the aid of the other in the event of hostilities affecting the interest of any one of them in the Pacific. Attlee summarised the British position on this for the Cabinet.

The English-speaking alliance

Introduction

1. On 12th February the Cabinet had before them a paper by the Minister of State [Kenneth Younger] . . . on the subject of proposals which had then been put forward by Mr. Dulles on behalf of the United States for a Pacific Defence Council consisting of the 'Island Chain' of the United States, Japan, the Philippines, Indonesia, Australia and New Zealand. That paper recognised that it was highly desirable that Australia and New Zealand should obtain a security guarantee from the United States but explained that there were a number of grave objections to the arrangements then contemplated. The Cabinet endorsed the views expressed in the paper and recommended that every effort should be made to find alternative means of meeting the Australian and New Zealand requirement for safeguards. The Governments of Australia and New Zealand and Mr. Dulles were so informed.

The Draft Treaty

2. We have received from the Government of New Zealand, and subsequently from the Government of Australia, a copy of a draft tripartite treaty between the United States, Australia and New Zealand which was prepared for consideration by the Governments concerned during Mr. Dulles' talks with Australian and New Zealand Ministers at Canberra on the 15th, 16th and 17th February. . . . It appears that the earlier 'Island Chain' proposals have been dropped in favour of this simpler and more limited agreement. We have, however, been informed that the United States may wish to press for the inclusion of the Philippines as a fourth party to the Treaty.

3. The United Kingdom High Commissioner at Canberra has received a letter from the Australian Prime Minister . . . in which Mr. [Robert] Menzies [the Australian Prime Minister] explains the very great importance which the Australian Government attach to the conclusion of such a treaty and makes it clear that his Government expect the United Kingdom Government to do their best to help the Australian and New Zealand governments to secure the completion of a treaty on the lines proposed. . . .

Views of the Chiefs of Staff

4. The draft treaty has been examined by the Chiefs of Staff. . . . In brief the Chiefs of Staff regard the treaty as generally acceptable.

They recognise that there is a danger that such a treaty might in some degree divert Australian and New Zealand interest from the defence of the Middle East to the Pacific, but they feel that such limited risks of this kind as there are should be accepted in view of the undoubted strategic advantage which an American guarantee of Australian and New Zealand security provides. The Chiefs of Staff take the view that, provided that the arrangements are confined to the United States, Australia and New Zealand, the United Kingdom need not be a party to the treaty or a member of the Defence council which it is proposed to set up. They add, however, that the United Kingdom should seek to be included should the treaty be extended to other countries, e.g. if the United States insist on the inclusion of the Philippines. The Chiefs of Staff also suggest that after consultation with the Australian and New Zealand Governments, Lord Tedder [Chief of the Air Staff] should be instructed to urge on the United States that the present agreed global strategy should not be prejudiced.

Political Comments
5. Having regard to these factors, I agree with the Chiefs of Staff that the treaty is generally acceptable.

6. As regards the risk of prejudice to our global strategy which might be involved, I endorse the Chiefs of Staff suggestion that Lord Tedder should be instructed to obtain an assurance about global strategy from the United States Chiefs of Staff, and that this should be done after the Governments of Australia and New Zealand have been consulted.

Inclusion of the United Kingdom
7. From the broad political view the question whether or not the United Kingdom should be included is a major one, and I should therefore like my colleagues to consider the arguments for and against.

8. *Arguments for the inclusion of the United Kingdom*

(a) Our exclusion might tend to give the impression, in countries in South East Asia and even possibly in Australia and New Zealand, that the United Kingdom was renouncing its responsibilities in the Pacific.

(b) It might even be argued that it was symptomatic of a rift in policy between the United Kingdom and the United States in that area, or of undue subservience by the United Kingdom to the United States.

(c) To give an impression of retreat in the Pacific would do harm to the United Kingdom's influence and credit in other parts of the world by seeming to diminish our stature as a world Power.

9. *Arguments against the inclusion of the United Kingdom*

(a) It is in our interests that a treaty should be concluded, since it meets Australian and New Zealand security requirements. But it is by no means certain that the United States Government or Congress will accept it. There will be greater prospects of success if we support Australia and New Zealand, as the Australian Government have strongly urged us to do, in backing the draft treaty as it stands. An attempt to secure our own inclusion might have the opposite effect.

(b) There are ways and means open to us which should forestall any false impressions such as those foreseen in the preceding paragraph – e.g. by way of a Governmental statement at the appropriate time on the analogy of the statements of friendly interest and welcome which were made by a number of other Commonwealth Governments when the United Kingdom entered Western Union.

(c) The inclusion of the United Kingdom would raise the same sort of difficulties as we foresaw in the 'Island Chain' proposals – the inclusion of Malaya and Borneo would emphasise the exclusion of other neighbouring territories and might be expected to provoke the French Government to press for the extension of the pact to their territories.

(d) As the Chiefs of Staff have pointed out, it is right that we should rely on the normal processes of Commonwealth consultation to ensure that our interests are represented. It is a specifically Australian view of the modern evolution of the Commonwealth that individual Commonwealth countries should take the lead on behalf of the whole Commonwealth in areas where they themselves are specially concerned. In line with this concept they recognise that the United Kingdom should take the lead in the North Atlantic and the Middle East and we have recognised that Australia is in the lead in relation to the occupation of Japan. It could be argued that this is not inconsistent with United Kingdom signature of the treaty since Australia would in any case take the lead in so far as arrangements under the treaty would be centralised in Canberra. But it would be appropriate, and helpful for our general relations with Australia, if, in the context of a Pacific pact, we were to indicate our acceptance of

Australian and New Zealand leadership in the Pacific and emphasise that we look to them to represent our own interests as well as theirs.

10. The problem would be more difficult if the United States were to insist on the inclusion of the Philippines. We should try to avoid this if we can. It raises difficulties not only for our own territories but also for other territories in South East Asia.

Public Record Office, London, CAB 129/45, fos 317–27, CP(51)64, Note by Attlee on Pacific defence and appendices, Secret, 27 February 1951.

2.28   *1951   July*   The Middle East Command

> About a month after the meeting of Commonwealth defence representatives in London in June 1951, Britain submitted a paper on the subject of a Middle East Command to the Standing Group of NATO. The history of the proposal is given by Alan Watt, the Secretary of the Australian Department of External Affairs. On 9 October 1951 Egypt denounced the Anglo-Egyptian treaty although it knew that the Middle East Command proposals were about to be presented.

This subject has been linked, naturally, with that of forces for the area and, more recently, with that of commitment of token forces in the Middle East in peace time.

2. It first arose for consideration specifically in a message received through the United Kingdom High Commissioner's Office which arrived after the Australian delegation had left for London. It was cabled to Sir Frederick Shedden [Secretary of the Australian Department of Defence] by Prime Minister's Department on 21st June. The message indicated that the United Kingdom government was discussing Middle East organisation with United States of America. It foresaw a Middle East Allied Command to be set up in peace and 'associated with' N.A.T.O. It should include Australian and New Zealand Headquarters Officers and Turkey and Greece should also 'be associated with' the Command. The position of Middle East States themselves also 'required examination'.

3. The London Conference was informed that the discussions with the United States of America were continuing and it was possible that 'the proposals might have to go before the N[orth].A[tlantic].T[reaty]. Council'.

4. The Conference Resolutions for consideration by Governments concerned included:

> '(i) It is *agreed* that in any comprehensive Command structure to be established in the Middle East, contributing countries of Commonwealth should be adequately represented.
>
> (The principle of associating the non-N.A.T.O. members of the Commonwealth with the higher direction of global war both political and strategic be accepted.)
>
> (j) Governments of Australia, New Zealand and South Africa will give consideration to the question of stationing token forces in the Middle East in peacetime.'

5. It does not appear that the Conference discussed the Middle East Command proposal any further. The resolutions were those proposed by the United Kingdom.

6. The question of token forces was referred by the Minister of Defence in a Cabinet Agenda which, it is understood, has been deferred. The Defence conclusion was that a token air force component should be sent in peace.

7. Apparently the question of Middle East Command next arose in a letter of 17th August from the United Kingdom High Commissioner enclosing a copy of a United Kingdom paper on the subject which was to be submitted to the Standing Group of N.A.T.O. It was later explained that the Standing Group would refer its own redraft to the Military Representatives' Committee on 23rd August asking for the Committee's comments by 31st August.

8. This paper of 17th August (which has been sent to the Minister by the Secretary, Department of External Affairs) was submitted to the Department of Defence. The Department of Defence prepared a draft reply. . . .

9. Meanwhile some changes in the situation appeared. A cable from the Australian Minister in Cairo on the breakdown of negotiations with Egypt stated (15th August):

> 'The British Government appreciates the position and [Sir Ralph] Stevenson [British ambassador in Cairo] has been given a most secret discretion which may be a trump card. He is authorised to announce to Egypt details of a Middle East defence scheme in which it is proposed Egypt will share as equal partner with Great Britain and other nations. It will be a Middle East command, and although at first naturally a British Commander will be in charge later on any other competent com-

mander of the new Allied Middle East Command could be in command.

'Stevenson will put the proposition to the Egyptians just before the proposed date of the announcement in the Egyptian Parliament of the abrogation of the Treaty.'

Australian Archives (ACT), A462/2, 439/1/10 part 1, Middle East Command – history, prepared by Alan Watt, Top Secret, 5 September 1951.

3

The Conservatives: deterrence and limitation, 1952–64

Shortly after becoming Prime Minister Winston Churchill entrusted his Minister of Defence, Earl Alexander of Tunis, with the task of investigating economies in Britain's military commitments. The 1952 Defence Policy and Global Strategy Paper outlined what the Chiefs of Staff regarded as 'reasonable' preparations for hot war. Their recommendations were undermined by the Treasury under R. A. Butler, who was concerned that the rearmament programme would reduce living standards in Britain. He was assisted by Duncan Sandys, the Minister of Supply, who attacked the navy's carrier and cruiser programme and argued for the strengthening of the strategic bomber and air defence fighter forces. But fears that the Royal Air Force's V bombers would be vulnerable to Soviet surface-to-air missiles, and NATO requirements for three carrier groups in the north east Atlantic, helped to save the navy. Sir Rhoderick McGrigor, the First Sea Lord, looked to the introduction of strategic ballistic missiles, atomic-powered submarines, destroyers and frigates equipped with missiles, and carriers with vertical take-off strike aircraft. The successful test of the American hydrogen bomb in November 1952 also contributed significantly to a further defence review which further undermined the 1952 Defence Policy and Global Strategy Paper. Churchill insisted that Britain needed a hydrogen bomb to remain a great power. Butler hoped that such a thermonuclear weapon would lessen expenditure on conventional forces. The Chiefs of Staff concluded that with thermonuclear weapons, provided the United States maintained its lead, another world war was unlikely, but the Cold War would go on. The main British deterrent should be nuclear forces.

When Anthony Eden became Prime Minister he outlined a British policy based on the proposition that the main threat to Britain's position was political and economic rather than military. In June 1956, before the Suez crisis, Eden instigated a review to take account of Britain's economic circumstances, to cover changes in domestic and overseas policy and adjustments in Britain's defence programme.

With his emphasis on improving the British standard of living Harold Macmillan, as Prime Minister, continued this policy. Macmillan restored the special relationship with the United States, hastened the British abdication in Africa with his 'wind of change' speech, and through his Minister of Defence, Duncan Sandys, initiated a defence policy based on the abolition of National Service, made possible with a reliance on nuclear weapons. In May 1957 the British hydrogen bomb was tested on Christmas Island in the Pacific. The American Congress further amended the McMahon Act in July 1958, and Britain moved towards reliance on American nuclear weapons in a relationship described as one of 'mutual interdependence'. Sandys hoped to replace the Royal Air Force's V bombers with the Blue Streak missile. This was, however, vulnerable to Soviet attack. Macmillan negotiated an alternative with Eisenhower in March 1960: in return for being allowed to purchase the American missile, Skybolt, Britain would permit the Americans to use Holy Loch in Scotland as a submarine base. Against the background of a threatened American cancellation of Skybolt, Macmillan met President John F. Kennedy at Nassau in December 1962 and, despite the opposition of American State Department and Pentagon officials, was offered the submarine-launched alternative, Polaris.

The development of the hydrogen bomb and the revised British defence policy and global strategy meant that the Middle East was no longer cardinal for Britain's security. With the negotiation of withdrawal from the Suez base it was hoped that personpower from there could be diverted to colonial wars in Kenya, Malaya and Cyprus. In January 1957 the Joint Planning Staff of the Chiefs of Staff Committee pointed to Britain's main interests in the area as being in the Persian Gulf and in East and Central Africa. The success of the Anglo-American military operation in the Lebanon and Jordan in 1958 led to the conclusion of the Joint Planning Staff that plans should be instigated with the United States to consider how to use force to prevent a Middle East country from falling under Soviet domination. In 1961, however, Britain mounted a successful military operation on its own to prevent the invasion of Kuwait by Iraq. In 1962 British forces were involved in quelling revolts in the Aden Protectorates and Aden, as well as in Brunei as the 'Confrontation' with Indonesia started. In 1963 British troops went to the assistance of Archbishop Makarios in Cyprus, and also helped to quell mutinies in the newly independent East African territories.

3.1   *1952   17 June*   Defence Policy and Global Strategy Paper

In 1952 the Chiefs of Staff revised Britain's global strategy. Far-reaching changes over the previous two years made this necessary. The allies were, in 1952, in a position to launch a devastating atomic attack on the Soviet Union at the very outset of a war. That had to be well known to the Kremlin. The Soviet Union with its widely spread frontiers and the vast expanse of its territories could not protect itself against an attack of this nature. So it was unlikely that the Soviet Union would deliberately start a war. Rather it would concentrate its efforts on a prolonged Cold War. But the West had to be prepared for a world-war since, even though the Soviet Union might not want one, circumstances could arise that would make war unavoidable. In considering what preparations to make for war, it was necessary to take into account three major developments: the increased accuracy and power of atom bombing; the advent of the small atom bomb for tactical use; and the economic situation. In its opening stages a world war was likely to be an all-out affair, lasting perhaps only a few weeks; during that time Britain, though not defeated, would be very seriously mauled by the Soviet Union's 'atom attack'. At the same time, the allied attack on the Soviet Union, which would be considerably more powerful, was likely to throw the Soviet Union into complete confusion and might well knock the Soviet Union out. But the Soviet Union would probably succeed in this stage in overrunning most of Europe. During the second stage, it was envisaged that those countries 'which had not taken a hammering', such as the United States, would 'turn the tables on Russia and in due course complete her defeat'. Australia would make a major contribution during the second stage. The Chiefs of Staff had decided that it was economically impossible to prepare and build up the necessary reserves for a prolonged war. Efforts had to be concentrated on producing forces and equipment for an intense, all-out conflict of short duration. In the view of the Chiefs of Staff in the Cold War period, the main effort had to be directed to the prevention of world war. In the Cold War, Europe had to be given top priority, with the Far East next and after that the Middle East. In a hot war Europe should remain a top priority, but the Middle East should be given priority above the Far East owing to the importance of communications through the Middle East, its oil and the 'necessity to prevent Communism from spreading throughout Africa'.

Section VIII. – Conclusions to Part I

Conclusions

71. We conclude as follows:

(a) The Free World is menaced everywhere by Russian and Chinese Imperialist expansion, working through and with Communism. All must be brought to recognise the danger and the need to take part in fighting it.

(b) The first aim of allied policy must be to prevent war.

(c) There is in the foreseeable future no effective defence against atomic attack.

(d) The knowledge that atomic attack would be swift, overwhelming and certain is the main deterrent that will prevent Russia risking world war.

(e) The Western Allies must keep their lead in atomic weapons and in the means of their delivery, and must retain the liberty to use them.

(f) As a subsidiary deterrent, and as an essential factor in the Cold War, the nations of the Free World must build up a sufficiency of land and tactical air forces at readiness in threatened areas, particularly in Western Europe.

(g) If these deterrent steps are taken, the likelihood of war is not great. The most likely prospect before the Free World is therefore a prolonged period of Cold War.

(h) War, if it nevertheless comes, is likely to open with an exceedingly intense but short phase of a few weeks' duration, probably followed by an intermittent struggle gradually spreading worldwide, during which the Allies will be recovering from the initial onslaught and redeveloping their war potential. Allied preparations for war should primarily be directed to ensuring survival in the short, initial, intense phase. It is in any case economically impossible for the Allies to provide and maintain the equipment and forces for a long war at a high tempo.

(j) Consequently, the Allies should now initiate a reassessment of the forces to be built up for war, particularly in Western Europe, taking into account the effect of atomic attack in Russia and also the tactical value of the small atom bomb.

(k) A further reason for this reassessment is the need to ensure that the forces demanded of the Allies are such that they can be raised and maintained for a long period without endangering the economic stability of the free countries. . . .

(m) The stabilisation of the Middle East States within the Western orbit is an essential measure in the Cold War. Any excessive reduction – let alone a complete withdrawal – of British military forces would result in the rapid spread of Russian influence throughout the area. If it proves possible to organise an Allied Defence Organisation in the Middle East with the support of the United States, Turkey and the Middle East countries, then Russia can be held at bay in the Cold War; it should also then be possible to organise an effective defence of the most important areas of the Middle East in war.

(n) Russia has, in accordance with her traditional policy, turn her main attentions for the present to East Asia, where an important new development is the rise of Communist China as a potentially great military Power. We do not regard China as a Soviet satellite, and allied policy should be directed to driving a wedge between Russia and China. The Allies must do all in their power to deter China from further aggression, particularly in French Indo-China, which is the front line of the Cold war in South East Asia.

(o) Should the Allies fail to deter China from further aggression, they should meet it only with such localised military action as may be practicable. Meanwhile the allied aim should be to build up a strategic reserve of land and tactical air forces for employment against Chinese aggression.

(p) The Allies must be prepared to adopt an increasingly stiff attitude towards Russian aggressive acts, provided action is not taken in places of traditional Russian interest. Opportunities for taking the initiative in the Cold War should be actively sought, but the premature stimulation of resistance in the satellites should be avoided.

(q) There is a real need for a world-wide strategic direction for both the Cold War and the planning of war preparations. The present disjointed efforts are uneconomical and largely ineffective. If this world-wide strategic direction is to be achieved, the first essential is full co-operation between the English-speaking nations. If the United States and Commonwealth agree on a policy, the rest of the Free World will fall in with it.

(r) Thought should be given to the possibility of removing the real danger arising from the division of Germany. The only way in which the Allies can reduce the heavy burden of maintaining large forces in

Europe is by the eventual achievement of a united Germany under the cover of an Anglo-American guarantee.

Public Record Office, London, CAB 131/12, Annex 1, D(52)26, Report by the Chiefs of Staff for the Defence Committee of the Cabinet on Defence Policy and Global Strategy, Top Secret, 17 June 1952. (References to paragraphs within the document have been omitted.)

> Clause l is deleted in the summary in CAB 131/12. It appears in the 'censored' version of the document in PREM 11/49:

(l) The Allies should not take up a position which would deprive them of the ability to use Bacteriological Warfare or Chemical Warfare in retaliation, if such was to their advantage.

> This is a summary of paragraph 42:

Other Weapons of Mass Destruction
42. We have considered what should be the attitude of the Allies to Bacteriological Warfare and Chemical Warfare, which the United Kingdom is at present committed by the Geneva Convention not to use except in retaliation. Research in Bacteriological Warfare has not yet gone far enough to enable us to decide whether or not it would be advantageous to the Allies to use it. The new nerve gases can, however, be used tactically to great advantage and would provide the Allies with weapons of real value against an enemy who relies on massed formations. The Allies should not take up a position which would deprive them of their ability to use Chemical Warfare or Bacteriological Warfare in retaliation if this were to be to their advantage.

Public Record Office, London, PREM 11/49, COS(52)362. fos 85, 80, Report by the Chiefs of Staff on Defence Policy and Global Strategy to be communicated to the Governments of the old Commonwealth Countries, and to the United States Joint Chiefs of Staff, Top Secret, 15 July 1952.

3.2   *1952   4 December*   Proposal to move British military headquarters in the Middle East

At the time of the election of the new Republican administration in the United States, British policy in the Middle East was being reassessed. On 4 December Anthony Eden, the new Conservative Foreign Secretary, told a meeting of the Cabinet, attended by Commonwealth Prime Ministers, that the accession of Turkey to NATO had changed the whole problem. It was also proposed to move the British military headquarters from the Canal Zone. Plans being contemplated envisaged the stationing of an armoured brigade in Libya, a brigade in Cyprus and possibly a brigade in Jordan.

Mr. Eden said that the accession of Turkey to the North Atlantic Treaty Organisation had changed the whole problem of Middle East defence. He also hoped that we should conclude a Treaty with Libya which would give us certain strategic facilities. It might well be possible to devise a successful form of defence for the Middle East, based on Turkey, Cyprus and Libya. Nevertheless, he had not given up hope that General [Muhammad] Neguib [Prime Minister] might be more forthcoming on defence problems. The General's main difficulty was that the economic position of Egypt was weak: the standard of living had fallen since his *coup d'état*, and his own political position was weakened in consequence.

Mr. Eden expressed his gratitude to Australia, New Zealand and South Africa for the practical assistance which they were giving in the formulation of plans for the defence of the Middle East.

Public Record Office, London, CAB 128/25, fos 344–5, CC102(52), 4 December 1952.

3.3   *1952   2 June*   Strategic policy for the Middle East following development of the hydrogen bomb

In 1953 and 1954 disturbances in Malaya, Korea, Kenya and then Cyprus and the need for British troops in those areas meant that the substantial British force in Egypt had to be reduced. Against this background on 2 June 1954 Sir William Dickson, the Chief of the Air Staff, outlined how the problems of the

Middle East had been changed by the development of the hydrogen bomb. On 3 October 1952 Britain had tested its first atomic device at Monte Bello, Australia.

The Chief of the Air Staff [Sir William Dickson] said that our defence problem in the Middle East had been changed by the development of the hydrogen bomb. In view of the weight of atomic attack to which they would be subjected in the opening stages of a major war, the Russians were now less likely to be able to develop a substantial offensive through the Caucasus and we had a better chance of holding them to the north-east of Iraq, possibly in the passes leading from Persia. This new strategic concept increased the importance of our air bases in Iraq, but gave us an opportunity for taking a more constructive line in proposing mutual defence arrangements with the Iraqis. The Chiefs of Staff therefore favoured the conclusion of a new defence agreement with Iraq, but they would prefer to see what progress could be made in the military talks before any offer was made to abandon our rights under the existing Treaty.

Public Record Office, London, CAB 128/27 Pt 1, fo. 284, CC37(54)3, 2 June 1954.

3.4   *1954   16 June*   Decision to produce hydrogen weapons

The Chiefs of Staff on 12 May 1954 discussed future weapon development and concluded that a British hydrogen bomb was vital because 'it would be dangerous if the United States were to retain their present monopoly since we would be denied any right to influence her policy in the use of this weapon'. The Defence Committee took the decision to build a thermonuclear weapon on 16 June 1954. The Cabinet discussed it on 7, 8 and 26 July 1954. On 7 July Churchill spoke to the Cabinet.

5. *The Prime Minister* [Winston Churchill] said that the Defence Policy Committee had approved, on 16th June, a proposal that our atomic weapons programme should be so adjusted as to allow for the production of hydrogen bombs in this country. His recent discussions in Washington and Ottawa had been conducted on the basis that we should produce hydrogen bombs. He therefore suggested that the Cabinet should now formally approve the proposal that

hydrogen bombs should be produced in this country, and should endorse the preliminary action which had already been taken to this end.

The Prime Minister said that we could not expect to maintain our influence as a world Power unless we possessed the most up-to-date nuclear weapons. The primary aim of our policy was to prevent major war; and the possession of these weapons was now the main deterrent to a potential aggressor. He had no doubt that the best hope of preserving world peace was to make it clear to potential aggressors that they had no hope of shielding themselves from a crushing retaliatory use of atomic power. For this purpose the Western Powers must provide themselves, not only with a sufficient supply of up-to-date nuclear weapons, but also with a multiplicity of bases from which a retaliatory attack could be launched. They must put themselves in a position to ensure that no surprise attack, however large, could wholly destroy their power of effective retaliation. These considerations, in his view, made it essential that we should manufacture hydrogen bombs in the United Kingdom so as to be able to make our contribution to this deterrent influence.

Public Record Office, London, CAB 128/27 Pt 2, fos 353, 355, CC48(54)5, Secret, 7 July 1954.

3.5   1954   7 July   Acceptance by Churchill of new British Middle East defence policy

> Churchill on 7 July 1954 confessed to the Cabinet that, despite his earlier doubts, he was now satisfied that the withdrawal of British troops from Egypt could be fully justified on military grounds.

The Prime Minister [Winston Churchill] said that the agreement reached with the United States Government in Washington was valuable both because it broadened the basis for the action which we now proposed to take, and because it would increase the chances that the Egyptian Government would abide by the terms of any agreement we might reach with them. In spite of his earlier doubts he was now satisfied that the withdrawal of British troops from Egypt could be fully justified on military grounds. Our requirements in the

Canal Zone had been radically altered by the admission of Turkey to the North Atlantic Treaty Organisation and the extension of a defensive Middle Eastern front as far east as Pakistan. Furthermore, the advent of thermo-nuclear weapons had greatly increased the vulnerability of a concentrated base area and it would not be right to continue to retain in Egypt 80,000 troops who would be better placed elsewhere. It was also relevant that the conditions in the Canal Zone were damaging both to the morale of the Forces and to recruitment.

Public Record Office, London, CAB 128/27 Pt 2, fos 350–1, CC47(54)2, Secret, 7 July 1954.

3.6   *1954   30 September*   British troops committed to Europe

Following the collapse of the proposed European Defence Community on which the American Republican administration had based its European policy, Eden, to allay American threats of a withdrawal from Europe and to calm French fears about German rearmament, announced that Britain would maintain for an indefinite period four divisions in Europe and the tactical air force.

1. *The Foreign Secretary* [Anthony Eden] reported to the Cabinet on the position reached in the discussions at the Nine-Power Conference now proceeding in London.

The Foreign Secretary said that at the present stage of the Conference it was most important that we should do everything we could to make it easier for Dr. [Konrad] Adenauer [Chancellor of the Federal Republic of West Germany] to secure the support of German public opinion for any settlement on which agreement might be reached. It was possible that the French Government would try to insist that their participation in a general settlement must be conditional on a prior solution of the problem of the Saar. He, therefore, proposed to tell M. [Pierre] Mendès-France [French Prime Minister] privately that, if the French Government were to do this, we should feel unable to adhere to the offer we had made about the maintenance of British forces on the Continent of Europe. It would, of course, remain open to the French Government to try to reach agreement with the Federal German Government about the Saar separately from any general European settlement.

The Foreign Secretary said that, if agreement were reached at the present conference, it would then be necessary to arrange a full meeting of the Council of the North Atlantic Treaty Organisation (N.A.T.O.). If the present momentum was to be maintained, this meeting should be held in Paris during the third week of October, which would involve his leaving London early on 20th October. In these circumstances a debate in the House of Commons on foreign affairs could not be held until the following week, although he could, if necessary, make a statement in the House on 19th October. The United Kingdom Government would become no more committed as a result of the meeting of the N.A.T.O. Council than they would be as a result of a successful outcome to the present Conference. The settlement as a whole would in any case remain subject to Parliamentary approval in due course. . . .

The Minister of Housing [Harold Macmillan] said that there were already signs that the Labour Party would take the line publicly that the commitment we had entered into to retain forces of a certain size on the Continent would preclude any reduction in the length of the period of National Service, and the Government must be ready to deal effectively with this accusation.

Public Record Office, London, CAB 128/27 Pt 2, CC62(54)1, Secret, 1 October 1954.

3.7 *1955 February* Nuclear deterrence and conventional forces in Europe

> Alongside the formation of a military alliance in the Middle East, the Baghdad Pact, British defence policy moved towards a global strategy based upon the nuclear deterrent alongside conventional forces stationed in Europe. British forces in the Middle East were reduced. This policy was outlined in the 1955 Statement on Defence.

Defence Policy

1. Overshadowing all else in the year 1954 has been the emergence of the thermo-nuclear bomb. This has had, and will continue to have, far-reaching effects on the defence policy of the United Kingdom. New and revolutionary problems are posed

requiring courage and imagination for their solution. Nevertheless our problem is still fundamentally a dual one. We have to prepare against the risk of a world war and so prevent it; it is on the nature of these preparations that the existence of thermo-nuclear weapons has its main effect. At the same time we must continue to play our part in the defence of the interests of the free world as a whole, and particularly of the Commonwealth and Empire, in the "cold war"; and we must meet the many other peacetime commitments overseas arising from our position as a great Power with world-wide responsibilities. . . .

The Cold War . . .
17. Our reduced commitments in Trieste, Korea and the Middle East now make it possible to rebuild a strategic reserve of land forces in this country. Coupled with the mobility of the Navy and increasing use of air transport, this will greatly increase our ability to exercise our world-wide responsibilities effectively and economically. . . .

II – The Programmes of the Services
33. This broad review of the strategic implications of the thermo-nuclear weapon does not radically alter the role of any of the three fighting Services. Each has a contribution to make to the three main aims of our defence policy – to build up the deterrent against aggression, to fight the cold war, and to prepare for a major war in case it should come to that.

34. Their roles in these three contexts are not competitive but complementary. Moreover, particularly in considering their preparations for a major war, we must always remember that we shall not fight alone but as a member, though a leading member, of a great alliance. Thus, within limits, the pattern of our own forces must conform to that of the whole.

35. The main contribution to the deterrent is made by the Royal Air Force whose primary task now is to build up the V-Bomber force, with its nuclear potential, to the highest possible state of efficiency and preparedness. The first squadrons of V-bombers will be introduced during this year.

36. The Navy also makes its contribution of heavy carriers to the allied striking fleet whose great mobility and offensive power, to be augmented by guided missiles and by the other modern equipment

which is under development, will add powerfully to our ability to hit the enemy either independently or in support of allied land forces and land-based air forces.

37. The importance of strong land forces prepared for instant action in the defence of Western Europe has already been explained. Elsewhere they are no less an essential part of the deterrent.

38. The main burden of the cold war and of our other peacetime military commitments in the Colonial Empire is borne by the Army whether in active operations against Communist guerillas in Malaya, in helping to restore law and order as in Kenya, or in maintaining confidence and stability elsewhere, for example in the Middle East. For these purposes conventional forces and conventional arms are required.

Cmd 9391, Statement on Defence 1955 (London: HMSO, February 1955), pp. 1, 6, 9–10.

3.8   *1955   23 June*   The Simonstown agreement

> The Cabinet decided to negotiate the return of the British-controlled Simonstown naval base to South Africa. It decided that South Africa would not agree to a firm commitment to Middle East defence, and that it would continue to press for an African defence organisation.

The Prime Minister [Winston Churchill] said that he would not put too high a value on a South African undertaking to contribute towards the defence of the Middle East. In the event, the decision whether or not South African troops should be sent to the Middle East in war would be taken by the Union Government of the day in the light of the circumstances then prevailing. Secret staff talks, to which Mr. [F. C.] Erasmus [the South African Minister of Defence] might be persuaded to assent, would give us almost as much assurance of eventual South African support in this area as any formal commitment by the present Government of the Union. He would therefore prefer to concentrate at this stage on securing the most satisfactory agreements that we could obtain on the Simonstown base and on naval co-operation. On the latter point the agreement which Mr. Erasmus was ready to sign met all our requirements. The South Africans were prepared to place in this country orders for naval vessels to the value of £18 million, and this would have the effect of linking the South African Navy to the Royal Navy for many years to come. As regards Simonstown, the agreement now proposed was defensible so far as strategic considerations were concerned. It was more open to criticism on grounds of discrimination against coloured workers, and we should try to improve the safeguards which it provided for them.

Public Record Office, London, CAB 128/29, fos 152–3, CM17(55)8, Secret, 23 June 1955.

3.9   1956   4 *June*   Reassessment of British defence policy in view of the changes of the objectives of the Soviet Union

> Before the nationalisation of the Suez canal and the Anglo-French invasion of Egypt the Eden government instituted a major review of British defence policy.

Note by the Secretary of the Cabinet [Norman Brook]
In the course of the next few weeks the Prime Minister proposes to consider, with the Ministers immediately concerned, what adjustments should be made in Government policy in view of changes in the methods, if not the objectives, of the Soviet Union. This review, which will take account of our own economic and financial circumstances, will cover changes in domestic and overseas policy and adjustments in our defence programmes.

Public Record Office, London, CAB 134/1315, PR(56)1, Note by Brook for the Policy Review Committee of the Cabinet, Secret, 4 June 1956.

Note by the Prime Minister
The Committee have approved the following as a basis for our military and political planning:
   1. Our political and military objectives are:
   (a) to avoid global war;
   (b) to protect our vital interests overseas, particularly access to oil.
   Attempts to secure these objectives are likely to fail unless we:
   (a) maintain North American involvement in Europe;

(b) maintain a large measure of identity between the interests of the United States and Canada and our own and develop closer co-operation with those countries;

(c) maintain the cohesion of the Commonwealth.

2. In our studies of future policy we must bear in mind that:

(a) The main threat to our position and influence in the world is now political and economic rather than military: and our policies should be adapted to meet that changed situation. Effort must be transferred from military preparations to the maintenance and improvement of our political and economic position.

(b) The period of foreign aid is ending and we must now cut our coat according to our cloth. There is not much cloth. We have to find means of increasing by £400 millions a year the credit side of our balance of payments.

(c) In our defence programmes generally we are doing too much to guard against the least likely risk, viz., the risk of major war; and we are spending too much on forces of types which are no longer of primary importance.

Public Record Office, London, CAB 134/1315, PR(56)11, Note by Eden for Policy Review Committee of Cabinet on assumptions for future planning, Top Secret, 15 June 1956.

3.10   *1957   24 January*   Post-Suez long term defence policy

> The Joint Planning Staff in recommending a long-term defence programme related to Britain's economic resources pointed out in January 1957 that Britain's main interest in the Middle East lay in the Persian Gulf area, and in East and Central Africa.

Long Term Defence Policy

Introduction

1. A long term defence programme is required which will be related to the economic resources of the country. The Minister of Defence in his memorandum to the Service Ministries, dated 21st December, 1956, directed that the armed forces be reduced to a total of about 450,000 uniformed manpower. He apportioned this manpower between the three Services and directed that the long term defence policy should be based on the principle of smaller forces

equipped with up-to-date weapons. He then called for proposals from the Service Ministries for the size, shape and deployment of their forces, and stated that these proposals were to be related to April, 1961. . . .

British Interests outside Europe

9. The United Kingdom has colonies, dependencies and other interests throughout the world. Nearly all these interests are coveted by other States and many of them by neighbouring States. The decision to defend or abandon these interests is politico-economic but we assume that it will be deemed necessary to afford at least a minimum level of defence. We are in no doubt that, failing this minimum defence, our interests will be taken over one by one and that this process, once started, will not take long to complete. . . .

Strategic background . . .

British Interests Overseas

18. Apart from support of the Pacts, important British interests lie to the south and east of the Suez Canal and the Middle East air barrier, particularly in the Middle East oil-producing areas, in Africa and in Malaya. The security of these interests can no longer be so readily ensured by reinforcement from the United Kingdom or the Mediterranean, owing to the length and uncertainty of the routes.

Reinforcement of the Far East

19. A further salient factor in United Kingdom world strategy is the relative inability to bring urgent and effective reinforcement of the Far East from the United Kingdom. . . .

Implications of proposed Size, Shape and Deployment of Forces

37. We consider that the main implications of the proposed size, shape and deployment of our forces would be as follows:

(a) It will no longer be possible for the United Kingdom to engage unilaterally in large-scale limited war with balanced forces.

(b) If world-wide internal security tasks remain at their past level, our ability, as allies, to make a rapid contribution of land forces to limited war will be curtailed.

(c) The actual United Kingdom contribution to NATO and the

potential United Kingdom contributions to SEATO [South East Asia Treaty Organisation] and the Baghdad Pact will be considerably reduced.

(d) The reduction of our fighter forces, even with the early addition of SAGW [Surface to Air Guided Weapons] may have an effect on the morale of our own people and on the prospective enemy's assessment of the risks involved in attacking this country.

(e) The reduction of forces and hence the United Kingdom's great reliance on centrally placed reserves enhances the importance of both air transport and stockpiling of heavy equipment.

Public Record Office, London, DEFE 4/94, fos 194–205, JP(57)8 Final, Top Secret, 24 January 1957.

3.11 *1957 March–April* Bermuda Agreements and the Sandys White Paper on nuclear deterrence

When Eisenhower became President he demoted Britain to the status of being one among a number of allies. There was no special relationship during the Suez crisis. In the aftermath of the Suez crisis Eisenhower revived the special relationship with Britain. Under the agreement he reached with the new British Prime Minister, Harold Macmillan, at Bermuda in March 1957 Britain was to receive sixty intermediate range ballistic missiles (IRBMs) from the United States. These Thor missiles were to be operated under a dual-key arrangement. In April, following the consideration of the Chiefs of Staff of long-term British defence policy, the White Paper on defence which became linked with the name of the Minister of Defence, Duncan Sandys, placed emphasis on the nuclear deterrent for the following five years. The Royal Air Force's V bombers, the Victor, Vulcan and Valiant, would be supplemented by ballistic missiles. Thermonuclear weapons (hydrogen bombs) would be developed. With the ending of conscription in 1962 service personpower would be reduced from 690,000 to 375,000. The smaller conventional forces would be better equipped and mobile. It was estimated that defence expenditure in 1957 would amount to £1,420 million, which was £180 million less than had been planned in 1956.

113

Need for New Approach . . .

2. The present shape of Britain's defence forces was largely settled by the rearmament programme launched in 1950 at the time of the Korean War. However, the ending of hostilities in Korea radically altered the position. The immediate danger of major war receded and was replaced by the prospect of a prolonged period of acute international tension. It was clear that the plan for a short intensive rearmament spurt no longer fitted the needs of the situation, and that for it must be substituted the conception of the 'long haul'. It also became evident that a military effort on the scale planned in 1950, which envisaged expenditure amounting to £4,700 million over three years, was beyond the country's capacity. In an endeavour to keep the cost within bounds, the programme was slowed down and spread out over a longer period. In addition, it has been examined each year and pruned back as far as possible.

3. However, the time has now come to revise not merely the size, but the whole character of the defence plan. The Communist threat remains, but its nature has changed; and it is now evident that, on both military and economic grounds, it is necessary to make a fresh appreciation of the problem and to adopt a new approach towards it.

Scientific Advances

4. In recent years military technology has been making dramatic strides. New and ever more formidable weapons have been succeeding one another at an increasing rate. In less than a decade, the atom bomb dropped at Hiroshima has been overtaken by the far more powerful hydrogen or megaton bomb. Parallel with this, the evolution of rocket weapons of all kinds, both offensive and defensive, has been proceeding apace.

5. It has been clear for some time that these scientific advances must fundamentally alter the whole basis of military planning. But it is only now that the future picture is becoming sufficiently clear to enable a comprehensive reshaping of policy to be undertaken with any degree of confidence.

Demands on Economic Resources

6. Britain's influence in the world depends first and foremost on the health of her internal economy and the success of her export trade. Without these, military power cannot in the long run be supported. It is therefore in the true interests of defence that the

claims of military expenditure should be considered in conjunction with the need to maintain the country's financial and economic strength.

7. Over the last five years, defence has on an average absorbed 10 per cent of Britain's gross national product. Some 7 per cent of the working population are either in the Services or supporting them. One-eighth of the output of the metal-using industries, upon which the export trade so largely depends, is devoted to defence. An undue proportion of qualified scientists and engineers are engaged on military work. In addition, the retention of such large forces abroad gives rise to heavy charges which place a severe strain upon the balance of payments. . . .

Nuclear Deterrent . . .

14. While comprehensive disarmament remains among the foremost objectives of British foreign policy, it is unhappily true that, pending international agreement, the only existing safeguard against major aggression is the power to threaten retaliation with nuclear weapons. . . .

Switch of Resources

67. The new defence plan set out in this paper involves the biggest change in military policy ever made in normal times. In carrying it through a certain amount of disturbance is unavoidable.

68. The large reduction in the size of the forces will inevitably create some surplus of officers and N.C.Os. The proportion will differ for each Service and for the various ranks and branches. Those whose careers have to be prematurely terminated will be given fair compensation and will be helped in every way possible to find suitable employment in civilian life.

69. The volume of defence work of many kinds will be curtailed and some establishments will have to be closed. The manpower and industrial resources released must be absorbed into productive use as quickly as possible; and the Government Departments concerned will do all they can to secure that this switch is effected smoothly.

Cmnd 124, Defence Outline of Future Policy (London: HMSO, April 1957), pp. 1–2, 3, 9–10.

3.12   *1957*   *24 October*   Atomic Energy agreements between Britain and the United States

Against the background of the shock in American circles following the launch by the Soviet Union of its satellite, Sputnik, Macmillan was invited to Washington and told by Eisenhower that the Anglo-American special relationship was based on mutual interdependence. Macmillan was presented with the effective repeal of the McMahon Act. The amendments later passed by Congress authorised the transfer of information, nuclear materials and non-nuclear parts of atomic weapons to any nation that had made 'substantial progress' in the development of atomic weapons capacity. Only Britain met this definition. Macmillan recorded that John Foster Dulles, the American Secretary of State, came to lunch in the British embassy and produced a draft of a declaration to be called the Declaration of Common Purpose. In his diary Macmillan noted:

I glanced at it, and saw, embodied in a lot of verbiage, para. 3 – the end of the McMahon Act – the great prize! [At 6.00 p.m. I] went to see Dulles in his house, for half an hour, before going to the White House for dinner. He said he got on much better now with Selwyn [Lloyd, the British Foreign Secretary], but would like to feel that he could sometimes approach me, either direct or through the President. He seemed very happy at the way the talks were working out. 7.00 p.m. at the White House – drinks and talks before dinner. All the same party as at the plenary session. Another committee (in addition to the two technical committees) had formed itself – Norman Brook and Livie Merchant [Livingston T. Merchant, United States ambassador to Canada]. By dinner, a redraft of the Declaration was available; and later (after dinner) the reports of the two technical committees, as well as one on *general* co-operation, through working parties, over the whole field of our relations – political, economic, propaganda, foreign policy, etc.

Harold Macmillan, *Riding the Storm 1956–1959* (London: Macmillan, 1971), p. 323, quoting Diary, 24 October 1957.

3.13 *1958 February* **Report on defence and Massive Retaliation**

The Sandys paper *Britain's Contribution to Peace and Security*, while pointing to the significance of Sputnik for mutual deterrence, suggested that 'invulnerable second-strike forces' could prevent a world conflagration 'through balancing fears of mutual annihilation'.

Balance of Arms . . .

3. Russia's successful launching of artificial satellites is evidence of her remarkable progress in rocket development. But it should not be thought that this has upset the balance of military power.

4. In fact, the overall superiority of the West is likely to increase rather than diminish, as a consequence of the advent of medium-range ballistic rockets. These weapons, against which there is at present no answer, could, from sites in Europe and elsewhere, dominate practically every target of importance in the Soviet Union. The possession by Russia of rockets of equal range will not, for reasons of geography, afford her any corresponding strategic advantage. It would be of no use to her to attack Western Europe unless she could simultaneously knock out the vital strategic air bases in the United States. She could at present have no reasonable hope of achieving this with manned bombers, and it will still take her several years to complete the development of an accurate inter-continental rocket and produce it in sufficient numbers. Even then, there could be no certainty of the success of an attack. Moreover, by that time the United States, which has now also successfully launched an artificial satellite, will have inter-continental rockets also; and strategic rocket weapons of all ranges will, in due course, be made relatively invulnerable by siting underground. Meanwhile, both sides are proceeding with the development of submarines, capable of firing nuclear missiles from under water.

5. There is thus no military reason why a world conflagration should not be prevented for another generation or more through the balancing fears of mutual annihilation. In fact, there is no reason why all this should not go on almost indefinitely. But that would indeed be a mournful prospect. To-day no country can hope to gain anything by war; and all would derive incalculable benefit from the restoration of mutual confidence and real peace. . . .

Disarmament . . .

12. The West ... relies for its defence primarily upon the deterrent effect of its vast stockpile of nuclear weapons and its capacity to deliver them. The democratic Western nations will never start a war against Russia. But it must be well understood that, if Russia were to launch a major attack on them, even with conventional forces only, they would have to hit back with strategic nuclear weapons. In fact, the strategy of N.A.T.O. is based on the frank recognition that a full-scale Soviet attack could not be repelled without resort to a massive nuclear bombardment of the sources of power in Russia. In that event, the role of the allied defence forces in Europe would be to hold the front for the time needed to allow the effects of the nuclear counter-offensive to make themselves felt. . . .

Nuclear Deterrent . . .

29. This continues to rest primarily upon the strength and constant readiness of the American Strategic Air Command, with its bases all round the world and its vast supply of megaton bombs. However, Britain is now making an increasingly significant contribution to the Western nuclear deterrent. She has a substantial and growing stockpile of kiloton weapons, the design of which is being steadily improved, as a result of the experience gained from the trials at the Maralinga proving ground in Australia. Following upon the successful thermo-nuclear tests at Christmas Island, British megaton bombs are now in production and deliveries to the Royal Air Force have begun.

30. The British strategic bomber force, which is equipped to carry these bombs, provides a mobile and flexible form of military power. While based in Britain its aircraft can be transferred within a few hours to stations overseas. The majority of the squadrons are equipped with Valiants; but the proportion of Vulcans and Victors, with their greater performance, is increasing. These can fly as high and as fast as any bombers in service in any other country; and their navigational and bomb-aiming equipment is of the highest accuracy. In addition, progress is being made with the development of propelled bombs, which can be released from a considerable distance, thereby making it unnecessary for the aircraft to fly into the more heavily defended target area. . . .

34. Now that Britain has a substantial strategic bomber force and a growing stockpile of nuclear weapons of her own, it has become

necessary to co-ordinate operational plans with the United States Air Force. . . .

36. The Western nuclear deterrent will shortly be supplemented by Intermediate-Range Ballistic Missiles, and Her Majesty's Government have accepted the offer of the United States Government to supply Britain with such weapons. . . .

37. A British ballistic rocket of a more advanced type is being developed on the highest priority, in close co-operation with the United States. This is being designed for launching from underground.

Conventional Forces

38. The strategic nuclear deterrent is the decisive factor in preventing major war. But it does not obviate the need for maintaining a substantial shield of land forces, with air and naval support, to defend the frontiers of the free world. Nor could it, of course, be used in localised emergencies, still less for preserving order and stability. For these tasks, which represent a large part of the present responsibilities of all three Services, conventional forces equipped with non-nuclear weapons are required. A high proportion of Britain's military effort will therefore, of necessity, continue to go into forces of this kind.

Cmnd 363, Report on Defence. Britain's Contribution to Peace and Security (London: HMSO, February 1958), pp. 1, 5, 6–7.

3.14   *1958*   *17 December*   **British defence policy designed for Cold War in the Middle East**

At the end of 1958 the Cabinet's Official Middle East Committee presented discussion papers on future British policy in the Middle East. These regarded the primary threat to British interests in the Middle East as being that of Arab nationalism. Soviet, or Communist, influence or control of Middle East countries was viewed as a secondary threat. The Middle East Committee concluded that it seemed probable that the use of force against Arab nationalism in the Middle East which involved bloodletting on any significant scale could not serve British interests. There was an opposing view that Britain, with the support of the United States if anything more serious than a police action were contemplated, should always be prepared to use military force to protect its interests. That view maintained that the Anglo-American action in the Lebanon and Jordan in July 1958 was proof of the effectiveness of such action. With this in mind the Joint Planning Staff of the Chiefs of Staff Committee recommended that London should be prepared to consider with Washington the conditions under which force could be used in the Middle East to prevent a country from coming under complete Soviet domination.

Our views

Nature of the Threat

We believe that there are two distinct threats to the United Kingdom's interests in the Middle East. The more immediate of the two is that of extremist Arab nationalism exploited by [President Gamal Abdul] Nasser, while the long term and ultimately greater threat is penetration by the Soviet Union of the Middle East and through the Middle East to Africa.

Countering the Threat

12. We incline to support the views of the Paper on the best counter-action to the immediate threat of Nasser inspired Arab nationalism for the following reasons:

(a) We believe that providing the United Kingdom does not appear to oppose the sentiments of Arab nationalism, a situation may be brought about in which it would be impossible for Soviet exploitation or penetration to take place.

(b) We consider that it will always be very difficult to determine the stage at which the internal situation of a Middle East country has reached the point at which the United Kingdom or the West should intervene with military force if not requested.

(c) If such intervention is to be effective, it must be very swift and take place before the local situation has crystallised. It must be in sufficient force to achieve its aim quickly. There are few places where these conditions could be fulfilled, even if one makes the most optimistic assumptions about availability of troops and aircraft and about speed in obtaining political and international agreement.

(d) Even should intervention be requested, there might not be a basis for the survival of the requesting government after the withdrawal of the United Kingdom or allied forces.

(e) In a country in which the situation has become so confused that intervention by request has become out of the question, the re-establishment after intervention of a viable government would also present the intervening powers with a problem of the greatest magnitude. Permanent occupation or control would, we believe nullify completely the advantages which would accrue from intervention in the short term.

13. However, in view of the great importance we attach to the longer term threat of Soviet penetration in the Middle East, we feel that:

(a) The United Kingdom should, where appropriate, be prepared to come to terms with Arab nationalism, even when controlled by Nasser, to counter Soviet penetration.

(b) The United Kingdom should be prepared to consider, with the United States, the conditions under which force could be used in the Middle East to prevent a country from coming under complete Soviet domination.

Public Record Office, London, DEFE 6/52, JP(58)169(Final), Top Secret, 17 December 1958.

3.15   1960   March–April   Skybolt agreement

> Following difficulties in the development of its own missiles Britain, in March 1960, was offered, by the Americans, Skybolt, which was designed to be a long-range missile fired from aircraft. It was thought that Skybolt could extend the life of the Royal Air Force's V bombers. Macmillan, however, preferred submarine-based missiles and wanted Polaris from Washington. The Prime Minister explained his philosophy to the Queen in a letter:

I was able, while in America, to get an assurance from the President that we shall be able to obtain either Skybolt or Polaris when we need them. This will enable us without further hesitation to put an end to Blue Streak, a weapon which the Chiefs of Staff now feel to be obsolescent and unsuitable. To finish it would cost us another £600 million, and by the time it was ready it would really be out of date. Moreover, for political and morale reasons I am very anxious to get

121

rid of these fixed rockets. This is a very small country, and to put these installations near the large centres of population – where they have to be – would cause increasing anxiety to Your Majesty's subjects. A bomber is somehow accepted on its bombing field; and a mobile weapon, either on a truck or better still in a submarine, is out of sight. It was made clear to me that no strings – to use the technical expression – will be attached. In other words, we shall be able to buy the vehicle and make our own warhead. We can thus maintain our independent deterrent, first by prolonging the life of the bomber force (if Skybolt proves satisfactory) and later by acquiring a mobile weapon in some form.

Harold Macmillan Archives, Macmillan to Queen Elizabeth II, 3 April 1960; quoted in Harold Macmillan, *Pointing the Way 1959-1961* (London: Macmillan, 1972), p. 253.

3.16 *1960 1 November* American Polaris submarine base at Holy Loch

Against the background of divisions within the Labour Party, evident at its conference in Scarborough over nuclear weapons, and marches by the Campaign for Nuclear Disarmament (CND), the decision to allow an American Polaris submarine base on the Clyde at Holy Loch was announced in the Queen's Speech to Parliament on 1 November 1960.

[*Queen's Speech*] The United States has made a significant advance in deterrent power. The first Polaris missile-firing submarine, the 'George Washington', will become operational before long. I am told that it will be quickly followed by other vessels now nearing completion. A new and flexible element will thereby be added to the strategic nuclear deterrent. There would be operational advantage and to that extent the deterrent would be strengthened if sheltered anchorage on this side of the Atlantic were available for a submarine depot ship and a floating dock. This Her Majesty's Government have undertaken to provide.

These facilities would be used by United States submarines on routine patrol in peace time. The anchorage will be provided in Holy Loch in the Clyde, and the depot ship should be established there during February of next year. The floating dock will follow later. Supporting facilities will be provided by the Royal Navy. . . .

The Prime Minister [Harold Macmillan] . . . The House will realise that it is impossible to make an agreement exactly on all fours with the bomber base agreement. The deployment and use in periods of emergency of the submarine depot ship and associated facilities in the United Kingdom will be a matter of joint consultation between the two Governments. . . .

As regards general control, therefore, we shall continue to rely on the close co-operation and understanding which exist between us and the United States in all these defence matters and which President Eisenhower has recently reaffirmed.

Wherever these submarines may be, I am perfectly satisfied that no decision to use these missiles will ever be taken without the fullest possible previous consultation, and, of course, it is worth recalling that these mechanisms have a greater degree of flexibility than perhaps some of the present methods of launching the deterrent. We therefore felt it right to conclude this agreement. It is in the tradition of Anglo-American co-operation in joint defence established in peace time more than twelve years ago and carried on by successive British Governments.

United Kingdom Parliamentary Debates, House of Commons, 1960–61, 5th Series, Volume 629 (London: HMSO, 1960), cols 37–8.

3.17   *1962   3 August*   Tactical nuclear weapons

Macmillan, following American concern about the spread of tactical nuclear weapons, raised the issue in Cabinet on 3 August 1962 as to whether Britain should continue to arm its forces with weapons of this sort.

4. *The Prime Minister* [Harold Macmillan] said that consideration of the broad issues of defence policy which would need to be settled before the Estimates for the forthcoming financial year were prepared had revealed points of such importance as to require the attention of the Cabinet. The most important of these concerned the future of the Army's nuclear weapon Blue Water.

The original intention behind the development of these so-called tactical nuclear weapons had been to interpose a stage between small-scale military aggression and the outbreak of strategic nuclear war. The British contribution to the Western strategic nuclear deterrent was assured, since the cancellation on military grounds of Blue Streak, by the deployment of Blue Steel, and subsequently Skybolt, with the V bombers of the R.A.F. The British Army of the Rhine had been equipped with the tactical nuclear weapons Honest John and Corporal, both of United States origin: the next generation of weapons was to consist of the United States Sergeant and the United Kingdom Blue Water, which although it would come into service later than Sergeant was certainly a better weapon.

It was becoming increasingly clear that the concept of a war of movement on the European front with the employment of modern nuclear weapons, but without the exchange of strategic nuclear weapons, was untenable. The scale of devastation which would be caused by the use of the thousands of so-called tactical nuclear weapons already at the disposal of Allied Command, Europe, would be comparable with the effects of strategic nuclear bombardment. If nuclear weapons were to be used for the purpose of enforcing a pause in hostilities and thus allowing time for negotiations even after war had broken out, this seemed to require no more than the provision of limited numbers of nuclear weapons under the direct control of the Supreme Commander. The President of the United States was known to be concerned at the possible consequences of his predecessor's policy of disseminating large numbers of tactical nuclear weapons in Allied Command, Europe, and of delegating authority for their use to subordinate commanders.

The first question for this country was whether we ought to proceed with the policy of arming United Kingdom formations with weapons of this sort, seeing that we doubted the validity of the military case for them and could expect that our allies would come to share these doubts before the weapons themselves came into service.

The second question was how best to present the case for dispensing with tactical nuclear weapons in view of the fact that most of our allies were already committed to them and that the British Army stood in line with other armies which expected to be equipped with Sergeants. . . .

Summing up the discussion the Prime Minister said that any public announcement of the cancellation of Blue Water at the present time must at least cast some doubt on the validity of the present strategy of the Alliance. It would however be unwise to announce that we should propose to acquire Sergeants in the event of our failure to persuade our allies of the rightness of our strategic concepts, because this would greatly strengthen the hands of those in the United States who were concerned to increase the sales of Sergeant. It would be better to insist on the capability of the TSR2 aircraft to discharge whatever role might remain to be performed by nuclear weapons in the front line. Any public announcement should include confirmation of the Government's decision to proceed with the TSR2, the third nuclear-powered submarine and the other important and expensive items in the defence programme which could be justified on wider considerations than applied to Blue Water. Ministers would wish to have further time for reflection on these matters before reaching final decisions: in the meanwhile drafts should be prepared of a public announcement on these lines and of a communication which he might make to the President of the United States, informing him of the Government's decision and of the reasons for it.

Public Record Office, London, CAB 128/36 Pt 2, CC53(62)4, Secret, 3 August 1962.

3.18 *1962 December* Agreement reached over Polaris at Nassau and the 'Special Relationship'

With the threat of the American administration to cancel development of the Skybolt missile, Macmillan led an angry British delegation to meet President J. F. Kennedy and his advisers at Nassau. Macmillan asked for Polaris as a substitute for Skybolt. Despite the opposition of advisers like George Ball Kennedy gave Britain Polaris at low cost and helped to preserve the British independent nuclear deterrent. This alienated the French and eased pressure on Britain to become part of a multilateral force (MLF). In his letter to the Queen from Nassau Macmillan paid tribute to President Kennedy:

It has been a hard and at times almost desperate struggle to maintain the two concepts of interdependence and independence. But I must pay tribute to President Kennedy's sense of fairness and willingness to be persuaded by argument and over-rule those of his advisers who were not sympathetic to our views.

Harold Macmillan Archives, Macmillan to Queen Elizabeth II, 21 December 1962; quoted by Alistair Horne, *Macmillan 1957–1986* (London: Macmillan, 1989), p. 443.

> There was a successful test of Skybolt the day after the Nassau conference ended. Macmillan speculated in his diary about American motives and British independence.

A very successful test was made on the day after our conference ended. Did the President and [Robert] McNamara [Secretary of Defence] know about this or did they expect another failure? But, whatever the test may have shown, it is clear that the American Defence Minister and the White House have decided – on wider grounds – to concentrate on Minuteman (the Intercontinental Rocket) and Polaris (the submarine weapon). It is also clear to me that they are determined to kill Skybolt on good general grounds – not merely to annoy us or to drive Great Britain out of the nuclear business. But, of course, they have handled things in such a way as to make many of us very suspicious. Nor do we yet know what will be the effect of the successful test of Skybolt in American politics. The President is clearly alarmed. The Air Force 'lobby' in Washington, as well as the 'Douglas' lobby, will be much strengthened. All this may have repercussions on the general agreement which we reached and published at Nassau on Friday, December 21st. . . .

Broadly, I have agreed to make our present bomber force (or part of it) and our Polaris force (when it comes) a NATO force for general purposes. But I have reserved absolutely the right of H.M.G. to use it *independently* 'for supreme national interest'.

These phrases will be argued and counter-argued. But they represent a genuine attempt (which Americans finally accepted) to make a proper contribution to *interdependent* defence, while retaining the ultimate rights of a sovereign state. This accepts the facts of life as they are. But I do not conceal from myself that the whole concept will be much knocked about by controversy at home. The Cabinet (which met on the Friday morning and was kept fully informed throughout) did not much like it, although they backed us up loyally.

Harold Macmillan Archives, Diary, 23 December 1962; quoted in Harold Macmillan, *At the End of the Day 1961–1963* (London: Macmillan, 1973), pp. 361–2.

3.19   *1963   20 March*   Debates over the Multilateral Force

The United States proposed a Multilateral Force as a means of coping with difficulties in NATO over West Germany. Britain saw a Multilateral Force as a challenge to its independent nuclear deterrent. Later the Conservative government of Sir Alec Douglas Home and the Labour government of Harold Wilson opposed the idea of a Multilateral Force. Britain agreed with the Soviet Union that a Multilateral Force could lead to nuclear proliferation. Britain did support the Americans in their attempt to secure Soviet agreement to an international non-proliferation treaty, as Britain did not want other countries to acquire nuclear weapons. On 20 March 1963, Edward Heath explained the British position to the House of Commons.

Mr Healey. Could the hon. Gentleman clear up the matter in relation to a multinational force? I understand that so far the Supreme Allied Commander Europe has never been given any control over strategic nuclear weapons. Is it intended that under Her Majesty's Government's proposals for a supranational N.A.T.O. force as put before the N.A.T.O. Council this morning, S.A.C.E.U.R. should be given direct control of a strategic nuclear strike force?

Mr Heath. I have already explained that these questions of the control of the force have got to be worked out by the Alliance generally, and I am not prepared to say what our proposals are going to be in the context of the general discussions in the Alliance. . . .

There are discussions going on at the moment inside the Alliance, in which all the countries concerned can take part, in order to try to work out the arrangements which should be made first for the multinational force and then for the multilateral force.

United Kingdom Parliamentary Debates, House of Commons, 5th Series, Volume 674 (London: HMSO, 1963), 20 March 1963, cols 375-6.

3.20   *1963   July*   **White paper on the Central Organisation for Defence**

The White Paper of July 1963 envisaged a single Ministry of Defence under a Secretary of State. The existing Service Ministries would become Army, Navy and Air Force Departments.

I. Introduction

On 4th March, 1963, the Minister of Defence in the House of Commons announced decisions in principle to strengthen the central organisation for defence.

2. A unified Ministry of Defence will be set up. Authority and responsibility will be vested in a single Secretary of State for Defence.

3. The new Ministry of Defence will absorb the present Ministry of Defence, Admiralty, War Office, and Air Ministry. New arrangements will be made for collaboration between the Ministry of Defence and the Ministry of Aviation.

4. The object is to improve the central control of defence policy without impairing the efficiency and morale of the fighting Services. Their separate identities will be preserved.

5. The arrangements set out in the 1958 White Paper (Command 476) have not in practice secured the degree of central control over defence policy which is necessary in the national interest. A unified Ministry of Defence is essential if the defence budget is to strike a proper balance between commitments, resources, and the roles of the Services.

6. Better arrangements are needed for formulating requirements for weapons and for controlling the defence research and development programme.

7. In certain fields of administration the three Services have different practices. Economy and efficiency may in the long run be improved by removing these differences wherever practicable. In some cases a common Defence approach will replace the practices of the individual Services. In others the procedure whereby one Service undertakes a task on behalf of all three will be extended.

Cmnd 2097, Central Organisation for Defence (London: HMSO, July 1963), p. 1.

3.21 *1963 5 August* Treaty banning nuclear weapon tests in the atmosphere, in outer space and under water

Faced with public demands at home, reassured by its nuclear relationship with the United States, and worried about the dangers implicit in nuclear testing, the Macmillan government worked for a nuclear test ban. Though London favoured a Comprehensive Test Ban Treaty (CTBT), it urged Washington to accept a Partial Test Ban Treaty (PTBT) and argued that verification was not critical. The governments of Britain, the United States and the Soviet Union signed the Test Ban Treaty on 5 August 1963.

Treaty
banning nuclear weapon tests
in the atmosphere, in outer
space and under water

The Governments of the United States of America, the United Kingdom of Great Britain and Northern Ireland, and the Union of Soviet Socialist Republics, hereinafter referred to as the 'Original Parties', . . .

Have agreed as follows:

Article I

1. Each of the Parties to this Treaty undertakes to prohibit, to prevent, and not to carry out any nuclear weapon test explosion, or any other nuclear explosion, at any place under its jurisdiction or control:

(a) in the atmosphere; beyond its limits, including outer space; or underwater, including territorial waters high seas; or

(b) in any other environment if such explosion causes radioactive debris to be present outside the territorial limits of the State under whose jurisdiction or control such explosion is conducted. It is understood in this connection that the provisions of the sub-paragraph are without prejudice to the conclusion of a treaty resulting in the permanent banning of all nuclear test explosions, including all such explosions underground, the conclusion of which, as the Parties have stated in the Preamble to this Treaty, they seek to achieve.

2. Each of the Parties to this Treaty undertakes furthermore to refrain from causing, encouraging, or in any way participating in, the

carrying out of any nuclear weapon test explosion, or any other nuclear explosion, anywhere which would take place in any of the environments described, or have the effect referred to, in paragraph 1 of this Article. . . .

United States Department of State, *Treaties and Other International Acts Series*, 5433 (5 August 1963).

4

Withdrawal from East of Suez and the European emphasis, 1964–79

Initially Harold Wilson's Labour government seemed determined to pursue a policy of world-wide influence, to maintain the nuclear deterrent, and to continue a British presence East of Suez. Faced immediately with economic crises, Denis Healey, the Secretary of State for Defence, initiated defence reviews which led to the cancellation of the British aircraft projects, including the TSR2, and of the CVA 01 class fleet carrier for the navy, and a British withdrawal East of Suez, to be completed by the mid-1970s, plans for which were accepted by the Cabinet in April 1967. Lord Carrington, as Conservative Secretary of State for Defence in the administration of Edward Heath, extended the life of the carrier fleet, but Britain did not sustain a presence East of Suez. It was during the premiership of James Callaghan that a report by Professor Ronald Mason, the Chief Scientific Adviser in the Ministry of Defence, and Sir Anthony Duff, Deputy Under Secretary in the Foreign Office, recommended that Polaris should be replaced with Trident submarines and C4 missiles. In January 1979, on the island of Guadeloupe, Callaghan met President Jimmy Carter, the French Premier, Valéry Giscard d'Estaing, and Chancellor Helmut Schmidt of West Germany to discuss Bonn's concern over the SALT (Strategic Arms Limitation Talks) negotiations and the Soviet deployment of intermediate-range SS-20 missiles which were targeted on Western Europe from a long way inside the Soviet Union. From this meeting evolved the NATO 'twin track' response to the SS-20 missiles. Firstly American cruise missiles would be deployed in Western Europe. Secondly, there would be negotiations with Moscow to eliminate all intermediate-range missiles. Carter also indicated that he was prepared to offer Britain Trident.

4.1   *1964   December*   American view of British assistance in defence

Richard Crossman recorded in his diary the account Harold

131

Wilson, the newly elected Labour Prime Minister, and Denis Healey, his Secretary of Defence, gave to the Cabinet of their visit to Washington and the Johnson administration's suggestion that British forces would be more useful to the alliance outside Europe than in Germany.

Friday, December 11th. We started with a Cabinet at which Harold Wilson reported on his Washington visit. . . .

Turning to Europe, he said the atmosphere was different from what he expected. The President feels as strongly as we do the danger of proliferation of nuclear weapons – and then Harold made a long reference to the problems of China and India, saying that the great watershed of proliferation would be if India were compelled to make a nuclear weapon under threat from China. The Indians, he said, could become a nuclear power in eighteen months once they had decided to do so. That is a very real danger.

Harold then turned to Vietnam and said that the President himself is deeply committed to Vietnam and asked him outright for a British military commitment. Harold had resisted, apart from offering the use of our jungle training team in Malaya and also our teams for anti-subversive activities. He didn't think the Americans really expected him to concede; they wanted not so much the presence of British soldiers as the presence of the British flag. He had persuaded the Americans not to embarrass our Foreign Secretary who, with the Russians, is co-chairman of the Geneva Conference. He ended up by referring to the importance of the communiqué and drawing attention to the last paragraph, emphasising continuing discussion at all levels so that we, the British, are to be in on all the transatlantic conferences. 'They want us with them,' Harold said. 'They want our new constructive ideas after the epoch of sterility. We are now in a position to influence events more than ever before for the last ten years.'. . .

I then asked about our world-wide role: 'If the Americans like us to have a world-wide role what does this mean for us in terms of military commitments?' Healey replied that what they wanted us to do was not to maintain huge bases but to keep a foothold in Hong Kong, Malaya, the Persian Gulf, to enable us to do things for the alliance which they can't do. They think our forces are much more useful to the alliance outside Europe than in Germany.

Richard Crossman, *The Diaries of a Cabinet Minister*, I, *Minister of Housing 1964–66* (London: Hamish Hamilton and Jonathan Cape, 1976), pp. 93–5.

4.2   *1964   16 December*   Labour and peacekeeping East of Suez

> Initially the Labour government decided to retain Britain's peacekeeping role East of Suez. Harold Wilson outlined this to the House of Commons on 16 December 1964:

[*Harold Wilson*] The problem we are facing derives from the fact that alone in the world – apart from the United States and the U.S.S.R. – we are trying to maintain three roles. There is the strategic nuclear role. There is our conventional role within N.A.T.O., our commitment to the defence of Europe, to which we are committed by interest and by treaty. And there is our world role, one which no one in this House or indeed in the country, will wish us to give up or call in question.

Let me say right away, because I do not think that these facts are fully realised here or abroad, how great is the burden we are carrying not entirely on our own account, nor for our own interests alone. We have a major role in the Middle East, defending interests which are not exclusively ours, at a cost of about £125 million a year. We have numerous other contractual commitments in the Middle East and in Asia. We have to be ready at a moment's notice – I fully endorse what the right hon. Gentleman said about Malaysia – to respond to the needs of our Commonwealth partners, not least some of the newest self-governing countries within the Commonwealth. All of us have lively memories of the successful operations mounted in the early months of this year – to the efficiency of which I paid my tribute at the time – though every one of us realised how desperately the thin red line – and what a former Minister called the thin blue line – was stretched. . . .

The Government's conclusion from the first long, cool look at this whole problem is that, on the interpretation so far put on our three roles, we cannot do all that so far has been thought ideally desirable without fatally weakening our economy and, correspondingly, weakening our real defences.

I want to make it quite clear that whatever we may do in the field of

133

cost effectiveness, value for money and a stringent review of expenditure, we cannot afford to relinquish our world role – our role which, for shorthand purposes, is sometimes called our 'east of Suez' role, though this particular phrase, however convenient, lacks geographical accuracy.

I was glad to see last week in Washington the full recognition the United States gave to our unique role as a world peacekeeping Power. They recognise, I know, the importance of the bases we provide in case of need, simply because, as I said, we are there. Our maritime tradition, our reputation, our mobility, despite inadequate equipment, above all our Commonwealth history and connections, mean that Britain can provide for the Alliances and for the world peacekeeping role a contribution which no other country, not excluding America, can provide.

United Kingdom Parliamentary Debates, House of Commons, 5th Series, Volume 704 (London: HMSO, 1964), 16 December 1964, cols 421, 423–4.

4.3   *1965   November–December*   **The TSR2, F–111 and British collaboration with other countries on weapons**

The cancellation of the British-developed TSR2 aircraft and its envisaged replacement by the American-built F–111 marked a British move towards interdependence in military equipment as a basis for defence policy. At the same time as Healey announced the envisaged purchase of the F–111s he indicated that Britain was investigating joint collaboration in defence projects with European partners. The order for the F–111s was cancelled. Collaborative projects with European partners were started in the late 1960s with the establishment of an Anglo-German-Italian consortium to build the Tornado aircraft, and the Anglo-French partnership to build the Jaguar aircraft. There was, however, very little collaboration between Britain and the United States over the building of aircraft in the 1960s and 1970s. The Harrier vertical take-off aircraft developed by the British firm of Hawker Siddeley in the late 1960s was popular with the American Marines, who ordered 114. The Harrier developed into a joint Anglo-American programme in the 1980s with the Americans in overall charge. On 24 November 1964 Healey explained to Enoch Powell the British government's need to make economies in the purchase of aircraft.

Mr. Powell. Does the right hon. Gentleman remember that he has undertaken to announce the Government's decision on the F111A before the end of the year?

Mr. Healey. I have told the House that the option on the F111A requires us to take it up by the end of the year.

Mr. Goodhew. The earlier part of my Question was simply how can the right hon. Gentleman say that he has made a saving on TSR2 when he does not even know what he is going to replace it with, if anything?

Mr. Healey. I am grateful to the right hon. Gentleman for reminding me of this point. The saving of £300 million is on the assumption of a full buy of F111A. We are already clear that the buy we would require of F111A would give us a larger saving than this. If it were decided to take another or cheaper aircraft the saving would be even larger.

United Kingdom Parliamentary Debates, House of Commons, 5th Series, Volume 721 (London: HMSO, 1965), 24 November 1965, col. 503.

4.4   1965   December   Announcement of purchase of F–111s

On 13 December Healey announced to the House of Commons the British intention to buy F–111 aircraft from the United States.

The Secretary of State for Defence (Mr. Denis Healey). On 6th April I informed the House that Her Majesty's Government had no intention of requiring our forces to forgo the aircraft then planned to replace the Canberra towards the end of this decade without making quite certain that they could carry out their operational tasks by other means. I also said that it would not be possible to define these tasks precisely until the Defence Review was completed.

Her Majesty's Government secured from the United States Government an option on the F.111A aircraft under an arrangement which did not require the option to be exercised until the end of this year. The arrangements made also provided that any initial order would be a very small one and that further orders would not be required until April 1967. As I indicated at the time, we wanted to be sure that we would not need to place even an initial order until we had completed the main work on our Defence Review.

I believe that it would be a mistake to take a decision on the Canberra replacement separately from other major decisions on the future structure of our forces. . . . I have therefore asked Mr. [Robert] McNamara [United States Secretary of Defence] to postpone the initial F.111A option for two months until 1st March, and I am glad to say that he has agreed to this request. I believe that this change will meet the convenience of the House.

United Kingdom Parliamentary Debates, House of Commons, 5th Series, Volume 722 (London: HMSO, 1965), 13 December 1965, cols 912–13.

4.5   1966   *February*   East of Suez strategy

In the Defence Review it was stated that Britain would retain a major military capability outside Europe, subject to limitations. The review outlined an East of Suez strategy for the 1970s.

II Britain's Military Role
3. . . . Above all, the Government can, and must, decide in broad terms what sort of role Britain should play in the world in ten years' time, and what part its military forces should play in supporting that role. In short, it has to decide what sort of military capability is likely to make political sense. . . .

N.A.T.O. and the defence of Europe
8. In such a world, the first purpose of our armed forces will be to defend the freedom of the British people. The security of these islands still depends primarily on preventing war in Europe. For this reason, we regard the continuation of the North Atlantic alliance as vital to our survival. . . .

Outside Europe
16. At first sight, a direct threat to our survival seems less likely outside Europe. Although we have important economic interests in the Middle East, Asia and elsewhere, military force is not the most

suitable means of protecting them, and they would not alone justify heavy British defence expenditure. We have, however, a number of obligations, which we cannot relinquish unilaterally or at short notice; some of these obligations will still exist in the 1970s. But, in addition, Britain shares with other countries a general interest in seeing peace maintained, so far as possible, throughout the world. It is this interest above all which justifies our military presence outside Europe. . . .

18. . . . Recent experience in Africa and elsewhere has shown that our ability to give rapid help to friendly governments, with even small British forces, can prevent large-scale catastrophes. In some parts of the world, the visible presence of British forces by itself is a deterrent to local conflict. No country with a sense of international responsibility would surrender this position without good reason, unless it was satisfied that other could, and would, assume a similar role.

19. Nevertheless, to maintain all our current military tasks and capabilities outside Europe would impose an unacceptable strain on our overstretched forces, and bear too heavily both on our domestic economy and on our reserves of foreign exchange. For all these reasons we have decided that, while Britain should retain a major military capability outside Europe, she should in future be subject to certain general limitations. First, Britain will not undertake major operations of war except in co-operation with allies. Secondly, we will not accept an obligation to provide another country with military assistance unless it is prepared to provide us with the facilities we need to make such assistance effective in time. Finally, there will be no attempt to maintain defence facilities in an independent country against its wishes. . . .

Middle East and Far East

22. Further east, we shall continue to honour our commitments to our allies and to play our proper part in defending the interests of the free world. But the load must be more equitably shared than in the past; and we shall aim to make significant economies by deploying our forces more realistically in accordance with the political circumstances in which they are likely to operate.

23. South Arabia is due to become independent by 1968, and we do not think it appropriate that we should maintain defence facilities there after that happens. We therefore intend to withdraw our forces

from the Aden base at that time, and we have so informed the Federal Government. We shall be able to fulfil our remaining obligations in the Middle East by making a small increase in our forces stationed in the Persian Gulf.

24. It is in the Far East and Southern Asia that the greatest danger to peace may lie in the next decade, and some of our partners in the Commonwealth may be directly threatened. We believe it is right that Britain should continue to maintain a military presence in this area. Its effectiveness will turn largely on the arrangements we can make with our Commonwealth partners and other allies in the coming years. As soon as conditions permit, we shall make some reductions in the forces which we keep in the area. We have important military facilities in Malaysia and Singapore, as have our Australian and New Zealand partners. These we plan to retain for as long as the Governments of Malaysia and Singapore agree that we should do so on acceptable conditions. Against the day when it may no longer be possible for us to use these facilities freely, we have begun to discuss with the Government of Australia, the practical possibilities of our having military facilities in that country if necessary.

Other Areas

25. It will be necessary for some time yet to retain substantial forces in Hong Kong, but we can look with some confidence to a reduction of our commitments for the defence of our smaller dependent territories, some of which will soon achieve independence. We do not plan to keep garrisons in British Guiana or the Southern African Territories for much longer. Protection for island territories in the Atlantic, Indian or Pacific Oceans can readily be provided from our major areas of deployment.

The Equipment of our Forces

1. Against the background of the political commitments and military tasks which it foresees, the Government has been able to take some major decisions on the equipment of our forces. The main object has been to strike a balance between quantity and quality. Our forces must always possess enough of the arms and equipment required for the day-to-day tasks of peacekeeping throughout the world: it is also essential that they should have some advanced weapons which can deter potential enemies from raising the level of a

local conflict to a degree which might threaten world peace. We are determined to maintain a proper balance of capability in both these fields.

The Navy of the 1970s

2. The Royal Navy will exploit the most modern technologies, particularly in nuclear propulsion and guided missiles. When the Polaris-carrying nuclear-powered submarine force becomes fully operational in 1969–70, the Royal Navy will take over from the Royal Air Force full responsibility for the British contribution to the nuclear forces of the N.A.T.O. alliance. The running cost of the Polaris force will be under 2 per cent of the total defence budget. By the early 1970s, we reckon to have in service also four nuclear-propelled hunter–killer submarines, which, with their long endurance and immunity to detection, will be a formidable part of our anti-submarine defences. . . .

3. The present carrier force will continue well into the 1970s; but we shall not build a new carrier (CVA 01). This ship could not come into service before 1973. By then, our remaining commitments will not require her, and the functions, for which we might otherwise have needed a carrier, will be performed in another way, as explained below.

The Future of Britain's Carrier Force

4. . . .Experience and study have shown that only one type of operation exists for which carriers and carrier-borne aircraft would be indispensable: that is the landing, or withdrawal, of troops against sophisticated opposition outside the range of land-based air cover. It is only realistic to recognise that we, unaided by our allies, could not expect to undertake operations of this character in the 1970s – even if we could afford a larger carrier force.

5. But the best carrier force we could manage to have in future would be very small. The force of five carriers, which we inherited from the previous Government, will reduce to three in a few years' time. Even if CVA 01 were built, the force would be limited to three ships through the 1970s. The total cost of such a force would be some £1,400m. over a ten-year period. For this price, we should be able to have only one carrier permanently stationed in the Far East, with another normally available at up to 15 days' notice. We do not

believe that this could give a sufficient operational return for our expenditure.

6. We also believe that the tasks, for which carrier-borne aircraft might be required in the later 1970s, can be more cheaply performed in other ways. Our plan is that, in the future, aircraft operating from land bases should take over the strike-reconnaissance and air-defence functions of the carrier on the reduced scale which we envisage that our commitments will require after the mid-1970s. Close anti-submarine protection of the naval force will be given by helicopters operating from ships other than carriers. Airborne early-warning aircraft will continue to be operated from existing carriers, and subsequently from land bases. Strike capability against enemy ships will be provided by the surface-to-surface guided-missile mentioned in paragraph 2 above.

7. In order to give time to reshape the Navy and to reprovide the necessary parts of the carriers' capability, we attach great impor-tance to continuing the existing carrier force as far as possible into the 1970s. The purchase of Phantom aircraft for the Navy will, therefore, go ahead, though on a reduced scale. The Buccaneer Mk. 2 will continue to enter service. H.M.S. Ark Royal will now be given a major refit in Devonport, starting later this year, to enable her to operate both these aircraft until 1974–75. . . .

Canberra Aircraft Replacement

8. The key to the deterrent power of our armed forces is our ability to obtain early warning of an enemy's intentions through reconnaissance and to strike at his offensive forces from a distance in case of need. This role has been assigned to the Canberra aircraft since the early 1950s; this aircraft cannot safely continue after 1970. By the mid-1970s, we intend that the Anglo-French variable-geometry aircraft should begin to take over this and other roles. Both operationally and industrially, this aircraft is the core of our long-term aircraft programme. But, if the Royal Air Force is not to be lacking in a most critical part of its capability for some five years, some arrangement must be made for bridging this gap. We have therefore decided to buy 50 of the F111A aircraft from the United States. Until the Anglo-French variable-geometry aircraft is avail-able, the F111A will be supplemented in the strike role by the V-bombers, which will cease to form part of our contribution to the

strategic forces of the alliance when the Polaris submarines come into service.

Conclusion . . .

3. As far as commitments are concerned, we shall be able to keep our contribution in Europe at roughly its present level, but only if some means is found of meeting the foreign exchange costs. We shall make substantial savings in the Mediterranean, but will discharge our commitments in the area, including those to Libya and CENTO [Central Treaty Organisation]. In the Middle East, we shall give up the base at Aden and disengage ourselves until we have reached the hard core of our obligations to the States in the Persian Gulf. In the Far East, we intend to play a substantial and constructive role in keeping the peace, always in close collaboration with our allies and Commonwealth partners: but some limitations will be applied to the scale and nature of our military effort there.

4. The forces which we shall get with the reduced defence budget will be modern, flexible and effective. We shall possess, with our aircraft and Polaris submarines, substantial strategic power to contribute to international arrangements. Our forces in Europe will enable us to share fully in supporting a realistic strategy in N.A.T.O. We shall be able to cover our defence and internal security tasks arising in protected and dependent territories, and to support United Nations operations when required. The nuclear-powered submarines, the Type 82 destroyers and the F111A and Phantom aircraft will be among the most advanced military equipment in the world and will act as a strong deterrent to limited war. Our Army units, helicopters, frigates and amphibious forces will have great value in the day-to-day task of keeping the peace.

5. In short, we have been able to make significant savings of money and foreign exchange in return for a comparatively small reduction of our military capacity. As the pattern of our commitments is adjusted, we shall relax the strain on our forces without sacrificing the speed of our reaction in a crisis. If the price of defence today is high, at least we shall be getting value for money.

Cmnd 2901, Statement on the Defence Estimates 1966, Part 1, The Defence Review (London: HMSO, February 1966), pp. 4–11, 14–15.

4.6   1967   18 July   The British withdrawal from the Middle East and the Far East

The Supplementary Statement on Defence Policy of 1967 revised commitments and deployment plans in the light of a British policy to encourage indigenous developments so as to enable the withdrawal of British forces from the Far East and the Middle East.

I Introduction ...

2. We announced in Part I of the Statement on the Defence Estimates 1966 (Cmnd 2901) the decisions which we had taken in order to carry us close to the financial objective for 1969–70. Since then, as part of our continuous review of defence policy and programmes, we have looked beyond 1969–70 to determine how much money and how many men we must plan to have in the 1970s both in relation to the commitments which we foresee and to the resources which the country can afford for defence. We have followed the broad approach to future defence policy described in the Defence Review.

3. But we have also taken account of major developments in the last twelve months: political – the evolution of Government policy towards Europe, progress in revising N.A.T.O. strategy, the Middle East crisis, and changes in South East Asia following the end of 'confrontation'; and economic – a more pressing need to reduce overseas expenditure, a slower rate of growth than expected in the British economy, and the consequent necessity to keep Government expenditure as low as possible. . . .

II Europe

1. The security of Britain still depends above all on the prevention of war in Europe. We, therefore, regard it as essential to maintain both the military efficiency and the political solidarity of the North Atlantic Treaty Organisation. For this purpose, we must continue to make a substantial contribution to N.A.T.O.'s forces in order to play our part in the defence of Europe and to maintain the necessary balance within the Western alliance. This contribution will become even more important as we develop closer political and economic ties between Britain and her European neighbours. . . .

III Outside Europe

1. The aim of our policy outside Europe is, as we said in the Statement on the Defence Estimates 1967 (Cmnd 3203), 'to foster developments which will enable the local peoples to live at peace without the presence of external forces', and thus to allow our forces to withdraw from their stations in the Middle East and Far East. . . .

6. In the Far East, we have decided to reach a reduction of about half the forces deployed in Singapore and Malaysia during 1970–71. The total number of men and women now working in or for the Services in Singapore and Malaysia is roughly 80,000. It includes servicemen stationed ashore and ships' companies on sea service in the Far East, together with both U.K. and locally-entered civilians. We estimate that by April 1968 the total will fall to about 70,000, reflecting the second stage of the reduction of 20,000 in the Far East as a consequence of the end of 'confrontation'. We expect that, between April 1968 and 1970-71, the numbers in Singapore and Malaysia will drop by a further 30,000. This will leave a total of about 40,000, of which about half will be civilians. The reductions will be so phased that, by the early 1970s, the British forces still stationed in Singapore and Malaysia will drop by a further 30,000. This will leave a total of about 40,000, of which about half will be civilians. The reductions will be so phased that, by the early 1970s, the British forces still stationed in Singapore and Malaysia will consist largely of naval forces (including an amphibious element) and air forces; there will still be some Gurkhas in Malaysia. Corresponding cuts will be made in our base facilities. In implementing the reductions, we shall work closely with the Governments of Singapore and Malaysia; and we shall help them to adjust their economies by the grant of financial aid. . . .

VI Conclusion

1. We have been working continuously for almost three years on a major review of defence, revising Britain's overseas policy, formulating the role of military power to support it, and planning the forces required to carry out this role. This Statement marks the end of that process. The decisions in it have been reached after extensive consultations with our allies, to whose views we have given full weight. They spring from the best assessment we can make of Britain's interests and responsibilities as they will develop in a changing world.

2. Substantial savings will be made in the demands of defence on the nation's manpower and financial resources. More of our forces will be based in Britain. We plan no major change in the size of our contribution of N.A.T.O. The savings will be chiefly obtained from a significant reduction in our military presence outside Europe, and from some changes in its deployment.

Cmnd 3357, Supplementary Statement of Defence Policy 1967 (London: HMSO, July 1967), pp. 1–2, 4–5, 12.

4.7   *1968   16 January*   British withdrawal from the Far East and the Persian Gulf

> Wilson devalued sterling on 18 November 1967. By the end of that year ten thousand British servicemen and women had returned from the Far East with the conclusion of the 'Confrontation' campaign in Borneo. Britain evacuated Aden on 29 November 1967 and the People's Democratic Republic of Yemen was established. On 16 January 1968 Wilson told the House of Commons that British forces would be withdrawn from the Far East and the Persian Gulf by the end of 1971.

11. . . .There is no military strength whether for Britain or for our alliances except on the basis of economic strength; and it is on this basis that we best ensure the security of this country. We therefore intend to make to the alliances of which we are members a contribution related to our economic capability while recognising that our security lies fundamentally in Europe and must be based on the North Atlantic Alliance. . . .

12. We have accordingly decided to accelerate the withdrawal of our forces from their stations in the Far East . . . and to withdraw them by the end of 1971. We have also decided to withdraw our forces from the Persian Gulf by the same date. The broad effect is that, apart from our remaining Dependencies and certain other necessary exceptions, we shall by that date not be maintaining military bases outside Europe and the Mediterranean.

13. Again, by that date, we shall have withdrawn our forces from Malaysia and Singapore. We have told both Governments that we do not thereafter plan to retain a special military capability for use in the

area. But we have assured them both, and our other Commonwealth partners and allies concerned, that we shall retain a general capability based in Europe – including the United Kingdom – which can be deployed overseas as, in our judgement, circumstances demand, including support for United Nations operations. . . .

20. *The Navy.* The aircraft carrier force will be phased out as soon as our withdrawal from Malaysia, Singapore and the Gulf has been completed. There will also be reductions in the rate of new naval construction, for example in the nuclear-powered Hunter/ Killer submarines.

21. *The Army.* There will be a considerable increase in the rate of run-down of the Army and in the disbandment or amalgamation of major units. As a result of our accelerated withdrawal from Singapore and Malaysia, the run-down of the Brigade of Gurkhas to 10,000 by the end of 1969 will continue at the same rate until 1971, bringing the total strength of the Brigade to 6,000. . . .

22. *The Royal Air Force.* We have decided to cancel the order for 50 F111 aircraft. . . .

United Kingdom Parliamentary Debates, House of Commons, 5th Series, Volume 756 (London: HMSO, 1968), 16 January 1968, cols 1580–1, 1583.

4.8   *1968   25 January*   The European emphasis

On 25 January Healey explained to the House of Commons that with the withdrawal from East of Suez Britain would have more forces for Europe.

Mr Healey. . . . As a consequence of our withdrawal we shall, despite the big cut in our expenditure, have available a bigger proportion of our defence resources for the defence of Europe than we have today, and an important part of those resources will be available for operations outside Europe – often, I hope, under United Nations auspices – in case of need. . . .

Big changes are on the way in Europe. Whatever our hopes may be, it is not possible now to foresee the precise nature of our relationship with the Common Market in 1972. But what is certain is that our political relations with our European neighbours will be even more important than they are today, and that the scale and nature of our military contribution to their defence may exercise a more important influence on those relations than it has in the last 20 years. . . .

Mr [George] Brown. . . . When we have carried through these cuts and changes we shall have, as my right hon. Friend said this afternoon, modern and powerful forces, powerfully equipped, based in Europe. This will give us – and I beg the Opposition, in their desire to score party points here, not to play us down abroad – a capability, a very powerful capability, which, as we have said, can be used anywhere in the world as we may determine.

United Kingdom Parliamentary Debates, House of Commons, 5th Series, Volume 757 (London: HMSO, 1968), 25 January 1968, cols 624–6, 727.

4.9   1970   20 July   Arms sales to South Africa

The newly elected Conservative government under Edward Heath announced in July 1970 that it was considering reactivating the 1955 Simonstown agreement and selling certain defensive and maritime arms to South Africa. In 1964 the then Labour government had stopped all arms sales to South Africa. New Commonwealth countries opposed this move by the Heath government. South Africa did receive a few Wasp helicopters and spare parts. Following the return of Labour to power in February 1974 Wilson stopped the sale of Buccaneer maritime strike aircraft to South Africa.

The Secretary of State for Foreign and Commonwealth Affairs (Sir Alec Douglas-Home) . . . Her Majesty's Government have an overriding duty to take account of present and future strategic needs, of the United Kingdom and, in that context, a particular concern for the free passage of ships in all circumstances on the vital sea routes round South Africa. It was to that end that the Simonstown Agreement was negotiated.

It is our intention to give effect to the purposes of that Agreement and we believe that, as a consequence, we should be ready to consider within that context applications for the export to South Africa of certain limited categories of arms, so long as they are for maritime defence directly related to the security of the sea routes.

The Government have made abundantly clear their fundamental

disagreement with the racial policies of the South African Government. In no circumstances would there be sales to South Africa of arms for the enforcement of the policy of *apartheid* or internal repression.

United Kingdom Parliamentary Debates, House of Commons, 5th Series, Volume 804 (London: HMSO, 1970), 20 July 1970, col. 49.

4.10   *1970   October*   Supplementary defence statement and the North Atlantic alliance

> In a supplementary statement the Conservative government in October 1970 announced changes in the defence policy pursued by the previous Labour administration. The Five Power defence arrangements for Malaysia and Singapore started on 1 November 1971. The Anglo-Malaysian Defence Agreement under which Britain had to assist either state if it were attacked was replaced by a new arrangement under which Malaysia and Singapore would consult with their Commonwealth partners, Britain, Australia, and New Zealand in the event of hostilities.

Strategic Priorities
4. The security of Britain rests on the strength of the North Atlantic Alliance. The maintenance and improvement of our military contribution to NATO remains the first priority of defence policy. Britain will continue to co-operate with her allies in order to enable the European members of the Alliance to take a fuller and more effective share of the common defence burden. The contribution of the British Polaris force to the Western strategic deterrent will be maintained.

5. But there are also serious threats to stability outside the NATO area. Britain will be willing to play her part in countering them by continuing:

– to honour her obligations for the protection of British territories overseas and those to whom she owes a special duty by treaty or otherwise;

– to support the efforts of the United Nations and other international authorities working to eliminate the sources of conflict between nations and to promote disarmament;

– to support CENTO and SEATO [South East Asia Treaty Organisation].

6. The Government intends in addition

– to contribute to 5-Power Commonwealth defence arrangements relating to Malaysia and Singapore;

– to continue discussions with leaders in the Gulf and other interested countries on how Britain can best contribute to the maintenance of peace and stability in the area.

Five Power Defence Arrangements

7. Britain has long-standing associations with the Commonwealth countries of South East Asia and she shares their interest in the stability of the area. The Government believes that the total withdrawal of forces planned by the previous Administration would have weakened the security of Malaysia and Singapore; and that a continuing British military presence on the spot will be valuable in helping to preserve confidence in the area. It has therefore proposed to the four Commonwealth Governments of Australia, Malaysia, New Zealand and Singapore that Five Power defence arrangements should be established as soon as possible, which would include a contribution of British forces.

8. These arrangements would be based on a political commitment of a consultative nature undertaken equally by all Five Powers, relating to the defence of Malaysia and Singapore. They would replace the bilateral Anglo/Malaysian Defence Agreement.

9. The Commonwealth Governments concerned have welcomed the British intention to maintain a military presence in the area and the contribution of forces which the Government has proposed. They have agreed to join in working out the new political arrangements which will replace the Anglo/Malaysian Defence Agreement. A meeting of Ministers of the five Governments is proposed for next year.

Cmnd 4521, Supplementary Statement on Defence Policy 1970 (London: HMSO, October 1970), pp. 4–5.

4.11 *1971 March* **British decision to withdraw from the Gulf**

In their election campaign the Conservatives had said that they would reconsider Britain's withdrawal from the Gulf and consult leaders in the area. After the Conservative victory the governments of Iran, Saudi Arabia and Kuwait indicated their opposition to a continued British military presence in the Gulf. Sir William Luce, the former Political Resident in Bahrain, consulted authorities in the Gulf and advised against reversing a decision that was seen as the end of British imperial policing in the Middle East. Sir Alec Douglas-Home, the Foreign Secretary, announced to the House of Commons on 1 March 1971 that the treaty relationships would finish at the end of that year. Following the independence of Bahrain and Qatar in August 1971, Britain in December signed new treaties of friendship with Bahrain, Qatar and the newly formed United Arab Emirates. Britain transferred the Trucial Oman Scouts to the United Arab Emirates as the foundation of its defence force. British forces were withdrawn from the area by the end of 1971.

The Secretary of State for Foreign and Commonwealth Affairs (Sir Alec Douglas-Home) . . . The Gulf is an area of outstanding strategic importance, not only to this country but also to Europe and the rest of the world. In January, 1968, the former Government announced their intention to terminate the treaties with Bahrain, Qatar and the seven Trucial States by the end of 1971 and to withdraw British forces from the region. These decisions taken by our predecessors created a new and difficult situation. They brought to the surface tensions which had hitherto lain dormant and led a number of countries which had previously accepted the British presence in the area to declare opposition to its continuance.

In these circumstances, Her Majesty's Government have given very careful consideration to the future relationship between Britain and the Gulf States. In accordance with their undertakings given before the General Election, they have held consultations with the Rulers to consider how best Britain could contribute in the future to the stability of the area.

Hon. Members are aware that the Rulers of Bahrain, Qatar and the seven Trucial States are continuing discussions among themselves about how an acceptable Union of Arab Emirates can be formed. The Saudi Arabian and Kuwaiti Governments are also involved in these negotiations. We do not yet know what decisions will be taken, so my statement today must be related solely to the situation as it stands at present.

Her Majesty's Government strongly support the development of a Union of Arab Emirates. The Rulers have recently been told what Her Majesty's Government are prepared to offer to a Union in the way of continuing links and assistance.

First, we are prepared to offer a Treaty of Friendship, containing an undertaking to consult together in time of need.

Secondly, Her Majesty's Government are willing to hand over the Trucial Oman Scouts, a force whose efficiency and value is well proven and to which I pay tribute today for its role in maintaining peace in the Trucial States, to form a nucleus of a Union Army. We are prepared to make available British officers and other personnel on loan to the Union's forces and to assist in the supply of equipment. The Union itself would naturally assume full financial responsibility for its own forces.

Thirdly, if the Union wishes, elements of British forces, including training teams to assist with the training of Union security forces, could be stationed there on a continuing basis to act in a liaison and training role.

Fourthly, training exercises involving British Army and Air Force units could take place regularly.

Fifthly, there would be regular visits to the area by ships of the Royal Navy.

Provisions would be made for the review of these arrangements where relevant.

On their side, Her Majesty's Government would expect the Government of the Union to continue to permit the overflying and staging of British military aircraft through Union territory on the lines of the present arrangements.

In addition, Her Majesty's Government are ready to consider ways of assisting local police forces if so requested. We are also prepared to help the Union in development and other appropriate fields.

The Rulers have been told that the Treaty of Friendship and these proposals would replace the existing Treaties between the United Kingdom and Bahrain, Qatar and the seven Trucial States. These Treaties, which are the present basis of the Protected status of these nine states and of Her Majesty's Government's right to conduct their international relations, will cease by the end of 1971.

I believe, Mr. Speaker, that arrangements of this kind will form a sound basis for a continuing and effective British contribution to the

stability of the area, and a new and up to date relationship between
Britain and the States concerned.

United Kingdom Parliamentary Debates, House of Commons, 5th Series,
Volume 812 (London: HMSO, 1971), 1 March 1971, cols 1227-9.

4.12 *1975 March* The second Wilson government's defence
review

When Harold Wilson became British Prime Minister for the
second time on 4 March 1974 he inherited a defence policy
from the Heath administration which on the one hand had
maintained a link with the United States: in December 1970
there had been a joint announcement by Washington and
London that against the background of a growing Soviet presence in the Indian Ocean work would start in March 1971 on an
Anglo-American base there to be financed by the Americans; in
April 1973 London, with the assistance of Washington,
initiated a programme to improve the Polaris missile. On the
other hand Heath had refused Washington the use of British
bases during the October War of 1973 between Israel and the
Arab countries. Heath also showed an interest in working with
Paris on the next generation of nuclear weapons. There was also
concern in Western Europe that, with the so-called *détente*
between the United States and the Soviet Union, the parity
established by the Strategic Arms Limitation Agreement of
1972 could weaken the ties between the United States and
Western Europe. Against this background Wilson initiated a
review of Britain's defence commitments which was outlined in
the defence estimates of 1975.

The Government's commitment
1. On 21 March 1974 the Government announced that it had
'initiated a review of current defence commitments and capabilities
against the resources that, given the economic prospects of the
country, we could afford to devote to defence'. . . . The aim of this
Review was to give effect to the Government's pledge to achieve
savings on defence expenditure of several hundred million pounds
per annum over a period while maintaining a modern and effective
defence system. . . .

The Government's Decisions

17. The Government has now taken the basic decisions on the Defence Review which are outlined in the following paragraphs. To achieve the economic as well as the military and political objectives of the Review, Britain's defence forces had to be concentrated on those areas in which a British contribution to collective defence would be most effective in ensuring Britain's security and that of her Allies. This meant that NATO – the linch pin of British security – should remain the first and overriding charge on the resources available for defence; that our commitments outside the Alliance should be reduced as far as possible to avoid overstretching our forces; and that general purpose forces should be maintained as an insurance against the unforeseen. . . .

Non-NATO Commitments . . .

34. We shall continue to maintain forces in the dependent territories of Hong Kong, Gibraltar, Belize and the Falkland Islands. In Hong Kong there will be some reductions in British Servicemen and locally-enlisted personnel; and we are seeking from the Hong Kong Government a larger share of the cost of our forces when the present cost-sharing agreement, which expires in 1976, is renegotiated.

35. The Five Power Defence Arrangements include a consultative commitment, but no obligation to maintain British troops in either Malaysia or Singapore. We shall maintain the commitment; but, with the exception of a small residual contribution to the Integrated Air Defence System, we will withdraw our forces, including the detachment of up to four Nimrods from the British maritime patrol force, by April 1976.

36. We will continue our membership of the South East Asia Treaty Organisation (SEATO), but will take part in fewer exercises in the future. We do not declare forces to the Organisation.

37. Subject to consultations with the Sultan we propose to carry out our 1968 decision to withdraw the Gurkha battalion from Brunei.

38. We plan to withdraw from the staging post on Gan by April 1976 and from the naval communications station on Mauritius. If there is any requirement for facilities in the Indian Ocean area in the future, we shall be able to use Diego Garcia where we have agreed to a modest expansion of facilities by the USA. We shall continue to aim

at realistic progress towards arms limitation in the Indian Ocean. Any such arrangements would clearly require the participation of the US and Soviet Governments; so we support the suggestion made by the Prime Minister of Australia that the US and Soviet Governments should consult together on the possibility of mutual restraint in the Indian Ocean.

39. Oman is fighting against a professionally organised and externally supported rebellion which threatens the stability of the Arabian Peninsula, an area of great economic importance to Britain and from which we receive a lot of our oil. We do not therefore think that it would be right in present circumstances to make any change in the arrangements we have with the Sultan of Oman. We shall, however, make some economies as our need for staging facilities at Masirah declines, and shall continue to keep the level of our military assistance to the Sultan under review.

40. In Cyprus we propose to make some early reduction in our forces stationed there. Meanwhile in order to ease the severe accommodation problems that have arisen within the Sovereign Base Areas (SBAs) since the events of last year, the squadrons of Lightnings and Hercules permanently based on the island, together with the Vulcan strike aircraft stationed there in support of the Central Treaty Organisation (CENTO), have been withdrawn and replaced by smaller numbers of aircraft on detachment from the United Kingdom. For the same reason there will be some reduction in Army personnel.

41. We will retain our membership of CENTO, but will no longer declare any forces to the Organisation: the CENTO-assigned Canberras and Nimrods will be withdrawn from Malta by 1979 and we will no longer permanently station Vulcans on Cyprus.

42. We have announced our intention to enter into discussions with the South African Government to terminate the Simonstown Agreements.

43. The permanent deployment of two frigates to the West Indies will cease in 1976 and the Senior Naval Officer West Indies will be withdrawn.

Cmnd 5976, Statement on the Defence Estimates 1975 (London: HMSO, March 1975), pp. 1, 7, 14–15.

4.13   *1976   March*   **Britain and *détente***

The 1976 statement on defence emphasised Britain's support of
NATO as an instrument of *détente* 'no less than of defence'. It
also stated that the Royal Air Force's early warning system
would be renewed with radars to be developed by the General
Electric Company in Britain.

The Conference on Security and Co-operation in Europe
3. The British Government played a major part in the negotiations of the Conference on Security and Co-operation in Europe
(CSCE) and will honour in full the various undertakings contained in
the Final Act (Cmnd 6198) signed by Heads of State or Government
in Helsinki on 1 August 1975. The successful conclusion of the
Conference does not mean that the divisions of Europe deriving from
the Second World War no longer exist or have become irrelevant;
but it does mark an important stage in the continuous process of a
search for *détente* through better political and military relationships
in Europe. The Final Act of the CSCE sets out an agreed code of
behaviour on relationships between all European States. An essential
part of this code is the undertaking to permit the freer flow of people,
ideas, and information and to promote co-operation of all kinds
between East and West. There is, of course, competition between the
political and social ideas held in different parts of Europe. But the
British Government believes that, if all governments make a real and
sustained effort to observe the standards of behaviour drawn up at
Helsinki, then the prospects of achieving increased co-operation and
confidence between East and West, based on tolerance and mutual
understanding, will have been valuably and visibly enhanced. The
thirty-five States who participated at the CSCE will meet again in
Belgrade in 1977 to review the progress made in implementing the
provisions of the Final Act, before going on to consider further ways
of improving security, developing co-operation, and furthering the
process of *détente*.
4. The Final Act of the CSCE also contained military measures,
designed to promote stability and security by reducing the risks of
misunderstanding and miscalculation. Although not mandatory,
they derive from a firm political decision on the part of all the
governments who participated in the CSCE. The measures include
the prior notification of major military manoeuvres exceeding a total

of 25,000 troops (including amphibious and airborne troops) independently or combined with any possible air or naval components. . . .

Mutual and Balanced Force Reductions

7. While the CSCE dealt in very general terms with some aspects of European security, other more specifically military problems in Central Europe are being covered in the mutual and balanced force reductions (MBFR) negotiations in Vienna, between members of NATO and Warsaw Pact nations. It is noteworthy that, in their speeches at the conclusion of the CSCE in Helsinki, all European leaders stressed that the next need was for progress in MBFR.

8. The agreed objective of the MBFR negotiations is to contribute to a more stable relationship between the Warsaw Pact and NATO and to strengthen peace and security in Europe. The participating States are seeking undiminished security at a lower level of forces in Central Europe. But this objective will not be achieved without a more even military balance between the two sides than exists at present. . . .

10. . . . In an important initiative designed to induce the Warsaw Pact to agree to the Western approach, Allied negotiators tabled on 16 December 1975 additional proposals which included an offer to withdraw a package of American nuclear weapons from the reductions area. In response the Warsaw Pact countries tabled a further proposal on 19 February this year. But this, like their previous proposals, is designed to preserve the disparities between the forces of the two sides. We and our Allies continue to believe that our own new proposals of 16 December, supplementing the West's earlier proposals, provide a reasonable basis for reaching an agreement which, while lowering the level of forces in Central Europe, would ensure undiminished security for all the countries concerned.

Strategic Arms Limitation Talks

11. Following the agreement in principle on the second stage of strategic arms limitation between President Ford and General Secretary [Leonid] Brezhnev in Vladivostok in November 1974, the United States and Soviet Governments have continued their negotiations of the detailed provisions of a new comprehensive agreement on strategic offensive weapons. Although not participants in the

negotiations, the European members of the Alliance are concerned with their outcome and are kept informed of progress through consultations with the United States in the North Atlantic Council. The British Government looks forward with keen interest to a successful conclusion of these negotiations, since strategic stability is essential for the continuance of *détente* in East/West relations. . . .

Expenditure on Equipment . . .
23. *Improvements to Aircraft in Service*
   a. *Nimrod*. Some of the additional Nimrod aircraft on order have been delivered and are being used to back the long-range maritime patrol force. A three-year programme to refit Nimrod with new and improved radio and telecommunications equipment is being undertaken. Its operational capability is also greatly to be improved by fitting better search radar, sonics and tactical systems, and new sonobuoys. These will enhance the capability of the aircraft to detect, classify, and attack submarines, and to detect and shadow surface vessels. The development of the new equipment is proceeding satisfactorily and installation will have been completed by the early 1980s. The modified aircraft will be designated Nimrod MR Mk. 2. The maritime crew trainers for the Nimrod will be modified to Mk. 2 standard at the same time.

Cmnd 6432, Statement on the Defence Estimates 1976 (London: HMSO, March 1976), pp. 1–4, 55.

4.14   1977   12 January   **Parliamentary criticisms of defence policy**

With the extension of the territorial waters of the United Kingdom to 200 miles from the coastline Enoch Powell argued in the House of Commons for a defence policy which gave primacy to the maritime element.

Mr. Powell. . . . I want only to draw attention . . . to a change that has taken place in the last few months, which is much more dramatic in its effect for the future than has yet been appreciated. I refer to the extension to 200 miles round these islands of the territorial waters of the United Kingdom. It is an act of State of profound importance, quite apart from the European Economic Community or the question of the common fisheries policy. We have deliberately made ourselves responsible for the policing of that vast area of our own waters, as we claim them to be, around these islands in the context of fisheries. But we cannot stop there. We are responsible for the policing of those waters in every aspect by which the economy or safety of these islands may be affected.

It is true that in the past – no doubt it would be true again – the decisive single naval engagements were fought at great distances from these islands. Yet the struggle which has been critical to our survival in war has been waged predominantly in, under and above those waters around these islands which we now claim exclusively as our own. We have in a sense entered into our own patrimony and rendered dramatic and tangible what has always been the prime responsibility of our national defence policy.

I believe that in this change there can and ought to lie the inspiration to remould the shape and philosophy of our defence forces as a whole, to establish the primacy of the maritime element – I include the air as well as the naval forces of all kinds – and to treat our domination over that air and sea area which is indisputably ours as the basis for thinking, for training, and for the military ambitions of our people.

United Kingdom Parliamentary Debates, House of Commons, 5th Series, Volume 923 (London: HMSO, 1977), 12 January 1977, cols 1468–9.

5
World-wide commitments, 1979–93

When Mrs Margaret Thatcher went to Washington in December 1979 as Prime Minister, she confirmed that Britain would accept cruise missiles. The debate over the replacement of Polaris by Trident was settled with President Ronald Reagan's decision to accelerate the development of the Trident II D5, which was designed to carry fourteen warheads, and offer it to Britain. The Thatcher government's acceptance of Trident II D5 was approved by victory in the 1983 general election, in which it had been a campaign issue. In January 1981 John Nott replaced Francis Pym as Secretary of State for Defence and instituted a review which enhanced the 'maritime-air and submarine effort' but reduced the size of the surface fleet and the building of new ships. The Falklands War in 1982 emphasised that Britain had world-wide commitments. It challenged a policy, initiated by the Sandys White Paper of April 1957, that moved away from a maritime strategy, towards emphasis on a continental commitment at the expense of safeguarding British interests outside the NATO area. The Chiefs of Staff developed plans for mounting operations outside the NATO area. Nott's successor, Michael Heseltine, through MINIS (Management Information Service), moved to strengthen the control of the Secretary of State over the Ministry of Defence. Heseltine also won the debate against the Campaign for Nuclear Disarmament, which had grown from a few thousand members in 1979 to around a quarter of a million in 1981 with its opposition to the siting of cruise missiles in Britain, and the Labour Party, with its unilateralist defence policy. This was reflected in the Conservative victory in the 1987 general election after a campaign fought mainly on defence policy. After that Labour moved away from unilateralism, and with the ending of the Iran–Iraq War in 1988, the breaking down of the Berlin Wall in 1989 and the collapse of Communism in Europe, as the state of the British economy deteriorated, defence expenditure was again challenged. The new Defence Secretary, Tom King, initiated the 'Options for Change' study to investigate a defence policy for the post-Cold War era which reflected a 'peace dividend'.

The promise of a new era of peace was challenged by Saddam Hussein's

invasion of Kuwait on 2 August 1990 and the subsequent Gulf War. The
defence White Paper of July 1992, while acknowledging Britain to be a
middle-ranking European power, outlined a budget of £24 billion to help
deploy around 80,000 service personnel in twenty-nine countries and
oceans, to buy four Trident nuclear submarines, to maintain three aircraft
carriers, and to develop a controversial European Fighter Aircraft. Britain
retained world-wide defence responsibilities. The July 1993 Defence
Review, while further reducing the armed services in line with 'Options for
Change', and acknowledging that a major external threat of Cold War
dimensions was unlikely in the foreseeable future, pointed to other areas
where risks and commitments had increased and ended the distinction
between 'in and out of area for defence planning'.

5.1   1980   15 July   Anglo-American strategic co-operation and Trident

> Following the election of Mrs Margaret Thatcher's Con-
> servative government in Britain in May 1979, the Secretary of
> Defence, Francis Pym, took soundings in Washington in July,
> and Mrs Thatcher asked President Jimmy Carter for help in
> defence. The two leaders agreed on the 'importance of main-
> taining a credible British strategic deterrent and US/UK stra-
> tegic co-operation'. Pym announced the agreement to buy the
> Trident American weapon system on 15 July 1980. He outlined
> this as follows:

Britain's Strategic Nuclear Force
The Choice of a System to succeed Polaris

On 15 July 1980 the Government published the texts of letters
exchanged between the Prime Minister and President Carter providing for the United Kingdom to buy from the United States the
Trident weapon system, comprising Trident I ballistic missiles and
supporting components for a force of British missile-launching submarines to replace the present Polaris-equipped force.

The new agreement is broadly similar to the 1962 Nassau
Agreement (Cmnd 1915). Following that Agreement and the 1963
Polaris Sales Agreement the United States sold to the United
Kingdom Polaris A.3 missiles and related equipment, together with
continuing spares supply and maintenance support. The four
nuclear-propelled submarines and the nuclear warheads for the missiles were designed and built in Britain. The Polaris force as a whole

is entirely owned by the United Kingdom, and final decisions on its operational use rest with Her Majesty's Government alone; but it is committed to NATO and targeted in accordance with Alliance policy and strategic concepts under plans made by the Supreme Allied Commander Europe (SACEUR), save where Britain's supreme national interests otherwise require. The new Trident force will be acquired, committed and operated on the same basis.

The Future United Kingdom Strategic Nuclear Deterrent Force, Defence Open Government Document 80/23, July 1980, fo. 1.

5.2   *1980 July*   Anglo-American agreement on Trident

Between 10 and 14 July Mrs Thatcher and President Carter exchanged letters of agreement on Trident.

Dear Mr. President,
As you are aware the United Kingdom Government attaches great importance to the maintenance of a nuclear deterrent capability. It will be necessary to replace the present Polaris force in the early 1990s, and having reviewed the options, the Government has concluded that the Trident I weapon system best meets the need to maintain a viable nuclear deterrent capability into the 21st century. I write therefore to ask you whether the United States Government would be prepared, in continuation of the co-operation which has existed between our Governments in this field since the Polaris Sales Agreement of 6th April 1963, to supply on a continuing basis, Trident I missiles, equipment and supporting services, in a manner generally similar to that in which Polaris was supplied.

2. The United Kingdom Government would wish to purchase sufficient missiles, complete with multiple independently targetable re-entry vehicles and less only the warheads themselves, together with equipment and supporting services, on a continuing basis to introduce and maintain a force of 4 British submarines (or 5 if the United Kingdom Government so prefer), close co-ordination being maintained between the Executive Agencies of the two Governments in order to assure compatibility of equipment.

3. The successor to the Polaris force will be assigned to the North Atlantic Treaty Organisation, like the Polaris force; and except

where the United Kingdom Government may decide that supreme national interests are at stake, the successor force will be used for the purposes of international defence of the Western alliance in all circumstances. It is my understanding that co-operation in the modernisation of the United Kingdom nuclear deterrent in this way would be consistent with the present and prospective international obligations of both parties. . . .

Dear Madam Prime Minister,
In reply to your letter of July 10, 1980 I am pleased to confirm that the United States attaches significant importance to the nuclear deterrent capability of the United Kingdom and to close co-operation between our two Governments in maintaining and modernising that capability. To further that objective, the United States is prepared to supply the United Kingdom Trident I missiles, equipment and supporting services, as you propose in your letter, subject to and in accordance with applicable United States law and procedures. . . .

Cmnd 7979, The British Strategic Nuclear Force (London: HMSO, July 1980) pp. 2–3.

5.3   1981   *June*   Conservative reappraisal: the need for flexibility

John Nott, the Secretary of State for Defence, in his White Paper, *The Way Forward*, pointed to the necessity of dealing with an international scene which was 'in several areas unsettled and even turbulent'.

1. The first duty of any British Government is to safeguard our people in peace and freedom. In today's world that cannot be done without a major defence effort. The international scene is in several areas unsettled and even turbulent. Soviet military power, already massive, continues to grow in size, quality and reach, and the Soviet leaders continue to demonstrate their readiness to use it brutally. The North Atlantic Alliance remains vital to us, and neither its strength nor its cohesion can be maintained without our crucial contribution. This is at the top of the Government's priorities.
2. Our policy is translated into practice initially through decisions

on resources. Britain already spends 5.2 per cent of its gross domestic product on defence – one of the highest figures anywhere in the Alliance, even though we are not among the wealthiest members and continue to face sharp economic difficulties. The Government attaches such importance to its security responsibilities within the Alliance that defence expenditure is already 8 per cent higher in real terms than three years ago. It was announced in March, and has recently been reaffirmed, that the defence budget for the next two years (1982/83 and 1983/84) will reflect further annual growth at 3 per cent, in full implementation of the NATO aim. The Government has now firmly decided to plan to implement the aim in full for a further two years – 1984/85 and 1985/86 – and the programme will be shaped accordingly. This may well mean that defence will absorb a still higher share of our gross domestic product. Defence, like other programmes, will now be managed in cash terms: the intention will be provision for 1985/86 21 per cent higher, in real terms, than actual expenditure in 1978/79. In a setting of economic difficulty, and given the Government's determination to hold down total public expenditure, there could be no clearer or more concrete demonstration of resolve to maintain our vital priorities and our Alliance contribution.

The Need for Change

3. The Government's appraisal of the defence programme therefore in no way rests on a desire to cut our defence effort. On the contrary, it reflects a firm resolve to establish how best to exploit a substantial increase, which will enable us to enhance our 'front-line capability' in very many areas. Defence spending on the scale we have decided is a heavy burden on the British people, but one which in our judgement they are prepared to bear. It is then however all the more incumbent upon the Government to ensure that resources are spent to the very best effect in terms of security. . . .

Britain's Defence Roles

7. We have now four main roles: an independent element of strategic and theatre nuclear forces committed to the Alliance; the direct defence of the United Kingdom homeland; a major land and air contribution on the European mainland; and a major maritime effort in the Eastern Atlantic and Channel. We also commit home-based forces to the Alliance for specialist reinforcement con-

tingencies, particularly on NATO's European flanks. Finally, we exploit the flexibility of our forces beyond the NATO area so far as our resources permit, to meet both specific British responsibilities and the growing importance to the West of supporting our friends and contributing to world stability more widely. . . .

Beyond the NATO Area

32. As the Alliance collectively has acknowledged, changes in many areas of the world, together with growing Soviet military reach and readiness to exploit it directly or indirectly, make it increasingly necessary for NATO members to look to Western security concerns over a wider field than before, and not to assume that these concerns can be limited by the boundaries of the Treaty area. Britain's own needs, outlook and interests give her a special role and a special duty in efforts of this kind.

33. Military effort cannot be the sole instrument, but it has inevitably a part to play. The Government intends to sustain and where appropriate expand our activities by way of military assistance, advice, training, loan of personnel and provision of equipment to friendly countries whose security benefits from our help. But help in these ways needs increasingly to be backed by the ability of our own forces to act directly if our friends need us. Many elements of our Services have basic characteristics of flexibility and mobility which make them well suited for this without need for much extra expense or expansion. The Government intends to exploit them more fully, and to make plans and provision accordingly.

34. The Royal Navy has a particularly valuable role. For example, since the conflict broke out last year between Iran and Iraq a maritime presence has been maintained continuously in the Indian Ocean, with warships on rotation supported by fleet auxiliaries. We intend to resume from 1982 onwards the practice of sending a substantial naval task group on long detachment for visits and exercises in the South Atlantic, Caribbean, Indian Ocean or further east. We intend to make particular use of the new carriers, with Sea Harriers and helicopters, in out-of-area deployment. We will co-ordinate all these deployments and exercises as fruitfully as possible with the United States and other allies, as well as with local countries with whom we have close defence relations.

35. Measures will also be taken to enhance the out-of-area flexibility of our ground forces. We will implement plans for a modest

163

extra stockpile of basic Army equipment held ready to support contingency deployments and exercises, and for the designation of headquarters Eighth Field Force to plan and command any operations of this kind. Measures to increase the airlift capability of our Hercules force by fuselage-lengthening are already far advanced, and we have decided to increase its flexibility by fitting station-keeping radar equipment which will enable the aircraft to carry out the co-ordinated drop of a parachute assault force, even in poor weather. We now maintain two battalions fully trained for this role.

36. Our forces will also continue as necessary to sustain specific British responsibilities overseas, for example in Gibraltar, Cyprus, Belize and the Falkland Islands. The Hong Kong garrison will be expanded by one infantry battalion in accordance with our agreement with the Hong Kong Government.

Cmnd 8288, The United Kingdom Defence Programme: The Way Forward (London: HMSO, June 1981), pp. 3–5, 11.

5.4 *1982 December* Lessons of the Falklands War

In May and June 1982 Britain successfully fought a war 6,000 miles away in the South Atlantic against Argentina to restore sovereignty to the Falkland Islands. A Command Paper considering the lessons of the campaign suggested the need to increase the mobility, flexibility and readiness of Britain's armed forces.

The Lessons . . .

203. The Campaign provided the Royal Navy's first experience of battle in the missile age. At San Carlos British forces undertook the first large-scale amphibious operation for many years. And in the land battles for Port Stanley they experienced an infantry battle at brigade strength and in extreme weather conditions. Our analysis of the Campaign is continuing; some new lessons have been learned; many more old lessons have been reinforced. . . .

Conclusion

313. The many useful lessons we have learned from the Falklands Campaign . . . do not invalidate the policy we have adopted following last year's defence programme review. The Soviet Union – its

policies and its military capabilities – continues to pose the main threat to the security of the United Kingdom and our response to this threat must have the first call on our resources. Following the Falklands Campaign, we shall now be devoting substantially more resources to defence than had been previously planned. In allocating these, we shall be taking measures which will strengthen our general defence capability by increasing the flexibility, mobility and readiness of all three Services for operations in support of NATO and elsewhere.

314. Above all, the success of the Falklands Campaign demonstrated conclusively the superb quality and commitment of British Servicemen. It also showed the crucial role of the Merchant Navy, of civil servants on Royal Fleet Auxiliary ships, in the dockyards and elsewhere, and of British industry, all of whom gave tireless and unstinting support to the task force. The quality and reliability of much Service equipment was proved, as was the ingenuity and capacity for improvisation of the Services, defence establishments, and British industry. Finally, the Campaign confirmed that the British people and their Government have the will and resolve to resist aggression and the fortitude to withstand setbacks and casualties. We and our NATO Allies can draw confidence from this: the deterrent posture of the NATO Alliance as a whole has been strengthened.

Cmnd 8758, The Falkland Campaign: The Lessons (London: HMSO, December 1982), pp. 15, 35–6.

5.5   1983   Control of cruise missiles

Following the collapse of the negotiations with the Soviet Union which took place between 1981 and 1983, London maintained its commitment to deploy cruise missiles in Britain, despite domestic opposition. When the first cruise missiles arrived at Greenham Common in October 1983 the government rejected the idea of dual-key control because of the cost, estimated at around £1 billion. The agreement between Churchill and Truman of 1952 was thought applicable. This revived debates about British independence. In February 1983 Mrs Thatcher told journalists:

I am satisfied that those arrangements would be effective. A joint decision on the use of the bases or the missiles would of course be dual control. Got it?'

> she added. But the *New York Times* claimed two months later that Mrs Thatcher wanted the Americans to make an unambiguous statement pledging that the missiles would never be used without British consent, or a clause to that effect in the 1952 Agreement. Richard Perle, the Assistant Defence Secretary, discounted the idea three days later saying he didn't think it was 'necessary to change existing procedures'. A month later Mrs Thatcher maintained that

[the] existing agreement means that no nuclear weapons would be fired or launched from British territory without the agreement of the Prime Minister. This is categorical.

> President Reagan attempted to help her out in a TV interview by saying:

I don't think either one of us will do anything independent of the other . . . er . . . this constitutes a sort of veto doesn't it?

New York Times, 14 April 1983; BBC TV *News*, 27 May 1983; BBC TV *Brass Tacks*, 30 May 1983; quoted by Christopher Grayling and Christopher Langoon, *Just another Star? Anglo-American Relations since 1945* (London: Harrap, 1988) p. 95.

5.6   1983   5 October   Callaghan's criticisms of Labour's defence policy

> Following the Conservative victory in the 1983 general election James Callaghan, the former Labour Prime Minister, on 5 October 1983, attacked his party's defence policy of unilateral disarmament at the Labour Party's annual conference.

What the movement has failed to understand is that it reversed the traditional policy of the Labour Party on which we had fought 11 succeeding elections without any real attempt to convince the British people that what we were doing was right. I happen to believe it is wrong. But you make a fundamental mistake by believing that by going on marches and passing resolutions without any attempt to try to tell the British people what the consequences were, you could carry their vote. And you lost millions of votes. (*Shouting*)

And let me say to Ron Todd, whose passion and sincerity I accept, as I hope he accepts mine on this – would he ever, when he was conducting his wage negotiations on behalf of the motor car workers, have gone into the negotiations and said 'we'll give up some of our cherished practices unconditionally'? Would he not have attempted to get a price for them? He always has tried to get a price for them. And we have got to try to get a price from the Soviet Union. If we are going to put the Polaris missile, which will be reaching the end of its life within a few years, we ought to try to get a price. Ron, that is an elementary element of trade union negotiations. Why do you forget it? (*Applause*)

Report of the Annual Conference of the Labour Party 1983 (London: Labour Party, 1983), pp. 160–1.

5.7 *1984* British reaction to disarmament talks and emphasis on competition in the equipment procurement process

> The 1984 statement of the defence estimates considered the policy introduced by Michael Heseltine when he became Secretary of State for Defence, the system of Management Information for Ministers System (MINIS). This stressed efficiency in management and looked at the functional and not the service divisions within the defence policy and planning structure. The statement also considered the need to promote effective competition in the supply of defence equipment, and British reactions to talks on weapons limitation.

112. We must hope that this demonstration of Alliance unity and resolve will bring the Soviet leadership to realise that they have miscalculated and that their own interests dictate that they should now pay serious attention to the arms control option. The West's position is clear: 1983 was in no sense a deadline for agreement in the negotiations. The NATO deployments are planned to be spread over a five year period and could at any time be halted, modified or reversed (that is, missiles already deployed could be removed) if there were a negotiated agreement in Geneva which provided for this. The

Alliance has already underlined its own commitment to the maintenance of security at lower levels of forces by its decision . . . to reduce
its nuclear warhead stockpile in Europe. If the Soviet Union chooses
to return to the negotiations, all the Western offers, including the
'zero option', remain on the table. A negotiated solution involving
substantial reductions in intermediate range nuclear weapons
remains possible, given the necessary political will on both sides. It
already exists on the NATO side.

113. The other principal negotiations on nuclear arms control are
the Strategic Arms Reduction Talks (START). Although Soviet
intentions towards these negotiations remain unclear following their
withdrawal from the INF talks, some progress was made during
1983 in establishing common ground. The Russians may now be
ready to accept the American premise that the first aim should be to
reduce and not merely to limit strategic nuclear arsenals.

114. In the area of conventional arms, agreement was reached at
the Madrid follow-up meeting of the Conference on Security and
Co-operation in Europe (CSCE) on a mandate for a Conference on
Confidence and Security Building Measures and Disarmament in
Europe (CDE). The first stage of the Conference, which opened in
Stockholm in January with all thirty-five signatory states of the
Helsinki Final Act participating, is devoted to the negotiation of
confidence- and security-building measures. The mandate of the
Conference, at Western insistence, requires that any such measures
should be militarily significant, politically binding, verifiable and
applicable to the whole of Europe up to the Urals. The Conference
offers the opportunity to negotiate measures designed to reduce the
risks of an outbreak of hostilities in Europe by accident or misunderstanding. The measures we and our Allies have proposed would
promote these aims by creating a greater openness and predictability
about normal military activities. We are making every effort to
ensure the success of the Conference.

115. The Mutual and Balanced Force Reductions (MBFR)
negotiations in Vienna resumed in March after some weeks delay
when the East refused to set a date for the next round. We, with the
rest of the Alliance, remain committed to achieving fair and
verifiable force reductions in Central Europe. But recent progress has
not been impressive. Eastern reactions to our comprehensive draft
treaty tabled in 1982 remain negative. An Eastern draft treaty tabled
in June of 1983, although it includes some positive elements relating

to verification, does not meet Western security requirements in a number of significant respects, particularly in its failure to tackle the dispute over data. . . .

Competition

234. The Armed Forces must be provided with the equipment and support services they need in the right quantities, at the right time and at a quality and price which represents value for money for the taxpayer. This means a sustained and vigorous pursuit of efficiency in the Procurement Executive and the supply and logistics organisations. Overheads must be reduced to the bare minimum. This applies equally to [the] defence industry – if it is to live in the keen and competitive international market place. With this in mind a number of recent initiatives to secure greater cost-effectiveness in defence procurement and supply have been taken.

235. Central to our strategy is the need to promote more extensive and effective competition in the supply of defence equipment. Competition is vital for the achievement of the best value for money, the most efficient use of industrial resources and the stimulation of innovation and new ideas. The achievement of more extensive competition between defence firms will bring benefits for the Ministry of Defence, the taxpayer and the firms themselves. There are inevitably some limits to the extent to which competition can be introduced. We need a strong indigenous defence/industrial base, as was illustrated vividly during the Falklands crisis; and the limited number of British suppliers of certain advanced defence equipment is also a constraint on competition within the United Kingdom. But we are nevertheless steadily succeeding in injecting an increasing degree of competition into the equipment procurement process.

Cmnd 9227–1, Statement on the Defence Estimates 1984 (London: HMSO, 1984), pp. 3, 17.

5.8 1985 Arms control, the British endorsement of the Strategic Defence Initiative, Trident, and the European dimension

The defence White Paper of 1985, while stressing Anglo-American co-operation, pointed to the benefits of a stronger and more cohesive European defence industry.

The Future

110. We have learnt the lessons of the 1930s and can today take comfort in the measures taken by successive Governments to sustain and improve our defence capability. This Government is determined that the improvements should continue. . . . the United Kingdom's defence expenditure at the end of 1985–86 will in real terms be some 20 per cent higher than in 1978–79, benefiting from an unprecedented period of seven consecutive years of real increases in spending which this Government has brought to fruition. We intend to capitalise on the higher level of resources now devoted to defence by means of increased value for money, improved efficiency, competition in procurement and the transfer of personnel from the support area to the front line. We shall continue to ensure that our forces are so structured and deployed that potential adversaries are in no doubt of the grave risk they would run in resorting to the use or threat of armed force against us.

111. In all this, we must work closely with our allies. Despite differences of emphasis among member nations, the prospects for the Alliance are good. NATO has been through many difficult periods in its history and has emerged from them stronger and more united. One such period was the 1960s, when the strategy of flexible response was being formulated; another was more recently, when the debate on intermediate-range nuclear forces (INF) was at its height. No doubt there will be more debate and more differences of opinion: there always have been and always will be in an Alliance of free nations. For in the words of the present Secretary General of NATO, Lord Carrington, when he was British Foreign Secretary: 'We have learnt to sing in harmony, whereas others – in the East for example – can only sing in unison.' We therefore welcome debate: it shows that we are facing, not avoiding, the issues. But we should not mistake legitimate differences of approach for any slackening in our unity of purpose in defending our freedom and democratic ideals.

112. One issue that will be the subject of continuing discussion within the Alliance is the Strategic Defence Initiative (SDI). This US programme is intended to investigate the technical feasibility of defence against ballistic missiles. Research in this area is permitted under existing treaties, and given the Soviet Union's own extensive and long-established research programme it is important that the West should not be left behind in this field. The NATO allies are consulting closely and will continue to do so as the US research

programme develops. . . .

113. Another subject that has recently received much public attention is the continuing validity of NATO strategy. . . . we see no convincing case for major changes in NATO's overall strategic concept. We believe that NATO's strategy of flexible response will continue to provide a sound basis for meeting the Alliance's security requirements in the years ahead. Our aim should be not to seek a new strategy, but to find more effective ways of implementing the one we have. A further important issue is Trident. . . . It is our firm belief that no alternative use of British resources would provide anywhere near such a strengthening of collective Alliance deterrence to aggression. . . .

Arms Control . . .

115. Britain has played a leading role in the search for greater international security and a reduction in tension. We have been in the forefront of all the multilateral negotiations in the field of arms control and disarmament since the Second World War, and have become a party to most of the treaties concluded. We have followed the step-by-step approach endorsed by the international community at the first United Nations Special Session on Disarmament in 1978. Our search for lower levels of armaments, and indeed for the abolition of certain types of weapon wherever practicable, has been serious and sustained.

116. A brief look at the period since the war shows that this approach has had some notable successes. . . . agreements reached include Treaties on the Antarctic, a Partial Test Ban, Outer Space, Nuclear Non-Proliferation, and the Sea-bed. We also strongly supported US and Soviet bilateral negotiations on strategic weapons, which led to the SALT I agreement, the Anti-Ballistic Missile Treaty and the SALT II agreement. A prime aim has been to reduce the risk of conflict and to strengthen international security. To this end Britain, France and the United States have each signed agreements with the Soviet Union on 'hotlines' and on the prevention of accidental nuclear war. In 1975, 35 countries adopted the Helsinki Final Act on security and co-operation in Europe; in continuation of this process, the Stockholm Conference on Confidence- and Security-Building Measures and Disarmament in Europe (CDE) opened in January 1984.

117. But these agreements were only made possible by the climate

of confidence existing at the time. Arms control measures are much more difficult to reach in a climate of mutual suspicion. That is why the British Government has been working actively to establish and foster better relations with the East. 1984 and 1985 saw visits by the Prime Minister and Foreign Secretary to Moscow and by the General Secretary of the Communist Party of the Soviet Union, Mr [Mikhail] Gorbachev, then a senior member of the Politburo, to this country as the leader of a parliamentary delegation. The Foreign Secretary visited several countries in Eastern Europe this spring; and Mr [Andrei] Gromyko, the Soviet Foreign Minister, is expected to come to the United Kingdom later this year.

118. Arms control negotiations touch the most vital areas of national security and therefore involve slow and painstaking work. We cannot expect immediate results. But the Government sincerely wants progress, and we are doing all that we can to bring it about. In the following paragraphs we look at the history of, and prospects for, the main arms control and disarmament negotiations of recent years.

119. The Strategic Arms Reduction Talks (START) began in June 1982. The United States' objective, which was strongly supported by the NATO allies, was to make deep cuts in both sides' strategic arsenals, and they put forward a number of proposals for doing so, emphasising the flexibility of their position. The Soviet Union put forward more limited proposals and held progress hostage to NATO's not proceeding with its INF deployments. At the end of 1983 the Soviet Union walked out of the negotiations.

120. The origin of the bilateral United States/USSR INF negotia-tions, which began in 1981, was NATO's decision in 1979 to modernise its longer-range INF forces by the deployment in Europe of ground-launched cruise and Pershing II missiles. This was needed because of the declining effectiveness of existing NATO longer-range INF forces (mainly United States F111 aircraft), and the increasing threat from the large numbers of SS20 missiles being introduced by the Soviet Union. At the same time as the deployment decision, the Alliance stressed its willingness to agree to limits on land-based missiles of this type. The United States, with the full support of the Allies, put forward the 'zero option', under which NATO deployments would not begin if the Soviet Union agreed to remove its SS20s; and offered flexibility in a number of respects in response to Soviet concerns. The latter's position was, however,

fundamentally inflexible. The underlying Soviet aim was to retain a substantial monopoly in longer-range INF missiles while preventing the West from deploying equivalent systems: the various offers they put forward would all have had this result. This approach was coupled with a propaganda campaign designed to influence Western public opinion. The Soviet Union walked out of the negotiations once NATO deployments began, despite the fact that the West had negotiated for two years while Soviet deployments of SS20s continued.

121. Another area of increasing importance is space, where we are anxious to prevent an arms race. Experience suggests that progress in arms control can be easier to achieve when the weapons concerned are still at an early stage of development. At their meeting at Camp David on 22 December 1984, the President of the United States and the Prime Minister agreed on four points, which were reaffirmed during their Washington discussions in February:

– the United States' and Western aim is not to achieve superiority, but to maintain balance, taking account of Soviet developments;

– SDI-related deployment would, in view of treaty obligations, have to be a matter for negotiation;

– the overall aim is to enhance, and not to undermine, deterrence; and

– East–West negotiation should aim to achieve security with reduced levels of offensive systems on both sides.

122. Against this background we very much welcomed the agreement in Geneva this January that the United States and Soviet Union would enter into negotiations on a complex of questions concerning both space and nuclear arms. They agreed that the objective of the negotiations would be to work out effective arrangements aimed at preventing an arms race in space and terminating it on earth, at limiting and reducing nuclear arms, and at strengthening strategic stability. The fact that renewed negotiations began on 12 March demonstrates that the firmness shown by the Atlantic Alliance over the last year has borne fruit; for, despite Soviet pressure, we did not make any one-sided concessions to bring the Soviet Union back to the negotiating table. The United States has made clear its commitment to consultation with its allies, and we shall play a full and constructive part.

123. As to conventional arms control, the scene has again been marked by strong Western efforts but slow progress. Soon after the

opening in Stockholm of the CDE the United Kingdom, together with its NATO allies, tabled a major set of proposals designed to create greater openness about normal military activities (for example, exercises) and thus reduce the likelihood of an outbreak of hostilities by accident, design or misunderstanding. Progress since then has been slow, but procedures have now been agreed which we hope will enable the Conference to get down to serious and constructive negotiations.

124. At the Mutual and Balanced Force Reduction (MBFR) talks in Vienna, the agreed negotiating goal is 900,000 ground and air forces on each side in an area of Central Europe covered by the two Germanies, Belgium, the Netherlands, Luxembourg, Poland and Czechoslovakia. The existing number from which the Eastern side claims it should start to reduce to this level is disputed by the West as a serious underestimate, and in April 1984 NATO took an initiative to break the deadlock by proposing a wholly revised format for the exchange of initial manpower data, concentrating on combat and combat support forces. This new initiative built on previous Eastern proposals and was intended as a response to Eastern concerns. It has, however, met only with a negative response from the Warsaw Pact, while an Eastern initiative tabled in February failed to address the real issues. We shall nevertheless continue to work in MBFR for a balanced agreement with satisfactory verification.

125. The United Kingdom's policy on chemical weapons (CW) has been to seek an arms control solution. We abandoned our chemical warfare capability in the late 1950s, and there has been no change of policy since then. The Soviet Union, by contrast, has continued with an extensive research and development programme, increased its CW stockpile, and maintains a formidable capability to wage offensive chemical warfare .... At the Conference on Disarmament (CD) in Geneva in 1984, further progress was made towards a comprehensive, world-wide and verifiable ban on the development, production, stockpiling, transfer and use of CW and the destruction of existing stocks – although this was slower than we would have wished. Several key problems of verification remain to be resolved. The urgency of a ban was underlined by the report of the UN investigation team of 26 March 1984, confirming the use of CW in the Gulf War. As a result the British Government imposed export controls on certain civil chemicals which could be misused to make chemical weapons; other OECD countries followed our lead. The

World-wide commitments

Geneva negotiations were taken an important step further in April 1984, when US Vice President Bush tabled a comprehensive draft treaty. The Soviet Union has yet to state its detailed position on a number of key verification issues, although it has accepted the principle of on-site inspection of CW stockpile destruction. The United Kingdom has played an active role in this and other negotiations at the CD.

126. Finally, our commitment to the maintenance and strengthening of the international nuclear non-proliferation regime has been demonstrated by the full part we have played in preparations for this year's Review Conference of the Non-Proliferation Treaty, of which the United Kingdom, together with the United States and Soviet Union, is a depository power. . . .

Trident

1. The United Kingdom has possessed nuclear weapons now for over 30 years. We have had a fully operational strategic nuclear capability since the entry into service in 1955 of the V-bomber, succeeded in the 1960s by nuclear-powered submarines armed with the Polaris ballistic missile bought from the United States. This force, now incorporating the Chevaline improvements to the front end of the missiles, will remain an effective deterrent until well into the 1990s. We do not, however, believe that it can be relied upon to provide an effective national strategic nuclear deterrent much beyond the mid-1990s, by which time it will also become increasingly difficult and expensive to maintain. Given the length of time needed to introduce into service a modern strategic nuclear deterrent force, we decided in 1980 to replace Polaris with a force of four nuclear-powered submarines equipped with Trident ballistic missiles. This will ensure the maintenance of an effective deterrent until at least 2020. . . .

8. Of the possible options for providing a ballistic missile, purchase from the United States has the advantage of building on the highly successful collaboration between the two countries on Polaris over two decades, and enables us to take advantage of the very advanced technology developed by the United States, at significantly less cost than if we developed it ourselves. There are, moreover, major operational and financial advantages in buying a missile that will be entering service with the United States Navy in the same timescale: to ensure commonality we have chosen the Trident D5

missile system. This missile is more expensive to buy than the Trident
C4, but, because we will enjoy access to United States through-life
logistic support, running costs will be much lower. In addition, the
D5 offers the best prospects of being able to penetrate Soviet anti-
ballistic missile defences in the face of possible improvements during
the lifetime of the system.

9. The Trident D5 has a greater range and accuracy than Polaris
and is capable of carrying more warheads. This has led to sug-
gestions that we are acquiring a force which is not only greater than
is required for deterrence alone but is also capable of mounting a
'first strike' against the Soviet Union. This is not so. A first strike
would involve a surprise attack intended to destroy the other side's
retaliatory capability before it could be launched. Such a concept
plays no part in the thinking of NATO, the United States, or the
United Kingdom: our policy is solely to deter an attack. A successful
first strike could not, in any case, be achieved by either NATO or the
Soviet bloc, because it would be impossible to detect and destroy
pre-emptively even a major part of the mobile and submarine-
launched systems available to both sides. For the United Kingdom
acting alone, a successful first strike would be impossible even
against just the Soviet silo-based ICBM force, which includes a far
greater number of missiles than the number of warheads available to
this country. We neither have nor seek to have a first-strike
capability; and we could not achieve it even if we wished. . . .

11. It would have been possible to maintain and re-furbish
Trident missiles in this country, as we do with Polaris; but the United
States is willing to make its own extensive facilities available, and we
have made arrangements to use them. Substantial savings will therefore be obtained both in capital and running costs by avoiding the
duplication in this country of facilities which – because of Trident's
requirements for less frequent servicing – would have been used
much less frequently than those currently used for Polaris pro-
cessing. This co-operation, which would not have been possible had
we not switched from Trident C4 to D5, will provide a satisfactory
and economical means of maintaining the missiles of the British
strategic deterrent. . . .

15. Like Polaris, Trident will be assigned to NATO and targeted
in support of the policy and strategic concepts that have been collectively agreed. Our strategic deterrent remains, however, at all
times under the independent control of the British Government and

could be employed independently of the Alliance should our supreme national interests so dictate. A British strategic nuclear deterrent force provides the ultimate guarantee of our national security and makes a unique contribution to the NATO Alliance. The question at issue is not whether this country should become a nuclear power. It is whether we should give up a major defence capability and role that we already possess. Critics of Trident must show that we would be less, rather than more, vulnerable to attack if we unilaterally abandoned a capability that has been an integral part of the structure of collective Western and European security for over 30 years; or else they must argue persuasively that an alternative system could provide a credible and cost-effective deterrent in the complex and demanding environment of the early decades of the next century. We are convinced that for Britain to abandon its nuclear deterrent would constitute a reckless gamble with the peace and security of future generations; and that the Trident D5 system is the best way of providing a credible deterrent into the 21st century. . . .

Strengthening the European Pillar

308. The substantial contribution that Europe already makes to collective security can be further strengthened and made more cohesive by greater co-operation between the European allies. The United Kingdom attaches great importance to the maintenance and development of bilateral relations with its European allies, and is also playing a leading role in the work of the major multilateral organisations devoted to European defence co-operation. The past year has seen the reinvigoration of these bodies, a process that we and our allies intend to take forward in the coming months.

309. The main multilateral forum within NATO for practical co-operation in this field is the Eurogroup, an informal grouping which includes all European members of the Alliance except France and Iceland. Training, logistics, communications, medicine and long-term operational concepts are some of the areas in which Eurogroup sub-groups are active. The Eurogroup is also doing valuable work to publicise current European defence efforts, particularly in North America. The biannual meetings of Eurogroup Defence Ministers both direct this work and provide an important opportunity for discussing major current issues in the Alliance. The United Kingdom chaired the Eurogroup during 1984.

310. Foreign and Defence Ministers of the Western European Union (WEU) countries (Belgium, France, the Federal Republic of Germany, Italy, Luxembourg, the Netherlands and the United Kingdom) met in Rome in October 1984 to celebrate the 30th anniversary of the modified Brussels Treaty. They stressed the importance they attached to the Treaty's goals of strengthening peace and security, promoting unity, and encouraging co-operation within Europe, and underlined the role that the WEU could play in helping to achieve them. Ministers acknowledged the significance of the WEU in promoting European defence co-operation by agreeing normally to meet twice-yearly in future; they also decided on a number of measures to reactivate the WEU and reform its institutions. The WEU is unique in having an Assembly specifically empowered by Treaty to discuss matters relating to the defence and security of Europe. It thus provides a forum for European political debate about issues of major concern to us, and makes it easier to achieve a consensus on them. It has an important role in stimulating greater public debate of security issues, and in generating greater public awareness of Alliance policies. It can act as a 'ginger group' giving political impetus to practical work in other groups aimed at improving European defence co-operation, and assists the development of a more unified, and thus stronger, European contribution to the Alliance. . . .

Equipment Collaboration . . .

314. Despite the problems, there is a creditable history of successful co-operation between NATO partners, going back some 20 years. . . . It includes some important European collaborative equipments that have been successfully brought into service: among them Jaguar, the Anglo-French helicopters, FH70 and Ronado. It also includes a number of projects in development or in earlier study phases in which the United Kingdom is involved, although in some cases decisions on our participation in full development and production remain to be taken.

315. The momentum is being maintained. In the past year there has been further production of the Tornado aircraft with our German and Italian partners. We have agreed with France, the Federal Republic of Germany and Italy the basis of work-sharing production arrangements for the Multiple-Launch Rocket system; and with France and the Federal Republic of Germany, together with the

United States, we have begun development in the high technology area of terminally-guided warheads for that system. The Anglo-Italian EH101 helicopter is now in full development. We expect soon to make a decision on full development of an advanced Anti-Tank Guided Weapon System (Trigat) with our French and German partners; other European nations (Belgium, Greece, Italy, the Netherlands and Spain) have asked to join the programme, and this proposal has been warmly welcomed. Norway has now joined the United Kingdom and Germany in the Advanced Short-Range Air-to-Air Missile programme. A multi-national industrial consortium is conducting feasibility studies for the NATO Frigate Replacement, working to a NATO Staff Target agreed between eight Alliance nations. It is encouraging, too, that Defence Ministers of the United Kingdom, France, Germany, Italy and Spain have agreed a European Staff Target for a European Fighter Aircraft for the 1990s and beyond. Defence industries of the five countries have undertaken feasibility studies in order to examine the basis for collaborative development and production, and the outcome of the studies is now being evaluated.

Cmnd 9430–1, Statement on the Defence Estimates 1985 1 (London: HMSO, 1985), pp. 2–3, 5, 6–8, 16–8.

5.9   1986   *July*   The Westland affair

> In response to the Westland helicopter company's financial straits Heseltine backed the concept of an Anglo-European consortium to make a rescue bid. Leon Brittan, the Secretary of State for Trade and Industry, opposed this, and supported a private enterprise scheme backed by the American Sikorsky helicopter company. In the ensuing fraças both Heseltine and Brittan resigned their Cabinet posts. Westland accepted the Sikorsky bid. Heseltine argued:

It is quite right that . . . there is practically nothing you cannot buy cheaper from the United States of America because they have huge production runs, huge resources, huge research programmes, funded by the taxpayer, and if we want to cut down Britain's industrial capability all we have to do is to go to the United States of America and they will enable us to buy the products cheaper, and they are very good products, which would satisfy most of our demands, I might add with defence as well. But it would be, in my view, totally unacceptable as a judgement, both in the strategic concept that you should never allow the strategic control of your essential defence requirements to be outside your hands, and, secondly, because the consequences in the acceleration of the brain drain, the loss of jobs, the destruction of the high technology base and the civil implications would be wholly unacceptable.

The defence implications of the future of Westland plc, Third Report from the Defence Committee, Session 1985–6 (London: HMSO, July 1986), para. 169.

5.10   *1987   January*   Trident and the alternatives

In January 1987 a Defence Open Government Document argued that Trident was the most cost-effective option to succeed Polaris/Chevaline.

Summary
23. The intrinsic characteristics of a cruise missile system make it less suitable than a ballistic system as the ultimate and only strategic deterrent for a medium size nuclear power. There is much evidence of sustained improvements in Soviet defences against cruise missiles used in the land attack role and for the current generation of cruise missiles the rate of attrition would be extremely high. To achieve the same striking power as Trident would therefore require a significantly larger number of sea based cruise missiles and submarines and would be twice as expensive in both capital and running costs. For similar reasons, an air launched cruise missile solution is likely to cost about double that contemplated for Trident. Furthermore, too much delay and uncertainty would be involved in resting this key procurement decision on future hopes for stealth technology.
24. Of the French ballistic systems, only the M5 is a possible contender as an alternative to Trident. However, its adoption would entail considerable cost penalties.
25. The shorter range of alternative sea based systems compared

with Trident creates operational penalties; in particular, the reduced sea room available makes them potentially more vulnerable to Soviet anti-submarine operations.

26. Both the SLCM [Submarine Launched Cruise Missile] and M5 solution would require complex modification programmes to both launch platform and weapon, resulting in several years delay in the deterrent modernisation programme. Any alternative to Trident would almost certainly demand a new warhead design taking several years. The mid 1990s in-service date would not be met which would mean running on an increasingly ineffective Polaris force or suffering a gap in our deterrent capability.

Conclusion
27. Trident still offers much the most cost effective option for meeting the UK's requirement for a minimum deterrent to succeed Polaris/Chevaline.

Trident and the Alternatives. Modernising the United Kingdom Strategic Nuclear Deterrent Force, Defence Open Government 87/01, January 1987, fos 8–9.

5.11   *1987   June*   Labour's rejection of the Trident option

In its manifesto for the June 1987 election Labour rejected Trident.

Labour's defence policy is based squarely and firmly on Britain's membership of NATO. We are determined to make the most useful possible contribution to the alliance. We can best do that by concentrating our resources on the non-nuclear needs of our army, navy and air force.

The Polaris system of nuclear delivery is ageing and will soon be obsolete. The Tories are buying the expensive American Trident system – a policy which increases nuclear armament without increasing security and, at the same time, diminishes our effective defences. Trident's cost of up to £10 billion will take up so much of our defence budget as to deny modern and necessary equipment to our front line forces. Indeed, this process is already happening.

Labour rejects this dishonest and expensive policy. We say that it is time to end the nuclear pretence and to ensure a rational conventional defence policy for Britain.

Britain will win. Labour manifesto June 1987 (London: Labour Party, 1987), p. 15.

5.12 *1987 28 October* Trident, the 'Moss Bros' missile

In September 1982 Nott had stated that Trident missiles would be serviced at King's Bay, Georgia, in the United States and that the envisaged servicing plant at Coulport in Scotland would be abandoned. A Ministry of Defence official, in a briefing to reporters in October 1987, implied that the Trident missiles were hired from the United States. Denis Healey raised the matter in the House of Commons on 28 October 1987.

Mr Denis Healey. . . . Because the Prime Minister has now made Britain totally dependent on the United States for the supply and maintenance of its strategic nuclear missiles and for the testing of its warheads, Britain is totally incapable of standing up to that great power on any major issue of defence or foreign policy. I suggest that that is something that should disturb Conservative Members as much as it disturbs us.

The long period during which this dependency on the United States will last is rarely recognised. According to the Government, the initial supply of Trident missiles will not be completed until the next century. Under the rent-a-rocket arrangement, we have to swap those Moss Bros missiles every seven or eight years for other missiles from the American stockpile. That will be so as long as the Trident force is operational, which I trust will be some 30 years from the launch of the first submarines. . . .

I conclude with this thought, and I hope that the Minister will give us his observations on it. We need Trident only if we cannot rely on the United States in a crisis, but if we cannot rely on the United States in a crisis, can we rely on the United States to provide us with Trident? There is a clear contradiction there which deserves to be explored. If we continue with the Trident programme, we risk crippling our expenditure on conventional forces for no real military advantage and with serious political disadvantage, which can be summed up as a period of prolonged and humiliating dependence on the United States that will corrupt the whole of our foreign and defence policies.

United Kingdom Parliamentary Debates, House of Commons, 6th Series, Volume 121 (London: HMSO, 1987), 28 October 1987, cols 326, 332.

5.13   *1989   7 March*   The zero option

At the Reykjavik summit of 1986 President Gorbachev accepted an offer, in principle, that President Reagan had made in 1981 which was known as the 'zero option', one which aimed to eliminate ground-launched Intermediate Nuclear Forces (INF). The INF treaty was signed in December 1988. Britain and West Germany objected that the zero option would mean imbalance in the shorter target systems to the advantage of the Soviet Union. Gorbachev subsequently extended the agreement to include systems with ranges between 500 and 1,000 km, as well as from 1,000 km to 5,500 km. This 'double zero' proposal led to questions being asked as to whether the Short-range Nuclear Forces (SNF) should stay in Europe, and over the credibility of flexible response, and raised the possibility of the denuclearisation of Europe. George Younger, the Secretary of State for Defence, told the House of Commons on 7 March 1989: 'none of us wishes to see a third zero in nuclear weapons in Europe'.

Mr Cohen. The Secretary of State says that Denmark fully subscribes to NATO strategy, but does it fully subscribe to the Prime Minister's plans for short-range modernisation in central Europe, as the Germans do not and most of Europe does not?

Mr Younger. None of those countries has yet been called on to make a decision on the matter. They will all have to decide in due course what their views are, but there is a wide measure of agreement on a number of important principles. They are, first, that if we are to have weapons we must keep them up to date; secondly, that the Lance system will be obsolete by 1995; and thirdly, that none of us wishes to see a third zero in nuclear weapons in Europe.

United Kingdom Parliamentary Debates, House of Commons, 6th Series, Volume 148 (London: HMSO, 1989), 7 March 1989, col. 742.

5.14   *1989*   Labour moves away from unilateralism

In its policy review for the 1990s Labour under the leadership of
Neil Kinnock moved away from its policy of unilateral nuclear
disarmament.

Immediately upon taking office Labour will adopt a policy of no first
use of Britain's nuclear capability. It is unthinkable that Britain could
take the first step in unleashing a nuclear holocaust on humankind.
Therefore, if a second stage of START has not begun by the time a
Labour government takes office, we shall as our highest foreign
policy priority take all immediate action open to us to initiate such
negotiations, involving the other nuclear powers. Labour will immediately seek to place all of Britain's nuclear capability – including
Polaris, and as much of Trident as has been completed – into international nuclear disarmament negotiations. The important objective
of early decommissioning, first Polaris and then of Trident, could be
pursued by Britain within the context of the START-2 negotiations,
depending on their pace and progress. If the beginning of START 2
[*sic*] is subject to long delay, and there is good reason to believe that
these negotiations will not make the progress we will require, a
Labour government will reserve the option of initiating direct
negotiations with the Soviet Union and/or with others in order to
bring about the elimination of that capacity by negotiated and
verifiable agreements. Our aim is to bring about the elimination of
that capability. Meanwhile on coming to office a Labour government will immediately end testing of all British nuclear devices.

*Meet the challenge. Make the change. A new agenda for Britain. Final report
of Labour's Policy Review for the 1990s* (London: Labour Party, 1989), p.
87.

5.15   *1990*   Labour and a political role for NATO

With the disintegration of the Soviet empire Labour supported
a political role for NATO.

Defence and Security

Labour's defence policy has been entirely vindicated by the events of
the last year. It will be a firm foundation for the new initiatives
required by the transformed map of Europe.

184

Many of the objectives we set out in our defence policy have already been achieved or are close to achievement. We opposed modernisation of land-based short-range nuclear weapons and supported the 'Third Zero' – in other words, the negotiated destruction of these weapons. Within NATO, only Mrs Thatcher's government supports modernisation. Now that President Bush has announced that modernisation will not take place, the Third Zero is implicitly accepted throughout the Alliance.

Last year, we also looked forward to huge negotiated cuts in conventional armaments. With the effective collapse of the Warsaw Pact and the planned withdrawal of Soviet forces from most of Eastern Europe outside the USSR's own borders, such international negotiation can make possible reductions in United Kingdom defence spending far beyond anything envisaged at last year's Labour Party Conference.

NATO's role

Formidable hazards remain. Turmoil in the Soviet Union and elsewhere on the issue of nationalities threatens the stability upon which all other progress depends.

Nonetheless, there is now no realistic threat of invasion from the East. NATO's doctrine of 'flexible response' based on nuclear weapons has collapsed. The role of NATO must therefore be fundamentally reassessed. We agree with James Baker, the United States Secretary of State, that NATO's role should be political rather than military.

There are two reasons why NATO will be needed for the foreseeable future. First, we in the West need an organisation to negotiate, implement and verify disarmament agreements. Second, NATO's existence makes it unnecessary for the European Community to have any military role – something which Labour would implacably oppose.

A military role for the EC [European Community] would make the position of Ireland as a neutral country very difficult – and make it impossible for Austria, Switzerland and Sweden, as neutral countries, to join. Moreover, the Soviet Union – which has braced itself for membership in NATO of a unified Germany – would feel threatened by the prospect of Eastern European countries joining a Community with a military role.

A unified Germany already poses difficult questions not only for

185

the Community, but also for NATO. Germany can, however, be regarded as a bridge across the divide once represented by the now demolished Iron Curtain. All the countries of Europe now need a forum for regular discussion. A basis is provided by the Helsinki Conference on Security and Co-operation in Europe (CSCE) process.

Looking to the Future (London: Labour Party, 1990), p. 46.

5.16   1990   25 July   Options for Change

> With the end of the Cold War Britain, in June 1990, at the Turnberry meeting of NATO foreign ministers, accepted that NATO should play a more political role. The subsequent British policy known as 'Options for Change' was outlined to the House of Commons on 25 July 1990. British armed forces would be reduced substantially.

The Secretary of State for Defence (Mr. Tom King). . . . In the defence debate last month, I set out the basis on which we have been considering options for change in defence. I would now like to advise the House of the broad proposals that we are considering and on which we will now be consulting with the NATO authorities and our allies, with the defence industries, and, most importantly, with all those directly affected in the armed forces and the MOD's civilian staff. My statement today follows the publication this morning of a valuable report from the Select Committee on Defence on the defence implications of recent events in eastern Europe and the Soviet Union.

The declaration issued at the NATO summit meeting here in London earlier this month said:

> 'Europe has entered a new, promising era . . . This alliance must and will adapt.'

The 'Options for Change' have identified the ways in which our forces might be restructured by the mid-1990s in the light of these developments. The pace of change will depend upon the signature and implementation of a Conventional Forces in Europe agreement, on the progress of the two-plus-four talks, and on how quickly Soviet troops leave eastern Europe and other Soviet forces are run down.

The precise shape of our contributions to NATO must reflect discussions yet to come with the NATO authorities and with our allies.

In the options for change studies, we have sought to devise a structure for our regular forces appropriate to the new security situation and meeting our essential peacetime operational needs. The framework that we have provided would be reinforced in a period of tension by drawing on volunteer reserves and reservists, who will have an important role to play. We have also allowed for the possible need to build back up our forces over a longer period should international circumstances ever require us to do so. . . .

Work remains to be done on detailed force structures and on changes in the support area, where we will be looking for substantial savings, before we can clarify the implications for individual units. We envisage in broad terms by the mid-1990s a Regular Army of about 120,000, Royal Navy/Royal Marines of about 60,000 and a Royal Air Force of about 75,000. On that basis, the overall reduction in regular service manpower would be about 18 per cent. We expect our civilian numbers to be similarly reduced. The volunteer reserves will continue to play a key role, and we wish to consider the appropriate numbers for the future, having regard to our needs and realistic levels of recruitment and retention.

United Kingdom Parliamentary Debates, House of Commons, 6th Series, Volume 177 (London: HMSO, 1990), 25 July 1990, cols 468, 470.

5.17   1992   7 July   **Britain, world-wide defence responsibilities, and global peacekeeping**

Malcolm Rifkind, in his first White Paper as Secretary of State for Defence, pointed by implication to the distinction between Britain's defence role and that of some of its NATO partners. Germany, for instance, indicated by its withdrawal from the production phase of the European Fighter Aircraft (EFA) that it probably did not envisage employing its fighter aircraft abroad. Britain, however, required fighter planes that could be used for global security purposes. The gist of the paper was that, despite the end of the Cold War, uncertainties and risks remained. Britain's obligations extended outside the NATO area: it continued to have world-wide commitments.

The Purpose of Britain's Defence Policy

5. Britain's defence policy forms a key component of our wider security policy. Its purpose remains to contribute to maintaining the freedom and territorial integrity of the United Kingdom and its dependent territories, and its ability to pursue its legitimate interests and activities at home and abroad. While there have been welcome reductions in the direct and immediate threat to our territory and that of our allies, Britain's armed forces are our insurance against the uncertainties of a rapidly changing world. As with any insurance policy, we must ensure that, within the resources available, the cover is right for the nature and the scale of the risks we may face, recognising that defence capabilities take time to develop, and must be matched to a realistic long term view of the potential for conflict.

6. Our security remains inextricably bound up with that of our partners in Europe and the Alliance. It remains a key security interest to sustain the present network of multinational Western co-operation and to avoid any reversion to nationally-driven defence. The principle of collective security within the North Atlantic Alliance remains a key element in providing stability and security in Europe.

Britain's Defence Roles

7. Since 1975 Britain's defence policy has been described in terms of four main roles: an independent element of strategic and theatre nuclear forces committed to the Alliance; the direct defence of the United Kingdom; a major land and air contribution to the European mainland; and a major maritime effort in the Eastern Atlantic and Channel. Specific British responsibilities and a contribution to world stability were to be met by exploiting, so far as resources permitted, the flexibility of our forces provided for NATO.

8. This framework was based on the broad areas in which we would provide support for NATO; the four roles did not in themselves provide a full basis for setting the objectives for the armed forces or the capabilities to be provided by the defence programme. There have always been tasks which our forces must be capable of meeting on their own under national command; those we planned to meet with allies; and a defence contribution to promoting the Government's broader security interests, where there were more choices to be made about the extent of any British military element.

9. Now, NATO has agreed a new Strategic Concept with

increased emphasis on flexibility and mobility to respond to risks to allied security which are multifaceted in nature and could arise from any geographical direction and area; our own contribution will be deployed throughout the Alliance area as necessary. Moreover, the distinction which tended to be drawn between Alliance tasks in Europe and other activities 'out of area' has become blurred; for example, we now foresee a requirement for military assistance, training and peacekeeping tasks both within and outside Europe. Finally, major examples of British military operations over the last 20 years, such as support for the civil power in Northern Ireland . . . , the defence of a dependent territory (the Falklands campaign), and the broader support of international stability (as in the Gulf campaign), fall outside the four roles.

10. For all these reasons, in the work on 'Options for Change' and subsequently we have looked again at our underlying defence needs, the strategy to achieve them and how this might be expressed in terms of future defence roles. There is no simple way of encompassing briefly all the tasks and activities of the armed forces; but we have concluded that defence policy would best be defined in terms of three overlapping roles:

– To ensure the protection and security of the United Kingdom and our dependent territories, even when there is no major external threat.

– To insure against any major external threat to the United Kingdom and our allies.

– To contribute to promoting the United Kingdom's wider security interests through the maintenance of international peace and stability.

11. Under the first role, the armed forces have day-to-day responsibilities for safeguarding our territory, airspace, territorial waters, and our dependent territories and, when required, support for the civil authority. Northern Ireland is the armed forces' largest peacetime commitment, and will remain of the highest priority. We intend that the second role should continue to be discharged through the collective security provided by the North Atlantic Alliance. In future, NATO may also act as an instrument in the third role, and more generally will continue to be the focus of our peacetime planning and training. Promotion of our wider interests can be achieved by a variety of means including military assistance and training, deployments and exercises and support for peacekeeping and other

operations . . . . Military operations could be conducted by NATO, WEU [Western European Union], the UN or ad hoc coalitions under UN or CSCE [Conference on Security and Co-operation in Europe] auspices. The participation of British forces in any particular operation will depend on the precise circumstances. The forces required to meet these requirements will be drawn from those with other roles. . . .

Defence Planning in a Changing World

1. Post-war United Kingdom defence policy has never been geared to a single threat. There have always been security responsibilities, though lighter now than they once were, beyond the NATO area. Since 1969 substantial fores have also supported the fight against terrorism in Northern Ireland. The dominant factor was always, however, the need to guard, with our allies, against a threat to European security and stability from a huge and highly militarised totalitarian power. Other tasks were mostly met from within what was provided for that central purpose.

2. The stability of Europe in freedom remains our fundamental security interest. But while it would be foolhardy to assume that what emerges from the wreck of Soviet communism can never again bear upon our defence needs, the risks as a whole are now much more diverse and uncertain. This transformation, vastly welcome in itself, sets new tasks for planners. What considerations should guide the shaping of our defence programme and the allocation of resources for and within it?

3. While our forces have increasingly been designed to contribute to total Alliance needs, with account taken of the effect of our choices on Allies, precise force levels and quality have always in NATO been a matter for national decision, largely reflecting how much of the burden each Government is prepared to carry. Moreover, even where a defence need is clear in a general way, the requirements in specific force terms are rarely obvious. No defence planner in the 1960s could reasonably have built plans around the sending of a task force to eject invaders from the Falklands; none in the 1970s could plausibly have argued the case for Tornado or a substantial armoured capability from the needs of a possible multinational operation in the Gulf. It is in fact dangerous to tailor our forces to highly specific scenarios. The expectation that we may increasingly be voluntary contributors to multinational efforts

compounds the problem of prediction; so does the fact that while major changes in international relations can come in weeks or months, the timescales for defence programme change, like acquiring new equipment, are far longer.

4. Nor, at the other extreme, can we hope to cater for everything that might happen. Defence is about insurance and deterrence, and rightly considers the darker possibilities, not the most agreeable or even the likeliest. But there is hardly any type or scale of military provision for which imagination cannot conceive a come-in-handy scenario; and we cannot afford everything. Even the Soviet Union, ruinously, could not. The discipline of resource constraint is inescapable.

Cm 1981, Statement on the Defence Estimates 1992 (London: HMSO, July 1992), pp. 8–9, 13.

5.18   *1993   5 July*   Elimination of the 'in and out of area' distinction

Rifkind's second defence White Paper, while further adjusting Britain's defence requirements in line with the Options for Change programme, adjustments which included reductions in the anti-submarine warfare capability and aircraft provided for Britain's defences, recognised the need for Britain to play a part in international peacekeeping missions and abolished the distinction between 'in and out of area' planning.

Introduction

Last year in the Introduction to my first Statement on the Defence Estimates, I forecast that changes in the strategic environment would continue. Events have borne out this judgement. Continued consolidation of the friendship and co-operation between the nations of NATO and the former Soviet Union, further democratic and economic progress in the countries of Central and Eastern Europe and the Baltic States, and broad implementation of both conventional and strategic arms control agreements, have significantly enhanced our security. On the other hand, tragic and dangerous conflicts have already broken out in the former Yugoslavia, the Caucasus, and many other areas. The potential for other disputes to deteriorate to open conflict is considerable, though whether we would choose to intervene would depend on the circumstances. . . .

This year's Statement on the Defence Estimates sets out our analysis of the implications of recent changes and the Ministry of Defence's response. The major restructuring begun following the 'Options for Change' review is on course and will be completed by the mid-1990s. In addition, the changes over the last 12 months led me to conclude that a number of further adjustments, both enhancement and reductions to the force levels and capabilities of the armed forces, are now appropriate. These adjustments, some of which have recently been announced, include an increase in Army manpower, improvements to our amphibious capability and the Army's anti-armour capability, and further investment in transport aircraft and support helicopters; as well as reductions in our anti-submarine warfare capability and the number of aircraft provided for the air defence of the United Kingdom.

In addition, this year's Statement contains a new and fundamental analysis of the way in which defence assets are, and will need to be, employed to meet our various commitments around the world. This makes explicit the links between policy, the tasks which our armed forces are called on to undertake, and overall force structures: a vital planning tool if we are to respond to the current, fluid strategic situation and future changes. This will provide a framework to ensure we can maintain a balance between policy, commitments and resources: a key objective if Britain's armed forces are to remain well-trained and equipped and fully able to meet the broad spectrum of operations which they might be called upon to undertake. Britain's defence industry continues to provide quality products and services for the Department, and has proved its international competitiveness by achieving record export orders in 1992. . . .

Increases in the Risks

114. There are however other areas where risks and commitments have increased and these must be reflected in our planned force structures and capabilities. There is considerable potential for conflict in which Britain's armed forces are or could be involved in a number of operations in both Europe and the wider world. The United Kingdom's contribution to United Nations peacekeeping and humanitarian operations. . . . In particular, the crisis in the former Yugoslavia has deepened and led to new commitments. . . . We have

also taken action with coalition allies in support of UN Security Council Resolutions (SCRs), to enforce the no-fly zones in Northern and Southern Iraq to deter repression of the populations in those areas by Saddam Hussein's forces. In Northern Ireland, the Provisional IRA [Irish Republican Army] and other sectarian groups maintain their campaign of terrorism, with scant regard for human life.

115. The potential for further conflicts in and around Europe is already apparent. The willingness of the UN and CSCE [Conference on Security and Co-operation in Europe] to become involved in seeking to prevent or contain such conflicts is welcome. NATO is now in a position to support UN or CSCE peacekeeping operations . . . . This has the full backing of the British Government. We must recognise that there will be pressure on the United Kingdom to play a part in any international response, and the Government may wish to do so where appropriate. The same is true outside Europe.

116. These developments mean that the old distinction between 'in' and 'out-of-area' is no longer relevant for defence planning. Instead the criteria will be the depth of British and allied interests involved and the implications of the crisis for international peace and stability, while recognising our continued commitment to collective defence through NATO. . . .

Force Restructuring

125. The threat to the United Kingdom itself is very much lower than during the Cold War. The increased commitments in Northern Ireland the Bosnia are of a different order of magnitude to the reductions we are able to make in the Central Region and for the defence of the United Kingdom. We are also making reductions in our commitments in Belize and Cyprus, and anticipate a further reduction as we withdraw from Hong Kong. Our measured response to these changes since 1991 means that the defence programme can be met from a reduced level of defence expenditure, as forecast in last year's Public Expenditure Survey. We anticipate that defence expenditure will be some 3.2 per cent of Gross Domestic Product by 1995/96 – still above the NATO average.

126. Britain's armed forces will remain well-trained and equipped, and fully able to undertake a broad spectrum of operations. Maintenance of a balance between commitments and resources, with robust, effective force structures appropriate to the

evolving strategic environment, is a key objective. We will continue to keep our plans, and defence policy as a whole, under review.

Britain's Nuclear Forces

The Strategic Deterrent

127. In common with our allies, we believe that nuclear forces will continue to play an indispensable role as part of NATO's strategy for the preservation of peace. While we continue to develop a co-operative relationship with Russia, the Alliance still needs to take account of the large nuclear arsenal Russia will retain even after implementation of the START agreements. The United Kingdom's independent nuclear forces remain the ultimate guarantee of our country's security, underpinning our defence strategy and providing a significant contribution to Alliance deterrent forces.

128. We have long emphasised that we will deploy only the minimum deterrent required for our security needs. Each Trident submarine will initially carry no more than 128 warheads; the exact number to be deployed – which may well be less than this figure – will be decided nearer the time. Factors to be taken into consideration will include the prospective major reductions in the US and Russian arsenals, the associated improvement in the strategic setting, and any improvements in defensive capabilities.

Cm 2270, Defending Our Future. Statement on the Defence Estimates 1993 (London: HMSO, July 1993), pp. 5, 10–11, 14.

Guide to further reading

British defence policy and strategy towards the Soviet Union, 1945–50

There are a number of relevant published documents in *Documents on British Policy Overseas*, Series I, Volume VI, *Eastern Europe, August 1945–April 1946*, edited by M. E. Pelly, H. J. Yasamee and K. A. Hamilton assisted by G. Bennett (London: HMSO, 1991); see in particular pp. 356–9, Report by the Chiefs of Staff Committee on the Strategic Position of the British Commonwealth, 18 April 1946. One of the earliest works in the field based on the documents in the Public Record Office is Victor Rothwell, *Britain and the Cold War 1941–1947* (London, 1982). See also Ritchie Ovendale, *The English-Speaking Alliance. Britain, the United States, the Dominions and the Cold War 1945-1951* (London, 1985), pp. 29–87; D. Dilks, 'The British view of security: Europe and a wider world, 1945–1948', in Olav Riste (ed.), *Western Security: the Formative Years. European and Atlantic Defence 1947–1953* (Oslo, 1985), pp. 25–59; Donald C. Watt, 'British military perceptions of the Soviet Union as a strategic threat, 1945–1950', in Josef Backer and Franz Knipping (eds), *Power in Europe? Great Britain, France, Italy and Germany in a Postwar World, 1945–1950* (Berlin, 1986), pp. 325–38; Anthony Gorst, ' "We must cut our coat according to our cloth": the making of British defence policy, 1945–8', in Richard J. Aldrich (ed.), *British Intelligence Strategy and the Cold War, 1945–51*(London, 1992), pp. 143–65.

The Middle East as one of the three cardinal pillars of British defence policy, 1945–60

For the evolution of the 'three pillars' strategy and the significance of the Middle East as a British and Commonwealth responsibility in allied defence policy and global strategy 1948-52 see Ovendale, *The English-Speaking Alliance*, pp. 91–142, 211-41, 273–89. For the importance of Palestine in British military planning 1945–8 see Ritchie Ovendale, *Britain, the United States, and the End of the Palestine Mandate, 1942–1948* (Woodbridge, Suffolk, 1989); Martin Jones, *Failure in Palestine. British and United States Policy after the Second World War* (London, 1986). For an account of the military campaign see David A. Charters, *The British Army and Jewish Insurgency in Palestine, 1945–47* (London, 1989). There is a discussion of British defence of the Middle East, 1945–51, based on the documents, in Wm. Roger Louis, *The British Empire in the Middle East 1945–1951. Arab Nationalism, the United States, and Postwar Imperialism* (Oxford, 1984). See also Richard J. Aldrich and John Zametica, 'The rise and decline of a strategic concept: the Middle East, 1945–51', in Aldrich (ed.), *British Intelligence*, pp. 236–74. The change in British defence policy towards the Middle East with the development of the hydrogen bomb is outlined in David R. Devereux, *The Formulation of British Defence Policy towards the Middle East, 1948–56* (London, 1990). For accounts of the British withdrawal from the Suez base based on the British documents see Ritchie Ovendale, 'Egypt and the Suez base agreement' in John W. Young (ed.), *The Foreign Policy of Churchill's Peacetime Administration 1951–1955* (Leicester, 1988), pp. 135–58; Wm. Roger Louis, 'The tragedy of the Anglo-Egyptian settlement of 1954', in Wm. Roger Louis and Roger Owen (eds), *Suez 1956. The Crisis and its Consequences* (Oxford, 1989), pp. 43–71. British defence policy with the formation of the Baghdad Pact is described in Brian Holden Reid, 'The "Northern Tier" and the Baghdad Pact', in Young (ed.), *Churchill's Peacetime Administration*, pp. 159–80. For the development of Anglo-American military plans to impose a settlement on the Middle East in 1955 see Shimon Shamir, 'The collapse of Project Alpha', in Louis and Owen, *Suez 1956*, pp. 73-102. A background to military considerations leading to the Suez crisis can be found in W. Scott Lucas, 'The path to Suez: Britain and the struggle for the Middle East, 1948–53', in Ann

Deighton (ed.), *Britain and the First Cold War* (London, 1990), pp.
253–72; see also Scott W. Lucas, *Divided We Stand: Britain, the
United States and the Suez Crisis* (London, 1991). The most compre-
hensive account of the Suez crisis including the military and defence
planning aspects can be found in Keith Kyle, *Suez* (London, 1991).
For aspects of British military planning see André Beaufre, *The Suez
Expedition 1956* (London, 1969); Robert Jackson, *Suez 1956:
Operation Musketeer* (London, 1980).

Cold War in Asia

For the planning of British strategy to cope with the joining of the
Cold War in Asia see: Richard J. Aldrich, 'British strategy and the
end of Empire: South Asia, 1945–51', in Aldrich (ed.), *British Intelligence*, pp. 275–307; Karl Hack, 'South East Asia and British
strategy, 1944–51', *British Intelligence*, pp. 308–32. For British
defence planning, and the views of the Joint Intelligence Committee,
with regard to the Cold War in South East Asia, particularly
Indochina, see Ovendale, *The English-Speaking Alliance*, pp.
145–84. British military planning including considerations of the
defence of Hong Kong with the rise of Communist China is considered in Ovendale, *The English-Speaking Alliance*, pp. 185–210.
See also Michael Dockrill, 'Britain and the first offshore islands
crisis, 1945–55', in Michael Dockrill and John W. Young (eds),
British Foreign Policy, 1945–56 (London, 1989), pp. 173–96;
Ritchie Ovendale, 'The Cold War, 1949–1951', in Carl Bridge (ed.),
*Munich to Vietnam. Australia's Relations with Britain and the
United States since the 1930s* (Carlton, Victoria, Australia, 1991),
pp. 87–98. Specialist studies on Britain's handling of the Communist
insurrection in Malaya include: Anthony Short, *The Communist
Insurrection in Malaya 1948–1960* (London, 1975); Richard
Clutterbuck, *The Long Long War. The Emergency in Malaya
1948–1960* (London, 1967); Richard Stubbs, *Hearts and Minds in
Guerrilla Warfare. The Malayan Emergency 1948–1960*
(Singapore, 1989); Derek McDougall, 'The Malayan Emergency
and Confrontation', in Bridge (ed.), *Munich to Vietnam*. See also the
relevant sections of John Cloake, *Templer, Tiger of Malaya. The Life
of Field Marshal Sir Gerald Templer* (London, 1985); Robert

Guide to further reading

Thompson, *Defeating Communist Insurgency. Experiences from Malaya and Vietnam* (London, 1966).

The development of Britain's nuclear weapons and the evolution of Britain's nuclear strategy

Published documentary material on Britain's atomic energy programme can be found in *Documents on British Policy Overseas*, Series I, Volume IV, *Britain and America: Atomic Energy, Bases and Food, 12 December 1945–31 July 1946*, edited by Roger Bullen and M. E. Pelly assisted by H. J. Yasamee and G. Bennett (London: HMSO, 1987); Series I, Volume II, *Conferences and Conversations 1945: London, Washington and Moscow* (London: HMSO, 1985), especially pp. 516–634. Parliamentary White Papers are referred to in the text. These include: *Cmd 9391, Statement on Defence 1955* (London, 1955); *Cmnd 124, Defence Outline of Future Policy* (London, 1957); *Cmnd 363, Report on Defence Britain's Contribution to Peace and Security* (London, 1958). An interesting account of the origins of Britain's nuclear programme by an American air force historian based on interviews with participants is Alfred Goldberg, 'The atomic origins of Britain's nuclear deterrent', *International Affairs*, 40, 1964, pp. 409–29. The classic official history commissioned by the United Kingdom Atomic Energy Authority is Margaret Gowing assisted by Lorna Arnold, *Independence and Deterrence. Britain and Atomic Energy, 1945–1952*, Volume I, *Policy Making* (London, 1974). The story is extended into the 1980s in John Simpson, *The Independent Nuclear State. The United States, Britain and the Military Atom*, 2nd edition (London, 1986). Nicholas Wheeler, 'The Attlee government's nuclear strategy, 1945–51', in Deighton (ed.), *First Cold War*, pp. 130–45, and Ian Clark and Nicholas J. Wheeler, *The British Origins of Nuclear Strategy 1945–1955* (Oxford, 1989), are accounts based on documents in the Public Record Office. An account of security leaks is given in H. Montgomery Hyde, *The Atom Bomb Spies* (London, 1980). For a discussion of the Sandys policy see Colin Gordon, 'Duncan Sandys and the independent nuclear deterrent', in Ian Beckett and John Gooch (eds), *Politicians and Defence. Studies in the Formulation of British defence Policy 1845–1970* (Manchester, 1981), pp. 132–53. For Sandys's successor's policy see his own

198

account: Harold Watkinson, *Turning Points* (London, 1986). See also R. N. Rosecrance, *Defense of the Realm. British Strategy in the Nuclear Epoch* (New York, 1968); Lawrence Freedman, *Britain and Nuclear Weapons* (London, 1980); A. J. R. Groom, *British Thinking about Nuclear Weapons* (London, 1974); Andrew J. Pierre, *Nuclear Politics. The British Experience with an Independent Strategic Force 1939–1970* (London, 1972); J. P. G. Freeman, *Britain's Nuclear Arms Control Policy in the context of Anglo-American Relations, 1957–68* (London, 1986); Greville Rumble, *The Politics of Nuclear Defence A Comprehensive Introduction* (Cambridge, 1985), pp. 78–101. Jeff McMahan, *British Nuclear Weapons. For and Against* (London, 1981) is a consideration by a professional philosopher of the controversy about British unilateral disarmament.

Britain and the formation of the North Atlantic Treaty Organisation

An account by a British participant in the negotiations is Nicholas Henderson, *The Birth of NATO* (London, 1982). The perspective of a Canadian delegate can be found in Escott Reid, *Time of Fear and Hope. The Making of the North Atlantic Treaty 1947–1949* (Toronto, 1977). For Montgomery's role see Nigel Hamilton, *Monty. The Field-Marshal 1944–1976* (London, 1986), pp. 725–78. John Baylis, *The Diplomacy of Pragmatism. Britain and the Formation of NATO, 1942–49* (London, 1993) includes four documents. Accounts based on the British documents include: Ritchie Ovendale, 'Great Britain and the Atlantic Pact', in Ennio Di Nolfo (ed.), *The Atlantic Pact Forty Years Later. A Historical Reappraisal* (Berlin, 1991), pp. 72–8; *The English-Speaking Alliance*, pp. 59–87; John W. Young, *Britain, France and the Unity of Europe 1945–1951* (Leicester, 1984), pp. 55–140; John Kent and John W. Young, 'The "Western Union" concept and British defence policy, 1947–8', in Aldrich (ed.), *British Intelligence*, pp. 166-92; Geoffrey Warner, 'The British Labour Government and the Atlantic Alliance, 1949–51', in Riste (ed.), *Western Security*, pp. 247–65. See also Don Cook, *Forging the Alliance. NATO, 1945-1950* (London, 1989). Peter Hill-Norton, *No Soft Options. The Politico-Military Realities of NATO* (London, 1978), is an account of how the organisation operated by a British Chairman of the NATO Military Committee.

The Anglo-American defence relationship

John Baylis, *Anglo-American Defence Relations 1939–1984. The Special Relationship*, 2nd edition (London, 1984), contains eighteen documents. Ian S. McDonald (ed.), *Anglo-American Relations since the Second World War* (London, 1974), also contains a collection of documents on defence. Christopher Grayling and Christopher Langdon, *Just Another Star. Anglo-American Relations since 1945* (London, 1988), offers important insights into the defence relationship as well as the defence industries. The nuclear relationship is discussed in Margaret Gowing, 'Britain, America and the Bomb', in Dockrill and Young (eds), *British Foreign Policy*, pp. 31–46, and 'Nuclear weapons and the 'Special Relationship', in Wm. Roger Louis and Hedley Bull (eds), *The 'Special Relationship'. Anglo-American Relations since 1945* (Oxford, 1986), pp. 117–28. See also Samuel F. Wells, Jr., 'The United States, Britain, and the defence of Europe', in Louis and Bull (eds), The 'Special Relationship', pp. 129–50; James Eberle, 'The military relationship', in Louis and Bull (eds), *The 'Special Relationship'*, pp. 151–60; Ernest R. May and Gregory F. Treverton, 'Defence relationships: American perspectives', in Louis and Bull (eds), *The 'Special Relationship'*, pp. 161–84. The history of American bases in Britain 1948–84 is examined in Simon Duke, *US Defence Bases in the United Kingdom. A Matter for Joint Decision?* (London, 1987).

The Korean War

Many of the documents concerned with Britain's role in the Korean War are published in *Documents on British Policy Overseas*, Series II, Volume IV, *Korea, June 1950–April 1951*, edited by H. J., Yasamee and K. A. Hamilton assisted by Isabel Warner and Ann Lane (London, 1991). The official history is Anthony Farrar-Hockley, *The British Part in the Korean War*, Volume I, *A Distant Obligation* (London, 1990). See also Ovendale, *The English-Speaking Alliance*, pp. 211–30; Peter Lowe, 'The significance of the Korean War in Anglo-American relations, 1950-3', in Dockrill and Young (eds), *British Foreign Policy*, pp. 126-48.

British attitudes to ANZUS

Documents on British Policy Overseas, Series II, Volume IV, contains material on the British attitude to the formation of ANZUS. See also *The ANZUS Documents*, edited by Alan Burnett with Thomas-Durell Young and Christine Wilson (Canberra, 1991). The British reaction is examined in Ovendale, *The English-Speaking Alliance*, pp. 230–41. See, generally, Trevor R. Reese, *Australia, New Zealand, and the United States. A Survey of International Relations 1941–68* (London, 1969); R. J. O'Neill, 'The Korean War and the origins of ANZUS', in Bridge (ed.), *Munich to Vietnam*, pp. 99–113.

South Africa and the Simonstown agreement

The Labour government's decision to further defence relations with South Africa, 1948–51, is examined in Ovendale, *The English-Speaking Alliance*, pp. 245–72. The Conservative government's policy is discussed in Geoffrey Berridge, 'Britain, South Africa and African defence, 1949–55', in Dockrill and Young (eds), *British Foreign Policy*, pp. 101–25; G. R. Berridge and J. E. Spence, 'South Africa and the Simonstown Agreements', in Young (ed.), *Churchill's Peacetime Administration*, pp. 181–206; Peter James Henshaw, 'The transfer of Simonstown: Afrikaner nationalism, South African strategic dependence, and British global power', *Journal of Imperial and Commonwealth History*, XX, 1992, pp. 419–44. See also G. R. Berridge, *South Africa, the Colonial Powers and 'African Defence'. The Rise and Fall of the White Entente, 1948–60* (London, 1992).

West German rearmament and the European Defence Community

A selection of the British documents is printed in *Documents on British Policy Overseas*, Series II, Volume III, *German Rearmament September–December 1950*, edited by Roger Bullen and M. E. Pelly assisted by H. J. Yasamee and G. Bennett (London, 1989). Saki Dockrill, *Britain's Policy for West German Rearmament 1950–1955* (Cambridge, 1991), is a study making extensive use of the Public Record Office material. See also Saki Dockrill, 'Britain' strategy for Europe: must West Germany be rearmed? 1949–51' in

Aldrich (ed.), *British Intelligence*, pp. 193–214; 'Britain and the settlement of the West German rearmament question in 1954' in Dockrill and Young (eds), *British Foreign Policy*, pp. 149–72; Matthias Peter, 'Britain, the Cold War and the economics of German rearmament, 1949–51', in Deighton (ed.), *The First Cold War*, pp. 273–90; N. Wiggershaus, 'The decision for a West German defence contribution', in Riste (ed.), *Western Security*, pp. 198–214. Britain's attitude to the proposed European Defence Community is examined in Edward Fursdon, *The European Defence Community. A History* (London, 1980).

Withdrawal from empire and the East of Suez defence policy

William Jackson, *Withdrawal from Empire. A Military View* (London, 1986), is a general account. Wm. Roger Louis, 'American anti-colonialism and the dissolution of the British Empire', in Louis and Bull (eds), *The 'Special Relationship'*, pp. 261–84, offers an interesting context. Philip Darby, *British Defence Policy East of Suez 1947–1968* (London, 1973), is a pioneering study. See also Philip Darby, 'East of Suez reassessed', in John Baylis (ed.), *British Defence Policy in a Changing World* (London, 1977), pp. 52–65; Coral Bell, 'East of Suez and the Guam Doctrine' in *Dependent Ally. A Study in Australian Foreign Policy* (Melbourne, 1988), pp. 87–113; John Darwin, 'Britain's withdrawal from East of Suez' in Bridge (ed.), *Munich to Vietnam*, pp. 140-58. C. J. Bartlett, *The Long Retreat. A Short History of British Defence Policy, 1945–70* (London, 1972) examines the East of Suez policy in the overall context of British defence policy. Julian Paget, *Last Post: Aden 1964–1967* (London, 1969), is an account of the British army's engagement in Aden; see also Karl Piergostini, *Britain, Aden and South Arabia. Abandoning Empire* (London, 1991). Glen Balfour-Paul, *The End of Empire in the Middle East Britain's relinquishment of power in her last three Arab dependencies* (Cambridge, 1991), covers military aspects of Britain's withdrawal from the Sudan in 1955, South West Arabia (Aden) in 1967 and the Gulf States in 1971. Brian Lapping, *End of Empire* (London, 1985), publishes many interviews with military personnel involved in the retreat from empire.

Guide to further reading

British sea power and the Falklands War

John B. Hattendorf and Robert S. Jordan (eds), *Maritime Strategy and the Balance of Power. Britain and America in the Twentieth Century* (London, 1989), contains important essays on post-1945 Anglo-American maritime strategy. Geoffrey Till (ed.), *The Future of British Sea Power* (London, 1984), includes historical essays on the development of the Royal Navy since 1945. David Brown, *The Royal Navy and the Falklands War* (London, 1987), is by the head of the Naval Historical Branch. See also Max Hastings and Simon Jenkins, *The Battle for the Falklands* (London, 1983); Paul Eddy and Magnus Linklater with Peter Gillaman with the *Sunday Times* Insight Team, *The Falklands War* (London, 1983).

The Labour Party and Defence

Dan Keohane, *Labour Party Defence Policy Since 1945* (Leicester, 1993), offers a brief history of the 1945–74 period and concentrates on the history of the divisions within the Labour Party over defence in the 1980s and early 1990s. Bruce George with Timothy Watson and Jonathan Roberts, *The British Labour Party and Defense* (New York, 1991), concentrates on the debates in the 1980s. See also *Sense about Defence. The Report of the Labour Party Defence Study Group* (London, 1977), the published recommendations of three years' work by a study group. Relevant Labour Party conference reports and manifestos are referred to in the text. These include: *Report of the Annual Conference of the Labour Party 1983* (London, 1983); *Britain will win. Labour manifesto. June 1987* (London, 1987); *Meet the challenge. Make the change. A new agenda for Britain. Final report of Labour's Policy Review for the 1990s* (London, 1989); *Looking to the Future* (London, 1990)

Defence Reviews in the 1960s and 1970s

Relevant parliamentary White Papers, Defence Reviews, and debates are referred to in the text. See especially *Cmnd 1639, Statement on Defence 1962. The Next Five Years* (London, 1962); *Cmnd 2270, Statement on Defence 1964* (London, 1964); *Cmnd 2592,*

Statement on the Defence Estimates 1965 (London, 1965); *Cmnd 3203, Statement on the Defence Estimates 1967* (London, 1967); *Cmnd 3540 Statement on the Defence Estimates 1968* (London, 1968); *Cmnd 3927, Statement on the Defence Estimates 1969* (London, 1969); *Cmnd 4290, Statement on the Defence Estimates 1970* (London, 1970); *Cmnd 6735, Statement on the Defence Estimates 1977* (London, 1977). Denis Healey, *The Time of my Life* (London, 1989), offers first-hand insights by Labour's Secretary of Defence. Michael Chichester and John Wilkinson, *The Uncertain Ally. British Defence Policy 1960–1990* (London, 1982), offers an overview. See also David Greenwood, 'The 1974 defence review in perspective', *Survival*, XVII, 1975, pp. 223–29; Peter Nailor, 'Denis Healey and rational decision-making in defence', in Beckett and Gooch (eds.), *Politicians and Defence*, pp. 154–78.

Defence debates in the 1980s and 1990s

Parliamentary White Papers, defence Open Discussion Documents, and parliamentary debates are referred to in the text. Amongst the most important are: *The Future United Kingdom Strategic Nuclear Deterrent Force*, Defence Open Government Document 80/23 (London, 1980); *Cmnd 7979, The British Strategic Nuclear Force* (London, 1980); *Cmnd 8288, The United Kingdom Defence Programme. The Way Forward* (London, 1981); *Cmnd 8758, The Falklands Campaign. The Lessons* (London, 1982); *Cmnd-1, Statement on the Defence Estimates 1984 1* (London, 1984); *Cmnd 9430–1, Statement on the Defence Estimates 1985 1* (London, 1985); *Trident and the Alternatives. Modernising the United Kingdom Strategic Nuclear Deterrent Force*, Defence Open Government Document 87/01 (London, 1987); *The defence implications and the future of Westland plc*, Third Report from the Defence Committee, Session 1985–6 (London, July 1986); *United Kingdom Parliamentary Debates. House of Commons*, 6th Series, Volume 177, 25 July 1990, cols 468–86 ('Options for Change'); *Cm 1981, Statement on the Defence Estimates 1992* (London, 1992). For the debate over Trident see Colin McInnes, *Trident. The Only Option?* (London, 1986); a CND case is given in Malcolm Chalmers, *Trident. Britain's Independent Arms Race* (London, 1984). On disarmament talks see Philip A. G. Sabin, 'Should INF and START be merged? A historical perspective', *International Affairs*, 60, 1984, pp. 419–28. On the Strategic Defence Initiative see Trevor Taylor, 'Britain's response to the Strategic Defence Initiative', *International Affairs*, 62, 1986, pp. 217–30. Lawrence Freedman, 'European collaboration and the British government. The case of Westland and the bias to Europe', *International Affairs*, 63, 1986–7, pp. 1–20. Peter Byrd (ed.), *British Defence Policy. Thatcher and Beyond* (London, 1991), and Stuart Croft (ed.), *British Security Policy. The Thatcher years and the End of the Cold War* (London, 1991), are collections of essays discussing issues relevant to British defence in the 1980s. The debates following the 'Options for Change' policy are considered in Christopher Bellamy, 'Soldier of fortune: Britain's new military role', *International Affairs*, 68, 1992, pp. 443–56; Philip A. G. Sabin, 'British defence choices beyond "Options for Change" ', *International Affairs*, 69, 1993, pp. 267–88; Len Scott, 'British perspectives on the future of European security', in Colin McInnes (ed.), *Security and Strategy in the new Europe* (London, 1992), pp. 178–96.

Defence organisation

Cmd 6923, Central Organisation for Defence (London, 1946) gave the newly created Defence Ministry executive authority. Mountbatten's challenge to this is discussed in Philip Ziegler, *Mountbatten. The Official Biography* (London, 1985), pp. 608–24. The subsequent reforms by Peter Thornycroft, the Secretary of Defence, and Mountbatten are outlined in *Cmnd 2097, Central Organisation for Defence* (London, 1963), and discussed in Michael Howard, *The Central Organisation of Defence* (London, 1970). William P. Snyder, *The Politics of British Defense Policy 1945–1962* (London, 1964), looks at the service departments, pressure groups and defence spending. The history of the Committee of Imperial Defence is covered in Franklin Arthur Johnson, *Defence by Committee. The British Committee of Imperial Defence 1885–1959* (London, 1960); that of the Ministry of Defence in Franklyn A. Johnson, *Defence by Ministry. The British Ministry of Defence 1944–1974* (London, 1980); and that of the Chiefs of Staff in William Jackson and Lord Bramall, *The Chiefs. The Story of the United Kingdom Chiefs of Staff* (London, 1992). Other books on planning and management include: Martin Edmonds (ed.), *The Defence Equation. British Military Systems Policy, Planning and Performance* (London, 1986); Malcolm McIntosh, *Managing Britain's Defence* (London, 1990); Andrew Cox and Stephen Kirby, *Congress, Parliament and Defence. The Impact of Legislative Reform on Defence Accountability in Britain and America* (London, 1986); Michael D. Hobkirk, *The Politics of Defence Budgeting. A Study of Organisation and Resource Allocation in the United Kingdom and the United States* (London, 1984). L. V. Scott, *Conscription and the Attlee Governments. The Politics and Policy of National Service 1945–1951* (Oxford, 1993), is an account of the continuation of conscription after the end of the Second World War.

Intelligence

An overall account of the workings of British intelligence in the post-1945 period can be found in Jeffrey T. Richelson and Desmond Ball, *The Ties that Bind. Intelligence Cooperation between the UKUDSA Countries – the United Kingdom, the United States of America, Canada, Australia and New Zealand* (London, 1985). Aldrich (ed.), *British Intelligence*, pp. 15–142, contains specialist essays.

Office holders' periods of tenure

Prime Ministers

1945–1951   Clement Attlee
1951–1955   Winston Leonard Spencer Churchill
1955–1957   (Robert) Anthony Eden
1957–1963   Harold Macmillan
1963–1964   Sir Alec (Alexander Frederick) Douglas-Home
1964–1970   (James) Harold Wilson
1970–1974   Edward Heath
1974–1976   (James) Harold Wilson
1976–1979   (Leonard) James Callaghan
1979–1991   Margaret Hilda Thatcher
1991–   John Major

Secretaries of State for Foreign Affairs

1945–1951   Ernest Bevin
1951–1955   (Robert) Anthony Eden
1955–1960   (John) Selwyn Brooke Lloyd
1960–1963   Earl of Home (Lord Home of Hirsel)
1964–1964   Richard Austen Butler
1964–1965   Patrick Chrestien Gordon Walker
1965–1966   (Robert) Michael Maitland Stewart
1966–1968   George Alfred Brown

Office holders' periods of tenure

Secretaries of State for Foreign and Commonwealth Affairs

1968–1970	(Robert) Michael Maitland Stewart
1970–1974	Sir Alec (Alexander Frederick) Douglas-Home
1974–1976	(Leonard) James Callaghan
1976–1977	(Charles) Anthony Raven Crosland
1977–1979	David Anthony Llewellyn Owen
1979–1982	Lord Carrington
1982–1983	Francis Pym
1983–1989	Sir Geoffrey Howe
1989	John Major
1989–	Douglas Hurd

Ministers of Defence

1945–1946	Clement Attlee
1946–1950	Albert Victor Alexander
1951–1952	Winston Churchill
1952–1954	Earl Alexander of Tunis
1954–1955	Harold Macmillan
1955	(John) Selwyn Brooke Lloyd
1955–1956	Sir Walter Monckton
1956–1957	Anthony Head
1957–1959	Duncan Sandys
1959–1962	Harold Watkinson
1962–1964	Peter Thorneycroft

Secretaries of State for Defence

1964–1970	Denis Healey
1970–1974	Lord Carrington
1974	Sir Ian Gilmour
1974–1976	Roy Mason
1976–1979	Fred Mulley
1979–1981	Francis Pym
1981–1983	John Nott
1983–1986	Michael Heseltine
1986–1989	George Younger

Office holders' periods of tenure

1989–1992 Tom (Thomas Jeremy) King
1992–   Malcolm Rifkind

Chiefs of the Defence Staff

1957–1959 Sir William Dickson (with no Defence Staff)
1959–1965 Earl Mountbatten (Defence Staff formed in
           April 1964)
1965–1967 Sir Richard Hull
1967–1971 Lord Elworthy
1971–1973 Lord Hill-Norton
1973–1976 Lord Carver
1976–1977 Sir Andrew Humphrey
1977   Sir Edward Ashmore
1977–1979 Lord Cameron
1979–1982 Lord Lewin
1982–1985 Lord Bramall
1985–1988 Lord Fieldhouse
1988–1991 Lord Craig
1991–1992 Sir Richard Vincent
1993–   Sir Peter Harding

First Sea Lords

1943–1946 Viscount Cunningham
1946–1948 Sir John Cunningham
1948–1951 Lord Fraser
1951–1955 Sir Rhoderick McGrigor
1955–1959 Earl Mountbatten
1959–1960 Sir Charles Lambe (retired in ill-health)
1960–1963 Sir Caspar John
1963–1966 Sir David Luce (resigned)
1966–1968 Sir Varyl Begg
1968–1970 Sir Michael Le Fanu (died in office)
1970–1971 Lord Hill-Norton
1971–1974 Sir Michael Pollock
1974–1977 Sir Edward Ashmore
1977–1979 Lord Lewin

Office holders' periods of tenure

1979–1982	Sir Henry Leach
1982–1985	Lord Fieldhouse
1985–1989	Sir William Staveley
1989–1992	Sir Julian Oswald
1993–	Sir Benjamin Bathurst

Chiefs of the Imperial General Staff

1941–1946	Viscount Alanbrooke
1946–1948	Viscount Montgomery
1948–1952	Viscount Slim
1952–1955	Lord Harding
1955–1958	Sir Gerald Templer
1958–1961	Sir Francis Festing
1961–1964	Sir Richard Hull

Chiefs of the General Staff

1964–1965	Sir Richard Hull
1965–1968	Sir James Cassels
1968–1971	Sir Geoffrey Baker
1971–1973	Lord Carver
1973–1976	Sir Peter Hunt
1976–1979	Sir Roland Gibbs
1979–1982	Lord Bramall
1982–1985	Sir John Stanier
1985–1988	Sir Nigel Bagnall
1988–1992	Sir John Chapple
1992–	Sir Peter Inge

Chiefs of the Air Staff

1945–1949	Lord Tedder
1950–1952	Sir John Slessor
1953–1955	Sir William Dickson
1955–1959	Sir Dermot Boyle
1960–1963	Sir Thomas Pike

Office holders' periods of tenure

1963–1967 Lord Elworthy
1967–1971 Sir John Grandy
1971–1974 Sir Dennis Spotswood
1974–1976 Sir Andrew Humphrey
1976–1977 Lord Cameron
1977–1982 Sir Michael Beetham
1982–1985 Sir Keith Williamson
1985–1988 Lord Craig
1988–1992 Sir Peter Harding
1993–   Sir Michael Graydon

Index